D1562926

David Hannay (Lord Hannay of Chiswick), one of Britain's most distinguished Foreign Office veterans, served in a number of key diplomatic posts and has been immersed in the conduct of British foreign policy relating to the UN, Europe and the Middle East over the last half century. He was Minister at the British Embassy in Washington, Ambassador to the European Communities from 1985 to 1990, and Ambassador to the United Nations from 1990 to 1995. Following his retirement from Britain's Diplomatic Service, he was the UK's Special Representative for Cyprus from 1996 to 2003. He is a member of the House of Lords' European Select Committee. He is the author of *Cyprus: The Search for a Solution* and *New World Disorder: The UN After the Cold War – An Insider's View* (both published by I.B.Tauris).

'British diplomats as a group are a clever bunch. David Hannay is one of the cleverest. It was his, and his country's, good fortune that his diplomatic career took him from Iran and Afghanistan to Brussels, Washington and the UN. This account of that journey is elegantly framed around the idea of a modern Britain in search of a role. As part of a generation of officials that enabled Britain to punch above its weight, he made the British case from EU accession to the UN Security Council. But the skill of his and his colleagues' performance has perhaps allowed their political masters to get away to this day without answering that tricky question about our country's role in the world.'

Lord Malloch-Brown,
Minister of State for Africa 2007–2009

'The real answer to Britain's quest for a role in the world is revealed time and again in the life and work of David Hannay and his colleagues so well described in this insightful and highly readable book.'

Tom Pickering,
US Ambassador to the United Nations 1989–1992

BRITAIN'S QUEST FOR A ROLE

A DIPLOMATIC MEMOIR
FROM EUROPE TO THE UN

DAVID HANNAY

I.B. TAURIS

LONDON · NEW YORK

Published and reprinted in 2013 by I.B.Tauris & Co Ltd
6 Salem Road, London W2 4BU
175 Fifth Avenue, New York NY 10010
www.ibtauris.com

Distributed in the United States and Canada Exclusively by Palgrave Macmillan
175 Fifth Avenue, New York NY 10010

ISBN: 978 1 78076 056 8

A full CIP record for this book is available from the British Library
A full CIP record is available from the Library of Congress

Library of Congress Catalog Card Number: available

Designed and typeset by 4word Ltd, Bristol
Printed and bound by CPI Group (UK) Ltd, Croydon, CR0 4YY

To all those members of Britain's Diplomatic Service, their wives and families, who participated in some of these experiences, and to my own wife and family who shared them all.

CONTENTS

ILLUSTRATIONS

*'Great Britain has lost an empire and
has not yet found a role.'*

Quotation from a speech by the US statesman and former
Secretary of State Dean Acheson at the United States Military
Academy at West Point on 5 December 1962

PREFACE

Sometimes a single sentence can sum up a whole, complicated series of historical developments. That, I personally have felt, was the case with Dean Acheson's lapidary comment, made not long after this memoir begins, that Britain had lost an empire and not yet found a role. Of course it is a wounding remark, and one only too likely to raise the hackles of those whom it described. But part of a diplomat's job is to discount the agreeable things that people say about your government and your country and to take seriously and to try to understand the less agreeable ones.

Looking back over the 50 years covered by this book, from the time I joined the Diplomatic Service soon after the Suez crisis shook Britain's diplomacy to its foundations, to the end of the first decade of the present century, it is striking how few fixed points remain. The Soviet Union has gone, and so has apartheid. The Cold War, whose frozen certainties dominated international affairs for so long, is no more. China has emerged from the horrendous convulsions of the Great Leap Forward and the Cultural Revolution to become one of the world's key players, a rising power par excellence, although by no means the only one. From the extremely modest beginnings of European economic cooperation, European integration has grown into something far more substantial, affecting pretty well every aspect of the public policies of its now 27 member states. Religion, for long discarded as a political factor, has come back with a bang to trouble international relations as it has not done for more than three centuries. Of course, some things have changed less. The United States remains for the time being top dog, the predominant military power in the world, although less able now to get its way than in the recent past. The Arab-Israel dispute remains unresolved, breaking out from time to time into open hostilities and circulating all the time as an insidious poison in the veins of the international body politic. So plenty of stuff has happened, some of it predictable, some of it actually predicted, and much completely unforeseen. It makes sense for those who have travelled through this rapidly changing landscape to set down what they saw and experienced and also to subject their experience to some critical judgements.

I have long hesitated before sitting down to write this memoir. Does the world really need another book of diplomatic memoirs, a genre which many may feel is already oversubscribed and which has a tendency to trivialisation and self-justification? This is a professional memoir, although one written from a personal standpoint and containing a certain amount of personal anecdote. But, as someone who still values what is no doubt regarded by many as old-fashioned reticence and who continues into the WikiLeaks age to defend the need for some discretion in revealing the details of dealings between officials and politicians and the advice they offered to them, I am not setting out to make waves or headlines, rather to cast some light on the complex developments and negotiations in which I have personally been involved. And then, during a life which left little or no opportunity to record these developments at the time, I am relying largely on memory and am courting the criticism of benefitting from hindsight in the judgements I make, although I have included a few contemporary documents which have not yet seen the light of day.

A number of factors have led me to overcome these doubts. My diplomatic career began with three years spent in Iran and Afghanistan, two exceptionally interesting countries, whose recent history and whose current role in world affairs has brought them much closer to centre stage than they have ever as nation states been before, and have made them the object of much, not always particularly well-informed or well-researched, comment. So an account of life in Tehran and Kabul some 50 years ago might contribute to achieving a better sense of perspective. Beyond that part of my career stretches a lengthy, almost unbroken, series of jobs dealing with multilateral organisations, first the Central Treaty Organisation (CENTO), then the European Community which metamorphosed into the European Union, and finally the United Nations. These multilateral organisations (or at least the second and third of them, CENTO is no more) have become an ever more important and more prominent part of the international landscape as the years have passed and have absorbed an ever greater proportion of ministerial and official time and energy. But their operations are not well understood nor, generally, well liked. Many people are put off by the alphabet soup of acronyms, by the obscurity of their decision-making processes and by the complete lack of televisual appeal of even the high points of their evolution. Many commentators do not make much of an effort to fight their way through this thicket of off-putting characteristics and to get to grips with what is really going on and why it is that governments worldwide, whether democratic or authoritarian, whether from developed or developing countries, attach so much importance to their activities. I was struck by the fact that, in a recently published anthology of valedictory despatches from British ambassadors over the last half century, only one out of a total of 91 (yes, I am afraid it was one of mine, although not the one I regard as the better of the two I wrote) was from an ambassador to a multilateral organisation. That surely is a balance that needs redressing.

And then, so far as Europe is concerned – and by far the largest proportion of my career in public service has been spent there – there is the domestic political dimension to the issue. Every one of the British governments which I served either aspired to join the European Community or was committed to making a success of our membership. And yet each of the two main parties which formed these governments was at various times split on European decisions (perhaps fortunately not at the same time), and the havoc that was wrought within them as they sought to grapple with those decisions is not yet by any manner of means spent. So a view of what this all looked like from the inside could be a useful corrective to some of the polemics which abound when European questions are discussed.

The UN is quite different, suffering more from attention deficit disorder than from the excess of ill-tempered attention that the EU attracts. But, as a rapidly changing world moves away from the bipolar realities of the Cold War and from the brief unipolar moment of US domination which followed it towards a more multipolar configuration, there needs, I believe, to be a better understanding of what the UN and other global multilateral organisations such as the IMF and the WTO are capable of and what we cannot reasonably expect of them; and that in turn requires a better understanding of how they coped with the post-Cold War world and of their capacity for adaptation and reform, both of which issues fall within the scope of the career covered by this memoir. Over the period ahead the choice between an increasingly rules-based international community and new world disorder will be posed again and again, by events as much as by conscious design; and it would surely be better if the responses were based on a better understanding of the recent past.

✳   ✳   ✳

Well, that is a view from one end of the half century. What about the view from the other end of it? I have to confess that I have no clear recollection and no record of precisely how and when the idea took root in my mind that I should aim for a diplomatic career. Somewhere along the spectrum of my last year or two at school (Winchester), my period of national service (mainly in Germany) and my university years at Oxford it became the clear focus of my ambitions. A passionate interest in the study of history certainly helped; and my choice at Oxford as my special subject of the diplomatic history leading up to the outbreak of the First World War for the first time brought me into contact with diplomatic material – telegrams, despatches and so on – although only at a most rarefied level and in a context far removed from the world of the 1950s in which my decision was made. So too did my fascination, fed by my New College tutor, Raymond Carr, with the events of the Spanish Civil War. But of diplomacy in practice I knew precisely nothing when I succeeded in the Foreign Office exam in the early summer of 1959. My parents knew no diplomats and nor did I; I had never, despite having travelled reasonably widely around Europe (to Germany, France, Italy, Spain and Greece), visited a British Embassy or a consulate. So it really was a leap in the dark when I presented myself in August of that year for the three-week introductory course which all new entrants at the that stage underwent. Nor was I much the wiser at the end of that course, since the Foreign Office in those days had not progressed far along the road of training and the inculcation of professional skills. I do remember a lecture by Harold Nicolson but that was of greater cultural than professional interest. It was on that blank sheet that the Foreign Office in its wisdom, and without paying any noticeable attention to my own wishes – I had actually volunteered to learn Arabic – inscribed the decision that I should study Persian for an academic year at the School of Oriental and African Studies in London, then going on to spend nearly a year as a language student in Tehran and finally ending up in my first proper diplomatic post, one with the fascinatingly anachronistic title of Oriental Secretary, in Kabul in the late spring of 1961.

1

IRAN 1960–1961

The drive from London to Tehran in the high summer of 1960 was a long, hot and hard one, but fascinating. We (I was accompanied for the journey to Tehran by a New College friend, Ian White-Thomson) had given ourselves a month to complete the trip, which left time for a week in Istanbul, a few days in Trabzon in eastern Turkey and some flexibility to allow for incidents or accidents along the way (there was in fact only one, when I clipped the wing of a taxi in Istanbul, detaching a mass of gaudy ornaments but doing no damage to my Land Rover which was made of sterner stuff). Nowadays a newly posted diplomat almost invariably arrives by air in the capital city of the country to which he is going and is plunged immediately into the routine of embassy work. I never regretted the more leisurely, but also much more educative, route by which I reached Tehran (and subsequently, the following year, Kabul also). It gave me some feel for the region and the countries where I was to spend the next three years. And that region was not, as it would now tend to be called, the wider Middle East, but rather Central Asia, which is historically and topographically much more apt.

We crossed Europe at a great pace, since we had to do a longish detour through Yugoslavia and Greece to reach Istanbul (the Foreign Office at that time did not allow its diplomats to go the more direct route through Iron Curtain countries like Bulgaria). But once we reached Istanbul we had some opportunity to explore what seemed to me at the time, and has seemed even more so ever since, one of the world's great cities, beautiful, picturesque and steeped in a complex history. It was of course a much smaller city then than the huge, sprawling megalopolis it has now become; there were no bridges across the Bosporus and one had to take one of the car ferries which criss-crossed the border between Europe and Asia at all hours of the day and night. It was in Edirne and Istanbul that I first came into contact with the mosques of the great Ottoman architect, Sinan; and thus laid the foundations of a lifelong passionate admiration of Islamic architecture, which was only strengthened as I moved further east and saw the great religious buildings of Iran, Afghanistan and north India. It was here too that the first, modest dents were inflicted on my hitherto totally Eurocentric historical world view; and I began to understand that there was a great deal more to the history and societies of these countries than their interaction with the dominant modern era world powers in Western Europe and North America, important though that interaction had been and still was to the way they conducted their affairs.

From Istanbul we passed as quickly as we could through Ankara, which seemed a graceless, rather lifeless modern city set in a singularly unappealing, tree-less Anatolian landscape (a poor impression which, I fear, no number of subsequent visits – frequent during the much later period when I was dealing with Cyprus – has done much to modify); passed along Turkey's Black Sea coast from Samsun to Trabzon; and then climbed up steep passes, to reach for the first time the Central Asian highland plateaus across which the rest of our journey took us. Passing Mount Ararat on our left, we eventually reached and crossed without incident the Iranian border.

I had done my best, during the academic year I had spent at the School of Oriental and African Studies studying Persian, to read widely on Iran's history and to read too the numerous travel books about the country, outstanding amongst them Robert Byron's *Road to Oxiana*. But no amount of reading can prepare you for the visual impact of a new country. The rough, unpaved road which sloped gradually down from the frontier watershed towards the city of Tabriz, and then on for hundreds more kilometres to Qazvin and Tehran, took us across a typical Iranian landscape, huge vistas of tawny-coloured plains, backed by bluish-grey mountain ranges; here and there a green blotch marking the site of a village, with in every case the otherwise featureless desert dotted with the lines of the air-holes of underground water channels, known as qanats, which brought water from the often quite-distant mountains to the small cultivated areas around the villages. The villages were poor, no signs of electricity; but at each end of every village, standing a little forlorn on dusty roundabouts, there would be a gold-painted plaster statue of the present Shah, Mohammad Reza Pahlavi, and at the other end of the village a similar statue of his father, the founder of the dynasty Reza Shah Pahlavi. The political statement was clear and unmistakable.

By this stage we were pressed for time if we were to arrive in Tehran by the date we had provided in advance and to avoid an embarrassing search for our whereabouts. But we did manage a small detour, to the dusty, run-down little village of Soltanieh, once, in the fourteenth century, the capital of the Il-Khan Mongol dynasty, (descended from Genghis Khan) from which a huge empire, stretching across Central Asia, was ruled. Now not a trace of that capital city was left apart from the Mausoleum of Oljeitu (the ruler who built it), a truly staggeringly beautiful building despite its advanced state of decrepitude. There it stood, a colossal egg-shaped, pale blue dome mounted on an octagonal base, with the remains of eight slender minarets, now truncated and resembling broken teeth, surrounding the dome – egg-shaped in the sense that it was more pointed than was normally the case in other great domes of that period but also resembling a cracked egg, with parts of the dome having collapsed and leaving gaps open to the sky and huge fissures threatening further dilapidation. Inside the mausoleum, whose dome soared more than 170 feet over our head, the floor was littered with broken tiles and other masonry. No building I had ever seen more merited the motto of Sir Christopher Wren's great cathedral 'si monumentum requiris, circumspice'. But it was also a reminder that between those two great Mongol destroyers of the world, Genghis and Tamerlane, came men of taste and culture.

A day later we drove, hot, dirty and exhausted, into the British Embassy's town compound in Tehran. This monument to an earlier age seemed like paradise. Huge, soaring oriental plane trees shaded well-tended gardens; in the centre was a large pool of translucent, greenish cool water fed directly from the mountains behind Tehran by underground channels, which served the dual purpose of irrigating the gardens and providing a swimming pool for those who worked there. Dotted around the compound were various offices and the houses of embassy staff. To one side stood the imposing cupola of the Ambassador's residence and a rather odd, stumpy campanile whose purpose I never did fathom. The residence (damaged by an invading mob in 2011) was a monument in its own right, its entrance hall bedecked with oriental-style mirror work (a reminder it had originally been designed by Indian Ministry of Works architects in the nineteenth century), its dining room containing a metal plaque detailing the seating plan for the dinner Winston Churchill had hosted there for Franklin Roosevelt and Joseph Stalin during the wartime Tehran conference in November 1943. It was all very grand; and just a bit out of tune with the spirit of the times and Britain's relative place in the world of 1960. But that was not my first reaction as we relaxed that evening, showered and well supplied with cold drinks, at an embassy party.

The Iran of 1960 was the Shah's Iran, and the Iranian government was, effectively, the Shah. The press was muzzled and even the mildest criticism of the regime was discouraged. Political opposition, insofar as it existed at all, was of a mild, carefully sanctioned variety, stage-managed by the authorities. The security police (Savak) were omnipresent. The disparity between rich and poor, although less than it was subsequently to become following the quadrupling of the oil price in 1973, was glaring. The great aristocratic landowners (many of whom regarded the Shah and his family as upstarts, although they were careful where and to whom they said that) possessed huge tracts of the fairly sparse cultivable land and many villages scattered around the huge country; corruption at every level of society was prevalent. Tehran, the most recent of Iran's several capital cities (Isfahan and Shiraz and other cities having been favoured by earlier dynasties) was already a vast, sprawling Third World city stretching for many miles along the foot of the Elburz mountains, whose 14,000 foot peaks (still in those days visible from anywhere in the city and not, as now, obscured by smog), towered over it to the north. The city was on a kind of slanted platform, the higher edge of which, right under the mountains, was more than 1,000 feet higher than the lower edge some 10 or 15 kilometres to the south. The city had no natural limits and was steadily creeping out into the desert which stretched away towards the south, towards the holy city of Qom and Isfahan. The rich and influential lived in the northern suburbs, as close as they could get to the mountains, where the air was cooler and the water more plenteous. The commercial centre of the city, the university (which was almost the only centre of open opposition to the Shah's rule) and the extensive bazaar came further down the hill, and beyond and below that came the teeming shanty-towns of the poor. It was a bit like a layer cake; it was not a recipe for social cohesion.

Britain's relationship with the Shah's Iran at that time was, on the surface, excellent. We were military allies in CENTO; through the Consortium, which had taken the place of the old Anglo-Iranian Oil Company following the fall of Mossadeq, BP continued to play an important role in Iran's one key industry, the production of oil, on which the whole economy crucially depended; we were an important commercial partner. But beneath that smooth surface there were plenty of cross-currents. No Iranian, and certainly not the Shah himself, had forgotten our manipulative role during the period of Iran's turmoil and weakness in the late nineteenth and early twentieth century, when we had played off one faction against another and, at first in competition and then in concert with Tsarist Russia, had actually divided the country up into spheres of influence. Nor had they forgotten that, in 1941, when Hitler invaded the Soviet Union, we had together occupied the country in order to secure it as a supply route for the Western allies to the Soviet Union, and had packed the abdicated Reza Shah off to exile in South Africa where he died. So although, subsequently, we and the Americans had helped the Shah to resist Stalin's post-war attempts to set up independent communist-dominated statelets in Azerbaijan and in Kurdistan, and although we had saved his bacon in August 1953 when we had encouraged General Zahedi's military coup which overthrew the elected government of Mohammad Mossadeq and enabled the Shah to return from brief exile, there was always a lack of trust there, the feeling that we could be up to our old tricks again, that our commitment to him and his regime might be less than total.

My own role in the nine months I was to spend in Iran had little to do with such high politics and everything to do with learning the language and familiarising myself with the country and its culture, the expectation, in fact never realised, being that I would return to the Embassy in Tehran some time after my first Persian-speaking posting in Kabul. The first stage of the process was to spend two months on my own in a provincial city where there would be almost no foreigners to distract me from total immersion in speaking the language. The city chosen for me was Mashhad, the capital of the province of Khorasan, in the extreme north-east of the country, sandwiched next door to the Soviet Union (since metamorphosed into Turkmenistan) and to Afghanistan; and it did indeed fulfil the desired criteria since there was, to the best of my knowledge, only one British family there, the British Council representative, who lent me a room in which to work. So, two weeks after arriving in Tehran, I set off for Mashhad by the more picturesque northern route which took one close to the Soviet frontier; on then through one of the very few patches of forest remaining in Iran, stopping off briefly at a small town, Bujnurd, inhabited by Kurds who had been settled there by Shah Abbas in the seventeenth century to hold off Turkomen marauders; and finally to Mashhad. Mashhad, like most Iranian cities, was steeped in history, having been, along with Samarqand, Bokhara and Herat, one of the chief urban centres of the Timurid empire; having also briefly in the eighteenth century been the capital of Iran during the reign of Nadir Shah, who looted the Peacock Throne from Delhi. For centuries it had been an important place of pilgrimage for Shi'a Muslims who came to worship at the shrine of the Imam Reza, the eighth Shi'a Imam, said to have been poisoned by the Arab Caliph Harun Al Rashid with a bunch of grapes. Now a city which had once been a hub along the Silk Road and then, in the late nineteenth and early twentieth centuries, a focus for the 'Great Game' between Tsarist Russian and Indian-based British representatives, lay isolated, close to two frontiers across which virtually no trade or other movements occurred, and dependent almost entirely on the pilgrim traffic.

Not much of the old Mashhad remained, but what little did – the golden domed shrine of the Imam Reza and, alongside it, the mausoleum of Gauhar Shad, the wife of Tamerlane's son Shah Rokh, with its elegant blue and green tiled dome, both embedded in a rabbit-warren of covered bazaars (since destroyed) – was both beautiful and picturesque. The second, but not the first, of those adjectives could have been applied to the British Council compound, where I studied. Formerly the base for the British Consul-General, from where were directed some of the complex intrigues of the Great Game it had once housed a squadron of Indian Cavalry. Now little remained other than an ornate but crumbling gatehouse and the Consul-General's residence, which was the British Council's cultural centre. I was lodged at first in a seedy hotel, and then, not without some difficult negotiation, in the house of a civil engineer in the bazaar quarter of the city. My two most regular interlocutors were my landlord and my teacher of Persian, but I gradually came to meet a number of their friends particularly on the evening strolls around the one dusty little park or out at the Coca-Cola bottling plant which had recently been built and had instantly become the main focus of Mashhad's social life – the inhabitants of Mashhad being as addicted to the Paseo as those of Madrid. But I also used to slip away most days to the covered bazaar around the shrine where the jewellers who set turquoises (much of the world's supply came from a medieval mine of the semi-precious stone near Nishapur, an hour or more drive west of Mashhad), and the carpet merchants, and the sellers of resplendent (if rather smelly) embroidered sheepskin coats seemed only too happy to engage in endless conversation. The bazaar around the shrine was also the only place from which a non-Muslim could see into the shrine, the shrine itself being off-limits. So I had to be satisfied with tantalising glimpses of the courtyards thronged with pilgrims, and the domes, seen from the back window of a stall in the bazaar.

Those two months in Mashhad left me with a number of impressions. The first was that the loyalty to the Shah's regime of the middle class, to which my two chief daily interlocutors and their friends belonged, was skin-deep at best – and yet these were the people who had probably benefitted the most from the relative stability and prosperity of those last few years. While I was in Mashhad the Shah's first son was born, thus, at least in his eyes and in those of his supporters, assuring the future of the dynasty by providing the male heir which two previous marriages had failed to do; and thus too a cause for rejoicing. But most of the talk I heard was about the decision for the baby to be delivered in a public hospital, which the Shah and his wife had no doubt intended to show a popular touch. Of course it had to be a boy this time, so having the birth in a public hospital made it easier to switch if it turned out to be a girl, went the whispered rumours. My second impression was less well formed than the first and consisted of a feeling that the impact of the West, its technology and its culture, was putting some heavy strains on Iran's traditional society. It seemed to me that many features of modern Western society as well as its values and institutions, our democracy and our respect for human rights which had taken us centuries and much strife to evolve, were being thrust at people who had had little preparation for them and whose basic culture provided little space or support for them. Yet I had no inkling that these strains might erupt at a later stage into a revolutionary religious uprising. Like many of my generation I suppose I simply could not envisage a situation in which religion made a major come-back into politics. The third impression was the extraordinary prevalence of the fantasy that Britain still pulled the strings worldwide, and most particularly in Iran – a myth which I did not again come across in such a virulent form until I became a frequent visitor to Cyprus in the late 1990s. I can remember arguing with my teacher in Mashhad that he had quite misunderstood the real balance of power in the modern world where the United States was now the overwhelmingly dominant force; to which he responded knowingly that all Iranians knew who really controlled US policy in Iran; at which point I gave up.

❊　　❊　　❊

Back in Tehran after my two months in Mashhad, although I had no formal function in the Embassy apart from doing some part-time work in the Chancery and translating some intelligence reports handed over to us by the Iranians about the Soviet penetration of Afghanistan, I was invited to join the weekly meeting of the Embassy's Persian speakers at which we pooled our information and discussed the trends that had been noted. At that time the Shah had not yet forced us to drop all our contacts with the opposition, as he was to do later under pain of Britain being cut off from profitable contracts. So our collective range of contacts was reasonably wide. I found my impressions were widely shared. The general view was that the Shah's regime was fragile; and that a political, economic or social shock could well bring it tumbling down. That view was not shared or welcomed by the Ambassador and other senior non-Persian speakers, and this created a good deal of tension over the Embassy's political reporting. However, all agreed that the Iranian tendency to attribute almost supernatural influence to Britain's policies in Iran was irremediable. This tendency was perfectly illustrated when from time to time there were stage-managed elections to parliament. Despite the fact that both government and opposition candidates were carefully chosen by the regime and vetted by Savak, these same candidates would one by one form up at the Embassy to ask for Britain's support. Invariably assured that we did not do that sort of thing any more, they would smile and say they knew we had to say that. Then, once elected, the successful candidates would appear to thank us for our support.

The remaining months of language study were interspersed with more travels around the country. Language students were encouraged to take two weeks to go to some remote area, thus improving the Embassy's geographical coverage, on the sole condition that we travel by public transport. So I set off by bus to the far south-east, tracing the southern edge of the huge central desert, through the architecturally and historically fascinating cities of Yazd (where a small Zoroastrian community still existed) and Kerman; then from Kerman my route went due south by a barely discernible road to Bandar Abbas, 24 hours of bone-jolting agony through largely empty, featureless country. Bandar Abbas was on the Gulf coast, at the Strait of Hormuz, the choke-point at its entry. This former trading post by now consisted of no more than a single row of dilapidated fishermen's houses; but a customs motor boat was made available to reach the island of Hormuz and the ruins of the Portuguese fortress which had briefly been the centre of Portugal's control of the area in the sixteenth century. Then an even more demanding journey, squashed in the cab of a rickety lorry, back from Bandar Abbas to Shiraz by a route which certainly could not be described as a road, if only judged by the number of times the driver lost his way. This was a journey which reminded me of the huge scale of Iran as a country, of its emptiness, and of the abject poverty that prevailed once one moved away from the bright lights of Tehran and the main cities; it also conveyed the faint rumbling of discontent among the mainly Baluch population of the south-east, who had their own language, were Sunni, not Shi'a, and felt closer kinship to their ethnic compatriots in Pakistan than to the Iranian state.

The Iranian New Year, which falls on the spring equinox, and which is a wonderful, ten day holiday full of pre-Islamic rituals, I spent with a friend from the Iranian Foreign Ministry, Yusuf Akbar, at his father's home in Rasht near the Caspian coast beyond the mountains that closed Tehran in from the north. There we explored the marshes along the coast that harboured the sturgeon fishery, the source of Iran's valuable caviar production. Yusuf's father was from a prominent local family. He recounted that in the past he would always be invited to the palace when he visited Tehran, to give the Shah a frank briefing on the state of opinion and grievances in the provinces along the Caspian coast; but those calls had now ceased, another sign of the increasing gap between the autocratic ruler and his subjects.

And then in the spring of 1961 the Queen and Prince Philip came on their first state visit to Iran. Part of this visit was to include a trip to Persepolis, the former capital of the Achaemenid Empire a few miles from Shiraz; and, as the only pair of hands who could be spared from the Embassy at that point, I was despatched to ensure that the preparations there were in good order. I am not sure that I contributed much; the local governor was tough and competent, if corrupt; his job security depended on there being no hitches; so everything passed off smoothly. There was one thing neither the governor nor I could do anything about: the weather was appalling. A gale was blowing the gritty sand of the Iranian plateau across the palace platform at Persepolis, freezing the Iranian courtiers in their Paris fashions and making the great pillars of the Apadana audience chamber look more like the ruined chimneys of some post-industrial landscape than the spectacular centre of one of the great empires of the ancient world. Still, a political point, to which the Shah attached an unrealistic degree of importance, had been made, that of the supposed continuity (and grandeur) of the Iranian monarchy; this in the teeth of the historical record which showed not continuity but rather a succession of dynasties each taking power from its predecessor by the use of force, as indeed the Shah's own father had done.

I had arrived in Iran a bachelor, but we left for Kabul a married couple, which I am delighted to say we still are some 50 years later. My future wife, Gillian, had been working in the embassy for a year before I arrived. She was due to return to Britain in May 1961 and I to go in the opposite direction to Kabul. Instead we were married on a glorious early summer day in Tehran; and, after a honeymoon in East Jerusalem (still then under Jordanian control) and Beirut, we set off by road for Afghanistan. I did make one serious mistake on my wedding day; it was not that I got married, but that I took the last paper of the Foreign Office's Higher Persian exam on the same day. This piece of hubris was duly punished.

Looking back on my relatively short time in Iran I often pose to myself the question whether British policy towards Iran could or should have been different. Could we have averted the damage, short-term commercial and long-term geopolitical, that occurred when the Shah's regime collapsed in January 1979 and the present theocratic authoritarian regime took its place? This memoir makes clear that awareness of the basically brittle nature of the Shah's regime was no last minute surprise. But I would hesitate to assume that that knowledge, even if it had not been discounted by London, could have led to a useful alternative prescription for policy. I say this for two reasons. The first was that, even those of us who were most convinced of the fragility of the regime, were unable to put any reliable kind of time estimate on when the regime might be tested and found wanting; most of us would have opted for a time frame much shorter than the further 17 years which it in fact survived. And secondly we were all looking the wrong way when it came to gauging the main threat. We were looking at the rising middle class and the many thousands of Iranian students returning from overseas, sickened by the poor job prospects and the repressive regime, as presenting the main threat – and so too were the Shah and his security apparatus. The possibility of a grassroots, genuinely revolutionary, religion-driven movement being the principal threat did not dawn until late in the day. So we were concentrating on the Kerensky figures and not the Lenins. In any case I would be very cautious about any suggestion that the principal job of diplomats is to predict the future. That is a part of the job, but often even successful prediction does not help much in the day-to-day shaping of policy. After all, in the case in point, the French certainly made a better job than we did of prediction and may indeed have known about the Shah's cancer since he was being treated by French doctors. They even attempted to hedge the future by allowing the Ayatollah Khomeini to operate from a district of Paris. But that did them little good in the event, when their interests suffered just as severely as those of other Western countries. It has also become fashionable in recent years to treat the US/UK-supported coup that overthrew Mossadeq as being the original sin from which all else followed. Again this seems to me a very bold assumption. Mossadeq's hold on power was precarious even without the intervention of the army; and the risk of an unstable Iran being drawn into a Cold War confrontation cannot be discounted. More fundamentally, does it really make sense to attribute a truly volcanic upheaval of the sort which shook Iran in 1979 as having emerged from one, single event? I doubt it.

2

AFGHANISTAN 1961–1963

The road from Tehran to Kabul began with a long stretch to Mashhad where we stopped for a couple of nights to see old friends; then on across hundreds of kilometres of featureless, stony desert towards the Afghan frontier and Herat. In the middle of this unforgiving landscape, and with no other habitation in sight, we approached a pole across the road and beside it a battered trailer caravan containing a couple of Afghan frontier police. There then ensued an extremely tiresome and lengthy impasse with the Afghans when it transpired that, although Gillian had been vaccinated, she did not have an international certificate to that effect. One of the border guards proposed to vaccinate her with a rusty pen-nib, using vaccine of unknown date and provenance but which had been cooking in the blazing heat. This seemed an unattractive proposition, as did returning to Mashhad to have it done there. Eventually some money changed hands and we went on our way to Herat. It had not been a promising start.

Herat, like Mashhad, had been one of the principal cities of the Timurid Empire, a centre of the arts; it had remained an independent, if moribund, principality well into the nineteenth century, when, somewhat improbably it was successfully defended against an invasion by the Shah of Iran by Eldred Pottinger, an enterprising lieutenant in the British Indian Army doing a bit of semi-authorised freelancing; it then became part of Afghanistan, but a part culturally and ethnically closer to the contiguous Iranian provinces than to the rest of Afghanistan. All that had been a long time ago. But some of the vestiges of its former glory were still there to be seen, albeit most of them in an advanced state of decrepitude. We spent a couple of days at the Park Hotel, a misleadingly Westernised name for an establishment which had sheltered Robert Byron on his travels in the 1930s described in *Road to Oxiana*, and did not seem to have been much cleaned since then and offered as the sole item on the menu chicken necks and feet. Herat in the early summer was, however, a joy. Well watered by the Hari Rud, which descends from the Hindu Kush mountains and ends up in the deserts to the west of the city, it was full of poplar and plane trees, orchards and vegetable gardens. We visited the crumbling citadel in the centre of the city; the large, colourfully tiled Friday Mosque; and, best of all, the wonderful mausoleum built by Gauhar Shad, one of the few melon-shaped, ridged domes surviving (others are at Balkh in the north of Afghanistan, and over the tomb of Tamerlane in Samarqand); and we went up in the hills a mile or two outside the city to Gazar Gah, where the former rulers of Herat are buried, a shrine and still an active religious community whose leader, the Mir, received foreign travellers as they passed through.

From Herat onwards it was three days hard slog over execrable roads, south to Farah and Kandahar and then north-east to Ghazni and Kabul. This circuitous southern route, skirting the tangled mass of mountains in the centre of Afghanistan, was the only option, apart from an even more demanding northern loop, which was at that time blocked by flooding after the spring rains and the melting of the winter snow. So we gritted our teeth and bounced our way along in a cloud of dust. Somewhere between Kandahar and Ghazni, as we were passing a battered bus halted at the side of the road to change a wheel, a man suddenly broke away from the huddle of tribesmen who had been travelling on the bus and ran straight under our wheels; his head struck the bonnet of the Land Rover with a thud (leaving a large dent) and he was thrown several yards down the road where he lay inert. My heart sank. All the advice we had had was that in such circumstances you should drive straight on; otherwise things could become ugly. Such advice is easier given than taken, and so we stopped to see what could be done. To our astonishment and relief the tribesman was staggering, dazed, to his feet (having apparently been saved from serious injury by his turban which had taken the main force of the blow to his head); and his fellow passengers were busy telling him what a fool he had been to have run out from behind the bus without looking. We took him on to the next teahouse, plied him with scalding tea, and went on our way deeply relieved.

*   *   *

To arrive in Afghanistan in 1961 was almost like coming to a lost world. This land which had so often in the past been a historical crossroads – when Alexander the Great used it as his route to the Indian subcontinent, when Buddhist pilgrims from China had passed through in their thousands on their way to visit the sites in India where the Buddha had preached, leaving behind the two colossal rock-hewn statues at Bamian, when the Silk Route crossed the north of the country – was now a road to nowhere which virtually no one was taking, or so it seemed at the time. For all the similarity to Iran in its look and feel and sound, it was a very different country, more mountainous, much poorer and with few material resources yet found or exploited. It had no sources of convertible currency apart from lapis lazuli, dried fruit, tribal rugs and the skins of unborn lambs. It had barely been touched by the twentieth century. No international airlines stopped there. The length of tarmac road could be measured in less than three figures. Even the capital had no hotels and no restaurants. Some of this isolation and appearance of backwardness was in reality a blessing. Opium poppies were not yet the main cash crop. While the poverty of Afghan villages was real and often cruel, with low life expectancy and high illiteracy, the mendicancy so evident in India and Pakistan was alien to the Afghans who were proud of their ability to survive; and the urban slums, so marked a feature of Iranian cities, barely existed in Afghanistan's few and much smaller centres of population. The extremes of wealth and poverty, so evident in Iran, did not exist to the same extent in Afghanistan; and even the small ruling class did not flaunt its power and relatively greater prosperity. Above all a country which had in the past suffered much from the meddling of its neighbours seemed somehow to be escaping the pressures of Cold War diplomacy and to be secure and respected in its non-alignment with the two great power blocks.

The Afghan body politic was a good deal less benign, but it did not have the same fragile feel I had detected in Iran. There had been a major upheaval in 1927 when the then king, Amanullah, had been chased into exile by a loose combination of conservative forces which resented his programme of modernisation (to some extent modelled on those of Ataturk and Reza Shah in Turkey and Iran respectively) and in particular his decision to allow women to appear unveiled in public. After an anarchical interregnum a new dynasty had seized power in 1929 and had ruled without serious challenge since then. The king himself, Zahir Shah, was little more than a figurehead, respected, but not the source of day-to-day government decisions. Since Zahir Shah came to the throne following his father's assassination in 1933, power had been first in the hands of two of his uncles and then, since 1953, of two brothers Prince Daud and Prince Naim who were first cousins of the king and also each married to one of his sisters. Daud, who was Prime Minister, was the dominant figure, his shaven, bullet-shaped head giving him a rather uncanny resemblance to Mussolini; while Naim, an altogether more suave figure, looked after foreign policy. The regime was autocratic and secretive; and it could be brutal. There was not even the pretence of a free press, and any form of political activity was forbidden. The huge, sprawling royal family, which was effectively an amalgamation of the previous, exiled king's relatives and those of the new dynasty, occupied many of the top ministerial and civil service jobs and was well entrenched in the armed forces. In that respect Afghanistan was more like Saudi Arabia than Iran. One of my jobs at the Embassy was to keep up to date the genealogical tree of this network since it was one of the ways of understanding what passed for politics in Afghanistan. Once a week King Zahir Shah held an audience at the Palace for all those even remotely connected to the family, and this was an occasion for much intrigue that it was extremely difficult for outsiders to comprehend or to penetrate.

By the time of our arrival in Afghanistan, Daud had already taken two far-reaching and fateful decisions. His uncles, who had held power for the preceding two decades, had continued the traditional Afghan policy of keeping in with both of Afghanistan's key neighbours, the Soviet Union and the ruling power in the Indian subcontinent (Britain until India and Pakistan gained their separate independence in 1947), playing them off against each other and relying on a mix of the two to equip and to train the Afghan armed forces. This was an astute policy if not a very efficient one so far as the armed forces were concerned. Daud, who was in some respects a moderniser, changed all that, and negotiated a series of agreements with the Soviet Union which resulted in both the Afghan army and the air force being solely armed with Soviet equipment and being solely trained either in the Soviet Union or by Soviet instructors. Two Soviet-built air-bases came with this deal, one at Bagram, just north of Kabul, and one at Shindand, south of Herat. Since the Afghans had no means of paying for all this, it was at least partly financed by maintaining a totally fictitious (and very favourable to the Afghans) exchange rate between the rouble and the afghani. All of this meant that Afghanistan's foreign policy non-alignment was more apparent than real, and that its potential vulnerability to any shifts in Soviet policy was profound. Daud's second decision was, if anything, even more reckless. He set about fomenting an insurgency in Pakistan's North-West Frontier Province whose population of Pashtun-speaking tribes straddled the Afghan-Pakistan frontier known as the Durand Line (after its British imperial progenitor) which had in any case never been recognised by Afghanistan. This Pashtunistan campaign, as it was invariably called in Kabul's state-controlled media, was promoted by Daud into Afghanistan's national cause to which all else was subordinated. It was enthusiastically supported, both rhetorically and with equipment, by the Soviet Union, which was only too pleased to see a Western ally, Pakistan, undermined and harassed. It ensured the worst possible relationship between Afghanistan and Pakistan, thus destroying the balance between Afghanistan's northern and southern neighbours which previous rulers of Afghanistan had striven so hard to maintain. And it had one other great fault. The Pashtunistan, which Afghanistan wished to see as an independent sovereign state seceding from Pakistan, would not have included the Pashtun tribes of Afghanistan. It only included those living in Pakistan, as well, rather oddly, as the Baluchis, who were not Pashtuns at all but whose agitation for autonomy or independence it suited the Afghans opportunistically to support. Why Afghan Pashtuns would not also wish to be a part of such an independent Pashtunistan was a question that was never allowed to be posed, let alone to be answered.

Britain's own relationship with Afghanistan had been nothing if not fraught, three wars having been fought between the two sides during the last century or so (although the third one, in 1919, hardly qualified for such a grand title, amounting as it did to little more than a few skirmishes along the Durand Line and resulting in British agreement that Afghanistan could conduct its own foreign policy and not remain in tutelage to the Viceroy in Delhi). The first two wars had been the occasion of a number of military disasters for the British side and the fundamental discrediting of what was called the 'forward' policy of direct British involvement in the governance of Afghanistan. As a result, the indirect approach to keeping the Russians out of Afghanistan, which was at every stage the British strategic objective, had been pursued in preference, that is to say promoting and supporting the emergence of an effective Afghan ruler who would keep Tsarist Russia (and subsequently the Soviet Union) at arm's-length. This indirect approach had been pursued consistently and effectively from the end of the Second Afghan War in 1880, when the Amir Abd al-Rahman emerged as an effective ruler on this model, until Britain withdrew from the Indian subcontinent in 1947. At that point Afghanistan simply disappeared off Britain's diplomatic radar altogether. I had some inkling of this void when trying, before I set out for Tehran in 1960, to locate and to consult whoever in London was responsible for relations with Afghanistan. This proved to be no easy task, complicated as it was by the division of responsibility between the then entirely separate Foreign and Commonwealth Offices. The Eastern Department of the Foreign Office, to which I had gone to talk about Iran, had no such responsibility; nor had the Commonwealth Office, which was, however, determined to ensure that Pakistan's views on Afghanistan (invariably hostile for the reasons stated above) should predominate in the formulation of British policy toward that country. Finally I ran to earth a desk officer in the Foreign Office's South East Asia Department (whose nearest geographical responsibilities to Afghanistan were Nepal, Burma and Thailand) who admitted that Afghanistan was a very small part of his job. So I had set off to my first diplomatic post with no exaggerated expectations of being close to the heart of Britain's diplomacy; and it did not come as much of a surprise when I got to Kabul to find that our reporting from there and any suggestions we might make for strengthening our relations with Afghanistan seemed to be being despatched into a vacuum.

✳   ✳   ✳

Soon after arriving in Kabul I had to perform an annual ritual which only the Oriental Secretary, as the sole Persian-speaker on the staff, could do, namely to stand just below the dais from which the Afghan Prime Minister would propose a toast (in fruit juice, of course, alcohol being banned on official occasions in Afghanistan) to the Queen on her official birthday and my Ambassador would reciprocate with a toast to the King of Afghanistan. My task was to translate the first into English and the second into Persian, not too demanding since the few words were carefully scripted in advance. The occasion took place on the lawn behind the Ambassador's residence. Scattered around the garden were the great and the good of Afghanistan, a cross-section of the Diplomatic Corps and the tiny British community including a few school teachers provided by the British Council to one of Kabul's four secondary schools (the other three being supported respectively by the French, the Germans and the Americans, while the Soviet Union subsidised the polytechnic institute). It was a perfect June day, not too hot since at 6,000 feet above sea level Kabul seldom got uncomfortably hot and the temperature always dropped sharply at night. In front of the dais stretched the lawns and terraces of the Embassy gardens traversed by irrigation channels fed from the neighbouring mountains. Beyond the gardens began the extensive plain north of Kabul, which was planted with vines, pomegranates, pistachios and mulberries; and beyond that, in the distance the sun glinted on the snow-covered peaks of the Hindu Kush. To the left and also in the distance could be seen the tips of the Paghman mountains, closer than the Hindu Kush and not so high, but providing in their foothills, and only a few miles from Kabul, a variety of green valleys fed by sparkling streams ideal for picnicking. Behind the dais towered the stucco-covered, neo-Palladian edifice of the Ambassador's residence, a splendid relic of the imperial era. However, it was not quite all it seemed to be. When it was first built in the 1920s the money had run out and as a result the second floor which had been designed for the house was never built; rather oddly the monumental internal staircase continued on up beyond the first floor but then came to a halt at the roof. Moreover, it did not belong to the British government, the Embassy in Kabul, like the consulates in eastern Iran and diplomatic posts in Nepal and Kuwait, having been the property of the (British) Government of India. After partition these properties were handed over to the governments of India and Pakistan where these two could agree on a division of the spoils; where they could not – and Kabul was one such instance – we stayed put (this temporary hiatus lasted in Kabul for 45 years and within a short time of the embassy being handed over to the Pakistanis in the early 1990s the residence was destroyed by the Kabul mob as a protest at the capture of Herat by the Taliban). So in that idyllic, if somewhat anachronistic, setting my two years in Kabul began.

A major part of my job was to travel widely around the country and to get some feel for developments and opinion in the provinces, many of which were cut off from Kabul for long periods of the year by climatic conditions and from none of which was it easy to reach the capital or vice versa. This was enjoyable but demanding, the roads being bad, the accommodation scanty and uncomfortable and the food dodgy. But the countryside was, almost invariably, spectacularly beautiful, with mountain scenery predominating, and valleys filled with poplar trees and orchards and rushing streams. The ethnic diversity was fascinating; Persian-speaking Tajiks in the north and north-east, Uzbeks and Turkmen in the north-west, Hazaras (descended from the Mongols, and Shi'a unlike most of the rest of the population who were Sunni) in the mountainous centre, and Pashtuns in the south. Diplomats were allowed to travel wherever they liked in most of the country, so long as they notified the Foreign Ministry in advance; and they travelled unescorted. A narrow strip along the long frontier with the Soviet Union was out of bounds at Soviet request; and the government discouraged visits to the Pashtun tribal areas in the south, since they did not want any foreigners prying into their activities there promoting the Pashtunistan campaign.

A duty visit to one of the remote parts of the country usually took ten days to a fortnight if one was not to spend most of the time on the road and was to have any chance of meeting a cross-section of the local government and notables. There was no alternative to driving yourself, since domestic air flights barely existed and were far from reliable or safe and buses were only for masochists. Our first major trip was to the extreme north-east of the country to the province of Badakhshan and its principal town Faizabad. The police chief there was the uncle of a friend of ours in Kabul (having been abroad for training by the Canadian police he had acquired some foreign habits, including a passion for playing bridge). He ensured we could travel freely, and we got as far as the bottom of the Wakhan corridor, the long panhandle which stretches hundreds of miles to the east of the rest of the country and which at its furthest point in the high Pamir mountains gives Afghanistan a frontier with China (this panhandle, while a geographical reality also had a political rationale having been designed, when Afghanistan's borders were first defined in the nineteenth century, to ensure that British India and Tsarist Russia at no point had a common border). The road finally petered out at Ishkashem, where one valley system ran up the Wakhan corridor and another led to the ancient, but still functioning, mine for lapis lazuli, from where much of the inlay of the Taj Mahal had come as well as the materials for Renaissance painting. It was there that we came across a sad, bedraggled caravan of some 50–60 refugees making their way down into Afghanistan. These, it turned out, were Uighur Turks from the Chinese province of Xinjiang, fleeing persecution by the Chinese authorities. So far as the Chinese were concerned they did not exist; and the Afghans were not keen to recognise their existence either since they had no desire to irritate a powerful, if remote, neighbour. So we never did find out what became of them.

Another journey took us to the north-west, through the provincial capital of Mazar-e-Sharif with its turquoise domed mosque and flocks of white doves, past Balkh, once one of the great cities on the Silk Route and still possessing a superb shrine with a melon-shaped dome, and on to Maimana, which was as close to the Soviet border as one was allowed to go and which had a mainly Uzbek and Turkmen population. This was a region where Soviet engineers had found gas deposits; and there was indeed a pipeline exporting gas to the Soviet Union. None of this provided much benefit to the Afghans, the area being too remote and on the wrong side of a formidable mountain range, and the proceeds going to pay down the arms purchases the government was making. The idea that this might be another Kuwait or Saudi Arabia did not survive a journey round an extremely poor, cut-off province whose population still depended more on selling the skins of unborn lambs.

Two long journeys with the Ambassador took us to the west. The first was to Herat through the tangled mass of mountains in the centre of the country known as the Hazarajat. The Hazaras were poor even by Afghan standards and made up much of the floating population of building labourers in Kabul; they were despised and discriminated against by other Afghans; but they were hospitable enough to visitors. We visited there the truly remarkable Minaret of Jam, built by the Ghorid dynasty, which had ruled an empire including most of north India in the twelfth century; one of the world's great architectural masterpieces (finer than its almost matching twin, the Qutb Minar in Delhi) it stood on the banks of a raging, mountain torrent without even a village, let alone a town anywhere near it. It is still unclear why or for what purpose it was built in this bizarre setting. The second western journey was down through Kandahar and the Helmand valley and across the stony desert that separates Afghanistan and Iran. Kandahar and the Helmand valley had been the focus of a major US aid programme in the 1950s but by this time it had all come to nought. Kandahar airport, with a runway capable of taking inter-continental jets, stood empty, its glittering modern terminal gathering dust; by the time it had been completed advances in aircraft technology had made an intermediate stop for flights going to India and the Far East unnecessary (it is now, at the time of writing, a major NATO military base). And the project to invigorate the valley of the Helmand and grow cotton there had turned into another white elephant, with salts being leached to the surface and damaging the crops (at that time you would have seen no opium poppies there). On the far side of the desert we went as far as the Iranian/Afghan border, which cut across a huge swamp formed by the lower waters of the Helmand River as they were swallowed up by the surrounding desert and never reached the sea. In the middle ages there had been a flourishing civilisation there, but Genghis Khan had put an end to that and all that remained were the ruins of great mud-brick forts, palaces and caravanserais.

And then for sheer pleasure we did much travelling closer to Kabul, camping near the great Buddhist statues at Bamian and fishing for trout in the sparkling river that flowed past them; visiting the azure mountain lakes at Band-e-Amir; camping too up the Panjshir valley, much later to become the centre of some of the most vicious fighting between the Soviet forces and the Mujaheddin.

What were the strongest impressions created by all these travels? The main one was the sheer tranquillity of it all, the complete absence of any feeling of being threatened or at risk as one travelled around, unescorted and unveiled. At that time the British press was filled with reporting on a peculiarly gruesome murder of a British family camping in the south of France; I can remember thinking how much safer one was in Afghanistan. There was great poverty, of course, but the Afghans seemed to bear their poverty stoically, as an invariable fact of life which had existed for hundreds of years. The ethnic diversity of Afghanistan was there for anyone to see but, apart from the ethnically diverse population of the area around Kabul, the different groups mainly kept to the regions they had inhabited for centuries. There were no obvious signs of tension between the different groups and certainly none leading to outbreaks of violence. Above all Afghanistan was quite evidently a real country, not simply an artificial political construct, of which its inhabitants were aware and proud. The regime was a tough, autocratic one, in many ways an unattractive one; but its writ did run from one end of the country to the other. All that is a far cry from the picture often painted now by superficial commentators.

*   *   *

Working in a country where what might be considered as normal domestic politics did not exist and such politics as there were lay well shielded from the prying gaze of outsiders, and a country so cut-off from events in the wider world and so isolated from global trends, life as a diplomat tended to be pretty uneventful. Three developments did stand out during the time I was there. The first was the decision by the government of Pakistan in September 1961, following the mutual breaking off of diplomatic relations between Afghanistan and Pakistan precipitated by increased Afghan activity on the Pashtunistan issue, to close their border with Afghanistan to all trade and traffic. Since a high proportion of Afghanistan's trade, as a landlocked country, traditionally passed through the Pakistani port of Karachi and through one of the two road crossings of their mutual border, one at the foot of the Khyber Pass and the other between Quetta and Kandahar, this decision had far-reaching consequences. Naturally there was a substantial increase in smuggling through the Pashtun tribal areas along the border. But the main effect was to make Afghanistan almost totally dependent on trade across its western and northern borders and to force it even further into the arms of the Soviet Union. Gradually trade adjusted to the higher costs and longer delivery times of the Soviet route (routes through Iran were impossibly arduous and expensive). The Afghan government was not noticeably deterred from its activities in the Pashtun tribal areas. So, while the Pakistan government had undoubtedly been much provoked, the action they took in closing the border was highly counter-productive and contrary to their own long-term interests. Sadly, Britain, Pakistan's ally in CENTO, was unwilling to bring this home to them, despite the urgings of those of us observing developments in Kabul. The second major development was the decision by the Soviet government to finance and construct the Salang Tunnel through the Hindu Kush. This not only, for the first time, provided an all-weather route between the north and the south of the country, but also cut many hours off the pre-existing route which had required a lengthy dog-leg detour. It clearly also had major strategic implications should the Soviet Union ever decide to get directly involved in Afghanistan. The enigma of the long-term direction of Soviet policy in Afghanistan (on which more below) remained unanswered at the time. But both these two developments sharply increased the potential for Soviet interference, as did the considerably later construction of a road-bridge across the Oxus River which formed the border between Afghanistan and the Soviet Union (now Uzbekistan). The third development, which came like a bolt from the blue, was the king's decision, in March 1963 to dismiss Daud and Naim and to call on a commoner technocrat, Mohammad Yusuf (previously Minister of Mines), who had no connection with the royal family, to take over as Prime Minister. This decision, which was seen at the time as an important step towards a more open and inclusive political system, turned out subsequently to be rather less far-reaching and significant than it had seemed, when the new constitution, promulgated in 1964, failed to legalise the formation of political parties or to provide for the establishment of any serious parliamentary control over the executive. It was a missed opportunity.

What then was the general view of diplomatic Kabul-watchers at that time as to the strategic objectives of the Soviet Union in Afghanistan? That it was a, if not *the*, key question over-hanging the future of Afghanistan was not seriously in doubt. The United States seemed to have lost interest in maintaining a serious position in the country. It did continue with a modest aid programme, although on a much smaller scale than in the 1950s. Nobody believed that a Soviet takeover of Afghanistan would provoke a fundamental, let alone a military, confrontation between the two superpowers. Afghanistan was not seen as an Asian Yugoslavia. No other Western country had any real influence in Afghanistan; and Pakistan, which could have inherited the balancing role that British India had played, was in baulk largely due to the Afghan government's actions and its own unwise policy response. There was certainly no military obstacle to a Soviet takeover. The Afghan armed forces made no pretence of being ready to defend their extremely long common frontier with the Soviet Union; all their efforts were directed towards the confrontation with Pakistan. But, despite all that, no one I met did believe the Soviet Union would move in. For one thing they seemed already to have a very satisfactory position. The Afghan government followed their lead pretty slavishly on foreign policy issues. The massive Soviet aid programme gave them access to every part of the country; and could be presented as a showcase for Soviet assistance to a non-aligned, Third World country. Their control over the equipment and training of the Afghan armed forces was an important trump card. Why then take on responsibility for 15 million or so of the poorest people in the world, Muslims with a long tradition of xenophobic reaction to foreign interference? The obvious answer to that question was assumed to be Afghanistan's real protection against a Soviet takeover. And so it was to be for some years to come. Why it ceased to be so remains a question on which historians have not yet thrown complete light.

Looking back on those two years in Kabul from a personal point of view, they were an idyllic time. A beautiful and fascinating country with an interesting history and a seemingly unexciting future; an eclectic but agreeable social life amongst a group of mainly foreign-educated Afghans; a diplomatic corps which bore more relation to that described in the picaresque short stories of Lawrence Durrell about life in post-war Belgrade than to that in more important centres of international diplomacy. Looking back there is no avoiding also a feeling of deep sadness at the appalling tragedies that have befallen Afghanistan over the last 40 years and a feeling that a people who deserved better have been miserably let down both by their own leaders and by those who have become involved in their affairs from outside. I would argue that Prince Daud bears a particularly heavy responsibility for what occurred. Not only was he the originator of two ultimately reckless and damaging policy decisions – the handing over of the equipment and training of the Afghan armed forces to the Soviet Union and the mounting of the Pashtunistan campaign – but he then added a third such decision when he took advantage of his cousin and brother-in-law the king's absence abroad in 1973 to mount a successful coup which left him as president of a new Afghan republic. This gratuitous act, which it is hard to attribute to anything other than frustrated personal ambition, removed from the Afghan political scene a public figure who was respected by all; and it destabilised Afghan politics, thus opening the way to Daud's own overthrow and death in the communist-led coup of 1978 and the many horrors that then followed. As to the outsiders, the Soviet role, whether or not they shared any responsibility for the communist coup, is a predominant one in Afghanistan's descent into chaos. As I have said, why they intervened as they did in 1979 remains something of a mystery which may gradually become clearer as time passes and more archive material becomes available. Other outsiders contributed; the West by over-equipping the Mujaheddin and being insufficiently cautious about whom they armed, the whole international community by turning its back on Afghanistan when the country subsided into anarchy and civil war following the withdrawal of Soviet troops and the collapse of the communist regime. All that produced an early example of the phenomenon of a failed state about which a good deal more will be written later in these memoirs.

3

LONDON 1963–1965

LEARNING THE ROPES

The move from Central Asia to the Foreign Office in London was something of a cultural shock, a move from the extreme periphery of Britain's foreign policy to the place where it was shaped. The fact that, when I went to work in the Foreign Office in the summer of 1963, some four years after joining the Diplomatic Service, it was the first day's work I had done there, reflected the still fairly amateurish approach taken at that time to training and work experience. Sending people out to the ends of the earth without the slightest idea of how foreign policy was formulated and directed at home was hardly the most professional way to mould careers. It was too close for comfort to the old, discredited pre-First World War system under which those who served abroad and those who served at home operated in water-tight compartments.

Nor was Britain's foreign policy in great shape. The aftershocks from the Suez crisis were still being felt, and the lessons from it had not yet been fully absorbed. More recently the collapse of the negotiations for Britain to join the European Community, following General de Gaulle's veto in January 1963, had left the government, at least temporarily, rudderless. A new Foreign Secretary 'Rab' Butler, had just, for the second time, been frustrated in his ambition to become Prime Minister and was clearly in the final stage of his political career. A general election was not far away, and the likelihood of its marking the end of a long period of Conservative government was evident. It was not a moment to expect either great initiatives or strong leadership.

The Foreign Office in which I went to work would have been more recognisable to those who served in it several decades earlier than to those who worked there a couple of decades later. The great Italianate building still retained something of its Palmerstonian grandeur. But it was shabby and run-down, a victim of planning blight, since the project was afoot to tear it down and replace it by a multi-storey, modern office block. Elderly messengers pushed trolleys of locked wooden boxes containing highly classified material around the corridors. Telegrams were circulated via a system of suction-operated pipes which would not have been out of place in a nineteenth century department store. The rooms were heated (if that was the right word) by smouldering coke fires. A faint smell of boiled cabbage percolated throughout the building from the canteen down in the basement. If Britain was about to experience Harold Wilson's white heat of technological revolution, it had certainly not yet touched the Foreign Office.

Not that I was too depressed by all this. Our minds were on other things, principally the arrival of our eldest son, born in my mother-in-law's flat in Exmouth, while I was, rather embarrassingly, marooned in a small dinghy in the Exe estuary unable to get back in time for the birth. The other great event of that autumn, the one which so many people still remember where they were when the news came through, was President Kennedy's assassination. We were unpacking our heavy luggage, just arrived back from Kabul, in our newly acquired flat overlooking the Regent's Canal in what was called Little Venice. The tragic impact of that event remains palpable, even nearly 50 years later, coming as it did so soon after the Cuban missile crisis had taken the world to the brink of a nuclear war and dissipating so many, no doubt excessive, hopes of a more promising future.

The job I took up in the Foreign Office was in the Eastern Department, at that time responsible for the region between Syria, Lebanon and Israel in the west and Afghanistan in the east. My own desk dealt for about three-quarters of the time with the business of the Central Treaty Organisation (CENTO) and for about the remaining quarter of it with Afghanistan. In those days the system was extraordinarily hierarchical. Above me came an Assistant Head and then the Head of my own department; then above that an Assistant Under-Secretary of State, a Deputy Under-Secretary of State and the Permanent Under-Secretary of State; and finally, in the stratosphere, the Ministers' offices. The saving grace of this potentially absurdly rigid set of arrangements was that the prevailing culture was to drive decision-making as far down the ladder as possible, with desk officers encouraged to take as much responsibility as they were willing to and with pretty well every proposal and idea starting at the desk level. My good fortune was to have as the Assistant Head of my department and the immediate supervisor of my work, Percy Cradock, later to become Ambassador to China and Margaret Thatcher's Diplomatic Adviser, who taught me all I ever learned about drafting documents clearly and in a compelling style and about how to survive in the Whitehall jungle; and to have as my Head of Department Willie Morris, later Ambassador to Egypt who was one of the service's outstanding and most subtly perceptive Arabists. Eastern Department was a wonderfully collegiate place, with everyone getting together for a quarter of an hour morning and afternoon over coffee and tea when one could escape from the stovepipe in which a desk officer existed and get a wider perspective.

✻   ✻   ✻

The work I did on Afghanistan was directed towards, at least in a modest way, filling that vacuum at the London end which had been so evident during my time in Kabul; and towards putting a little bit of substance into Britain's relationship with Afghanistan. There were some modest successes. The British Council opened an office in Kabul with a resident representative; in my experience the Council's ability to contribute to what is now called Britain's 'soft' power is unparalleled. We also began to provide the Afghan government with technical assistance, including advice on how to diversify the sale of their gas reserves away from total dependence on the Soviet market. Some aid was offered to help build a beet-sugar processing plant in the north of the country. A junior Foreign Office minister (Lord Walston) was persuaded to go on an official visit to Kabul, thus opening a first, tenuous dialogue with the Afghan government. In Afghanistan itself the process of modernisation and of very limited democratisation which had begun with the dismissal of Daud began to drift and stagnate, with the new constitution promulgated in October 1964 making no very marked progress and with any form of genuinely independent political activity still banned. The extension of Soviet influence continued, with the opening of the Salang Tunnel through the Hindu Kush in August 1964, a rather important landmark, although not yet a qualitative shift in that relationship. There seemed no reason to believe that Afghanistan could not continue to live in a kind of no-man's land created by the Cold War, which was moving into an intensive phase many thousands of miles to the east, in Vietnam.

My principal job, however, was to try to breathe some life into the comatose, not to say moribund, body of the Central Treaty Organisation. CENTO consisted of three regional members (Iran, Pakistan and Turkey), one non-regional member (Britain), and one observer which acted for all intents and purposes as a full member (the USA) – the USA's status being a function of problems in getting Congress to ratify the treaty founding the organisation rather than any lack of enthusiasm for its existence, for which it was largely responsible in the first place. The rationale for CENTO lay in the US policy of containment of what was still then thought of as the Sino-Soviet bloc. President Eisenhower's Secretary of State, John Foster Dulles, had pursued the idea of complementing the already existing NATO alliance in Europe with a string of further alliances, CENTO and SEATO (the South East Asian Treaty Organisation) around the southern borders of the bloc. The British government had eagerly supported that policy, motivated also by a desire to restore some of its influence in the Middle East which had been so severely shaken by the Suez crisis. But this latter objective, and indeed the basic viability of CENTO, had been badly undermined from the very outset of its existence when, in 1958, the only Arab regional member, Iraq, withdrew from the alliance following a coup in Baghdad and the overthrow of the monarchy.

The problems of CENTO went rather deeper than the early loss of one of its regional members, because each of the remaining regional members in their different ways contested the basic rationale of the alliance and had other purposes that were not shared or supported by the two non-regional powers. Thus Turkey, while a stalwart supporter of NATO, saw no added benefit to it from being also a member of another Cold War alliance and one which made no provision, as NATO did, for an integrated military command. Of far greater immediate interest to Turkey were the problems arising in Cyprus from the tensions between the Greek Cypriots and the Turkish Cypriots following the granting of independence to the island in 1960. But Turkish attempts to direct CENTO's attention to this problem by depicting President Makarios of Cyprus as a Soviet surrogate, were not acceptable to either Britain or the USA whose aim was to dampen down not to exacerbate tensions in the NATO alliance between Greece and Turkey. Iran for its part did not regard the principal purpose of CENTO to be defence against the Soviet threat. The Shah had no illusions about Iran's ability to withstand a Soviet military onslaught and pinned his faith more on an active diplomacy designed to avoid that eventuality which was hard to reconcile with membership of a robust Western security alliance. His main preoccupation, and the one to which he wished to direct CENTO's efforts, was preventing the spread of Arab nationalism, under either the leadership of President Nasser of Egypt or of the new rulers of Iraq, into the Gulf region which he regarded as Iran's backyard and over which he dearly wished to exercise a degree of control. Again neither Britain, which was still responsible for the external relations of many of the Arab Gulf states, nor the USA, whose relationship with Nasser was part of a delicate balancing act designed to avoid another Arab-Israel conflict, were prepared to see CENTO used in that way. As to Pakistan it was, as ever, completely obsessed by its vision of what it regarded as the threat to its existence from India and considered any alliance that did not address that threat as virtually worthless. Moreover, it was just beginning to develop, under the aegis of President Ayub's brilliant and imaginative young Foreign Minister, Zulfiqar Ali Bhutto, a relationship with China which cut right across the Cold War rationale of CENTO and which was gradually to become the sole fixed point in each successive Pakistani government's foreign policy. Neither Britain nor the USA was willing to see CENTO used against India and neither at that stage approved of any rapprochement with China.

Such then was the remarkably dysfunctional state of the alliance which confronted me on arrival at the CENTO desk; and it did not change noticeably during the two years I was there, these strategic fault lines not being the sort of thing which a lowly desk officer could hope to put to rights. Any discussion of policy in a CENTO forum tended to bring these tensions out into the open and so was better avoided to the degree that this was possible. The best form of displacement activity was to concentrate on the alliance's programme of aid and technical cooperation which was designed to strengthen the regional members' capacity to resist Soviet subversion and to build up their defences. These included projects such as the building of a rail-link between Iran and Turkey and the construction by Britain of a string of radar stations across the north of Iran to provide advance warning of a Soviet attack. But even these activities were not free of tension. The Iranians did not really want radar stations in the north of their country to warn of a Soviet attack; they wanted them in the south to warn of an attack from their Arab neighbours. And no amount of tinkering with economic cooperation could conceal the fact that this was an alliance which had no teeth, since no military forces were committed specifically to it and it had no command structure.

One occasion when the tensions invariably surfaced was at the annual ministerial Council meeting which rotated between the capitals of the members. The first of the two I attended was in Washington in the early summer of 1964, the British delegation being led by the Foreign Secretary, Rab Butler. This was Bhutto's debut as Pakistani Foreign Minister and he certainly put on a bravura performance for the occasion, regaling the assembled company with a lengthy but scintillating harangue against Indian policy which culminated in his betting anyone present one of his expensive silk shirts if India did not attack Pakistan in the near future. Butler was enchanted by this performance, even if he did not agree with its thrust. The former Parliamentary Under-Secretary for India who had taken the legislation to give India dominion status through the House of Commons with such difficulty in the 1930s could not get over his pleasure that a representative of one of the successor states now proved capable of putting on a rhetorical display of that nature. Following the Washington Council meeting the delegations were treated to a tour of some of the Unites States' main defence installations – Strategic Air Command at Omaha, the North American defence headquarters (NORAD) at Colorado Springs, and the space-rocket launch site at Cape Canaveral. To someone like myself, whose military experience had been confined to commanding a troop of tanks in north Germany, this tour was an eye-opener. The scale of the American defence effort was staggering; and the ability of the US military to present clearly and cogently what they were up to both tactically and strategically, in terms which were comprehensible to a group of civilians was impressive. The 1965 Council meeting, in Tehran, was a good deal less exciting, and not only because the leader of the British delegation, Michael Stewart, the new Labour Foreign Secretary was about the quietest, most understated minister for whom I ever worked.

Towards the end of my two years on the CENTO desk I sat down and wrote a paper that I entitled 'After CENTO'. The paper examined in detail what was wrong with the alliance and why its failings and weaknesses were not likely to be remedied. It pointed out that not only was the alliance ineffective and a source of irritation rather than one of security to its own members but that it actually had a negative impact on Britain's relations with other countries which were not members. Thus every public manifestation by CENTO, every military exercise or high level meeting, was greeted by protests and adverse publicity in India, Afghanistan, the Gulf region, Egypt, Cyprus and the eastern Mediterranean. My conclusion was that we should be seeking to wind up the alliance. The only country that would not then be covered by a Western security assurance (since Turkey would remain in NATO and Pakistan in SEATO) would be Iran, and that gap could be filled by a US bilateral assurance to that country. The analysis was broadly shared within Eastern Department, but it did not get far outside it, being considered far too adventurous and risky. So CENTO lingered on until 1979, unloved by its members and of dubious utility, succumbing finally to the Iranian revolution.

The later stages of my career were almost exclusively devoted to working in other international organisations; and I suspect that some of my colleagues and critics may have thought that I never met an international organisation that I did not value and promote. Not quite true, as this account will have shown; and surprising in a way that my first brush with multilateral diplomacy did not leave me more of a sceptic.

4

BRUSSELS (EUROPEAN COMMUNITY) 1965–1970

THE APPROACH MARCH

The news in early 1965 that I was to be sent to Britain's small permanent delegation to the European Community in Brussels struck me as underwhelming and I said so to those who were sending me there. I had no economic knowledge or experience; I had not served in any of the European Six's component member states; and, so far as I could tell from a reading of the press, the organisation itself had just been dealt a possibly fatal blow by France's decision to pursue an 'empty chair' policy, as a result of which business in Brussels had ground to a compete halt. All of which was true, but to no avail. In those days the wishes of individuals counted for little in decisions on future postings; nor was there any process by which people put their own names forward (or did not do so) when jobs became vacant. In truth I was protesting too much, and it was certainly ironic to have resisted so vigorously a move which was to provide the leitmotif for the rest of my professional life.

In reality I had spent quite a bit of my time at university studying European history, both that of the eighteenth century leading up to the Napoleonic wars and, as my special subject, the diplomatic history of the making of the Anglo-French and Anglo-Russian Ententes and the period immediately preceding the First World War; and I had followed the suggestion of my tutor at New College, Raymond Carr, to delve into the events surrounding the Spanish Civil War. So I had a serious grounding in the political background to the post-Second World War establishment of the European

Communities even if I knew little or nothing about trade, agriculture or competition policy, which at that stage were the bread and butter of European integration. From that grounding I had drawn clear conclusions that the intra-European wars of the twentieth century had been a catastrophe for all the peoples of Europe, for the victors as well as for the vanquished, and must not be allowed to happen again. However, Britain's own troubled relationship with the institutions and the members of the European communities – the refusal to join first the European Coal and Steel Community and then the European Economic Community and EURATOM as a founding member at the outset of their existence, and the failed attempt to negotiate a Europe-wide free trade area – had largely passed me by. When the news of General de Gaulle's veto of Britain's accession application in January 1963 reached the embassy in Kabul I can, however, remember being rather uncharacteristically enraged that anyone should suggest that Britain was in some way not qualified to be regarded as a properly European country. The reasons given, and often embraced subsequently by Britain's own Euro-sceptics, that Britain was somehow completely different and un-European because of its links with the outside world and in particular with the United States, seemed to me a peculiarly odd reading of the history of a continent whose worldwide colonial and trading links had been a general European phenomenon and all of whose countries, including Britain, had just emerged from two world wars, enormously costly in terms of lives lost and material damage, whose origins lay in European rivalries and disputes. In the weeks remaining before departure to Brussels I set about remedying the gaps in my knowledge, in particular focussing on the negotiations during our first attempt to join the European Community.

*   *   *

The Brussels in which we arrived in September 1965 would be hard for any present day visitor to the European institutions there to recognise. In place of the myriad ministerial Council meetings, working groups, consultations with commercial interests, and the permanent negotiations going on daily between the member states, the Commission and the Parliament, which characterise today's Brussels, there was precisely nothing happening. No Council meetings;

no meetings of the Committee of Permanent Representatives and its subordinate working groups; no proposals coming from the Commission. The other five member states and the Commission had taken the view that to hold any meetings in the absence of a French representative would be to exacerbate an already major crisis. But none of them was prepared to resile from the positions they had taken before the crisis in support of the impending shift to qualified majority voting on a limited range of issues – which was an integral part of the treaty which all Six had signed and ratified – and the proposal to give the European Assembly (as it was then more correctly called) some modest say over the European budget. So there was deadlock, and morale was low. The Commission and the Parliament continued to meet and to wring their hands at the state into which things had got; but neither of them was in a position to do anything about it. If a way was to be found out of the impasse it was going to be through inter-governmental contacts and negotiation between the six member states; but of that there was, as yet, no sign.

So we had arrived in a Brussels where there was little professionally to be done. We were able to settle comfortably into a terrace house not far from the Cinquantenaire, the grandiose archway marking 50 years of Belgian independence, and not far too from the, in those days quite modest, headquarters of the European institutions. Though we did not know it, this was to be our home for the next eleven and a half years; and a couple who arrived with one son were to leave Brussels with four. Unlike Iran and Afghanistan there was nothing particularly exciting about Belgium, although there was plenty to explore. But it was a pleasant, tranquil place to bring up a family of young children; Brussels was a relatively small European city lacking the traffic and pollution of London or Paris. The slow pace of the work to start with proved a major blessing as I immersed myself in the longest, most complex tutorial I had ever received. Commission officials, who had virtually nothing to do all day long, were only too willing to welcome a new arrival and to regale him with detailed accounts of their work and what they hoped to achieve if ever some handsome prince could liberate Sleeping Beauty from the tower in which she was imprisoned. And in the British delegation itself was a colleague, John Robinson, who had been through the first, failed accession negotiation, and who was generously prepared to pass on his encyclopaedic knowledge and experience of the European

Community. I learned much of what I know about Europe from him. So, by the time political and bureaucratic life did resume, I was much better equipped to understand, to report on and to explain it.

All through the autumn of 1965 the deadlock between the French government and the governments of the other Five remained unresolved. President de Gaulle continued to launch verbal thunderbolts at the Commission, whose President, Walter Hallstein's perceived presumption in mimicking the ceremony for receiving credentials from ambassadors in a nation state he particularly resented – the choicest epithet he employed was to call the Commission an 'areopage apatride'. And then the French presidential election in December 1965 changed everything. Contrary to earlier expectations de Gaulle did not win on the first round; and he was pushed into a humiliating run-off not by the official, socialist opposition candidate but by the third party, centrist candidature of Jean Lecanuet whose campaign focussed heavily on criticism of France's 'empty chair' policy in Brussels and the damage it was doing to the European Community, whose future Lecanuet argued it was in France's interest to be promoting not undermining. Once de Gaulle had won a second round victory, cracks began to appear in the impasse and one grey, gloomy February day the Foreign Ministers of the Six met in Luxembourg and reached a deal, which brought the European Community back to life. This deal, which has ever since been known as the Luxembourg Compromise, was in truth as much an agreement to disagree as it was a compromise. On the main institutional issue at stake, the introduction of qualified majority voting as specified in the founding treaty, the French stated their position which was that, where a member state regarded a vital national interest to be at stake, the discussions should continue until a consensus could be reached, and the Five reiterated theirs that, while any such matter should be discussed exhaustively, a vote could then be taken. The Commission suffered some collateral damage from the outcome, although not of a fatal or long-lasting kind; Hallstein was not reappointed when his term expired shortly afterwards and the low-key, more emollient Belgian, Jean Rey, succeeded him. The genuine compromise element in the deal was agreement that the two top priorities for business in the months ahead were to be completion of the individual market regulations of the Common Agricultural Policy (CAP) (a French objective) and the successful conclusion of the Kennedy Round of world trade negotiations in the General Agreement on Tariffs and Trade (GATT) (a German, Benelux objective).

At the time this settlement of what had clearly been an existential crisis for the European Community was seen as something of a draw. But in a longer perspective it is hard to score it as other than a defeat for the French, or rather for the Gaullist interpretation of France's national interest. Very gradually, majority voting began to be used and to take root; and its application to new areas of policy was agreed by all in successive revisions of the founding treaties. Budgetary powers of a limited kind were granted to the European Parliament, which became an elected rather than an appointed body and which also gradually acquired legislative authority. And the Commission re-emerged as a power-house for new policy measures including the conversion of the common market into a single market. No member state ever tried again the 'empty chair' policy, apart from a feeble half measure by Britain in 1996 over the ban on its beef exports to other parts of the European Union. Other consequences were clear at the time. The first was that the resilience of the European Communities had been severely tested and proved. All six member states had made it clear that its future development was a top priority of their nations' policies. The two policy objectives identified for the immediate period ahead (completion of the CAP and of the Kennedy Round) were achieved without undue friction or any further confrontation, as was the negotiation of a treaty merging the executives, the judicial bodies and the parliamentary institutions of the three, original Communities (the Coal and Steel Community, the Economic Community and EURATOM) – although not their founding treaties – into a new, streamlined set of institutions. And while what was loosely known as the Luxembourg Compromise – or veto – hung for many years over the negotiating table, its use was infrequent and its credibility a wasting asset particularly once it had been overridden in 1982 (on which see the events described in Chapter 8). None of those consequences were lost on a British government which was finding its current relationship with the European Community, following the breakdown of accession negotiations in 1963, unsatisfactory, and its attempts to remedy this ineffective.

At the time of my arrival in Brussels in September 1965 neither of the main political parties in Britain had shown any enthusiasm for renewing the attempt to join the European Community, the Conservatives remaining in principle in favour, the Labour government, which had come to power in October 1964, not wishing to re-open the divisions in its ranks which had arisen during the 1961–3 accession negotiations. Our policy was described as 'bridge-building' between the European Free Trade Area (EFTA), of which we were a member, and the European Community, although there was not much clarity of thought about what traffic was meant to cross that bridge. The idea of a Europe-wide free trade area, which had been championed by the Macmillan government before it applied to join the European Community, had been decisively rejected by the Six and was no more likely to be agreed now. And EFTA as a free trade area and not, like the European Community, a customs union, had no common policies on the basis of which cooperation between the two organisations could be developed. So bridge-building boiled down to cooperation in no doubt worthy but highly technical areas such as patents and customs facilitation. Moreover, the land at both ends of the proposed bridge was distinctly boggy. The European Community was at first entirely preoccupied with its own, internal crisis; thereafter its priorities were the objectives agreed at Luxembourg in February 1966 (completion of the CAP and the Kennedy Round) and the fusion of the executives, and they had little time or energy to devote to relations with EFTA. Meanwhile, EFTA had been dealt a near-mortal blow by the Wilson government's decision in October 1964 to impose unilaterally and without prior consultation an import surcharge. This move, quite apart from being of dubious legality under the Stockholm Convention founding EFTA, was bitterly resented by the smaller members; and they were subsequently loath to follow a British lead on the bridge-building policy, in which they had little confidence or interest and which at least one of them (Denmark) regarded as a far lower priority to reviving their membership bid which had foundered with ours in 1963. So exploratory talks between the two organisations on bridge-building continued in a desultory way until they were overtaken by a shift in British policy over accession. Attending meetings of the EFTA ambassadors in Brussels to be briefed on these talks and to attempt to concert our support for them was one of my early tasks and a peculiarly dispiriting one.

Following the British general election in March 1966, which gave the Wilson government a sizeable overall majority, our policy on accession began to shift. John Robinson, who had returned to London, and Sir Con O'Neill, previously Ambassador to the European Communities, were soon engaged in a major, preparatory exercise on the basis of which the Cabinet would be able to decide whether or not to reapply for accession. This exercise was almost exclusively a London affair, with posts like ours being required to provide factual material about the development, both past and prospective, of European Community policies, but not being much involved in policy formulation. My own principal preoccupation during that period was with the Kennedy Round of trade negotiations, on which I was the eyes and ears in Brussels of our small negotiating team in Geneva, headed by Roy Denman, who almost single-handedly fought Britain's corner in a negotiation which was effectively a three-sided one between the United States, Japan and the European Community. It was a salutary lesson in how Britain's exclusion from the European Community and the weakness of our economy had left us with a very diminished capacity to influence the outcome of major international negotiations. We were of course highly interested spectators of the internal debate going on in London as it gradually swung ever more decisively towards Britain making a new application. The debate was driven as much as anything by the fading attractiveness of all the alternatives, or rather by the realisation that they were not viable alternatives at all. In the Commonwealth, Britain was engaged in a divisive debate over its handling of Rhodesia's Unilateral Declaration of Independence (UDI); with the United States we were conducting an equally divisive dialogue over Vietnam and our unwillingness to commit any troops there; the status quo, based on a resentful partnership with EFTA, lacked substance. The decision to reapply, when it came in May 1967, was thus welcome to those of us working at the coal-face in Brussels, even if we had no illusions about how straightforward it was going to be to realise. Even more welcome was the decision on the occasion of this second attempt to submit a simple, one sentence application for membership, with no ifs and buts, a contrast with the 1961 approach which, in the obscurity of its language, had seemed more like the initiation of a fishing expedition than the reflection of a strategic choice.

The submission of the new application had been preceded by a tour of the capitals of the member states by the Prime Minister (Harold Wilson) and the Foreign Secretary (George Brown). This had revealed that five of them warmly welcomed the prospect of renewed negotiations; the French position remained a lofty enigma, but was not yet cast in totally negative terms. The first step the Six took was to ask the Commission to give its 'opinion', as provided for under the Rome Treaty. So we set out to provide the Commission with all the material they needed to put this together. This was not yet in any way a real negotiation; and we had to be careful to avoid revealing what our negotiating positions would be; but at the same time we began to prepare for those negotiations, which we hoped would start after the Commission had submitted its 'opinion' to the Council. As we followed the Commission's preparatory work carefully – and that was an important part of my own job – it became clear that the most problematic section of the 'opinion' was likely to be that dealing with Britain's economic and monetary position and policies, a section whose preparation was in the hands of Raymond Barre, Vice-President of the Commission and no fan of British membership. By this stage in the early autumn of 1967 the sustainability of the sterling exchange rate, while still an act of faith for the British government, had steadily weakening credibility in the markets, so Barre had plenty of material to work on. When Tony Crosland, the President of the Board of Trade, came to Brussels just a day or two before the 'opinion' was completed and transmitted to the Council, I was asked to brief him on what it was likely to say. I said, hoping I would survive mentioning the unmentionable that it would add up to saying we should devalue. 'Quite right too', said Crosland. The 'opinion', when it appeared, went a great deal further than that, making a major issue out of the sterling balances which Commonwealth and some other countries held in London and which the Commission argued could be a serious source of instability and were a sign that we had not yet definitively cast in our lot with Europe. It was immediately clear that the 'opinion' contained plenty of material for anyone who wanted to prevaricate and obfuscate over the application.

The next two and a half months were spent in a desperate and eventually unavailing attempt to persuade the French to agree with the Five that negotiations should be opened. The sterling exchange rate problem solved itself when, in November, Britain's currency was devalued. But that did not alter by one scintilla the French policy of stalling and raising any number of pre-conditions before any decision to open accession negotiations could be taken. There was little we in Brussels could do during this period. Our principal interlocutors, the Commission, were not the problem. But, reasonably enough in the circumstances, they were not prepared even to begin informal pre-negotiations, having no mandate to do so. Our contacts among the Five were entirely supportive but pessimistic as to the outcome. Eventually, faced with an endless drip of negative comment in the press, the British government decided that matters must be brought to a head even if that resulted in another French veto. That was the message that the Foreign Secretary gave his colleagues of the Five when he came to Brussels in December for a NATO ministerial meeting, and they agreed that further prevarication was worse than a showdown. The latter duly took place at a Council meeting just before Christmas, the French being forced to make it clear that they were not prepared to allow negotiations to begin, the Five that they were not abandoning their support for our application. It was a miserable occasion for all but the most hardened opponents of British accession, but not one that seemed likely to be changed any time soon, de Gaulle having five more years of his presidential mandate to run. All our own preparations for installing a negotiating team in Brussels, of which I might have been a part, were put on hold.

✣   ✣   ✣

On this occasion, unlike the first French veto in 1963, the British government had had plenty of time to consider the line it should take, if and when the axe fell. 'We will not take no for an answer', became the mantra of the moment and for a substantial period ahead. For all its slightly plaintive cadence it served far better than might have been expected. It made it clear that we were not ready to accept the French veto as the final word and thus encouraged the supporters of British accession amongst the Six to keep up the pressure on the French; and it also emphasised that we were not interested in halfway houses or diversions. This was important, because the pressure, under which the French felt themselves to be, led to their bringing forward the idea that the European Community should offer Britain a 'commercial arrangement'. This weird animal never formally saw the light of day since there was no agreement amongst the Six as to what it might contain, let alone on whether to put it to us. The French appeared to envisage a package of mutual industrial tariff cuts falling well short of a free trade area, for which we would be asked to pay with substantial concessions on agricultural trade. Among other drawbacks it was hard to see how this could possibly qualify for a waiver from the obligations under the GATT to Most Favoured Nation treatment. My job was to encourage the principal critics of this idea within the Six (the Germans, Dutch and the Commission) to maintain their objections and to keep it bottled up. This they did with a will, and there then ensued a period of trench warfare between the member states which suited our purposes well since it continuously reminded everyone concerned that the British application was not about to go away and that its capacity to snarl up the business within the Council was considerable.

Then in February 1969 the French tried a second diversion. At a tête-à-tête lunch with the British Ambassador in Paris (Sir Christopher Soames) President de Gaulle floated the idea that Britain, France and Germany should start to cooperate on foreign policy issues in what came to be called a 'directoire'. This was a good deal trickier to handle than the 'commercial arrangement', since it had been put directly to us and we could not simply duck it. But, even if it had not come relatively soon after France's break with NATO and the removal from France of its headquarters, it did not have much appeal. To have shown any interest in it, let alone to have embraced it, would have embroiled us with those members of the Six who were not included in the proposed 'directoire'; and it would have enabled the French to say that there was no need to lose any more sleep over our membership application since we were now participating fully in a much more interesting form of European cooperation. The decision was taken in London to inform the other members of the Six of the approach that had been made to us and, since leaks were then certain, to go public with the story and our reservations. There then ensued a major Anglo-French slanging match in what came to known as the 'affaire Soames' with much bad blood on both sides. While there was some criticism in the British press and political circles of the way this had been handled, those of us in Brussels who were involved in our membership application were totally supportive. For once fortune smiled on us, since, a few weeks later, following the loss of a referendum in France on regional government and the powers of the Senate, President de Gaulle resigned. His successor, Georges Pompidou, soon began to take a much less aggressively negative line on the possibility of British membership. And, when the Heads of State and Government of the Six met in The Hague in December 1969 – in those days an unprecedented gathering – a deal was struck. Agreement would be reached in the first half of the year on the treaty amendments needed to provide for the financing of the CAP from what was called the European Community's 'own resources' – customs duties, agricultural levies and a percentage of VAT – and the Six would prepare to open negotiations with Britain and the other applicants (Denmark, Ireland and Norway) in June 1970. This linkage was by no means fortuitous since the French were becoming increasingly nervous about the chances of getting German agreement to agricultural financing – the Germans being by far the biggest net contributors to the system – so long as the deadlock over enlargement persisted; nor was it without serious consequences for us since the agricultural financing settlement was likely to impose a heavy burden on Britain. So far as I was concerned the most immediate consequence was that I was appointed to be one of three First Secretaries at the Brussels end of the Negotiating Team which began to take shape in the first half of 1970 as our preparations for the opening of negotiations moved into top gear.

5

BRUSSELS (EUROPEAN COMMUNITY)
1970–1972

THE ACCESSION NEGOTIATIONS

The accession negotiations with the four applicant countries (Denmark, Ireland, Norway and the UK) opened in Luxembourg on 30 June 1970, on the last day of the Belgian Presidency and only weeks after Britain's general election had returned a Conservative government led by Edward Heath in place of the Labour government of Harold Wilson which had submitted the application some three years before. The speeches were formulaic in the extreme, with no surprises and no attempt at negotiation. Each party knew what the other was going to say before they said it. Two questions were no nearer being answered at the end of the day than at the beginning. How long would the negotiations last; and would they succeed? So a certain feeling of anti-climax was inevitable, even if it clearly was a moment of considerable historic importance; and, for those of us who had been labouring on these issues for a long time (five years in my case), the occasion for a bit of euphoria. It was one of the first occasions and, although we were not to know that then, one of the last, on which a major development in Britain's difficult relationship with the European Community enjoyed, across the board, bi-partisan support at home for the step being taken. The opening speech that Tony Barber, the Conservative cabinet minister who was to lead the negotiating team (replaced within weeks by Geoffrey Rippon, following the Chancellor of the Exchequer, Iain Macleod's, sudden death and Barber's promotion to succeed him), gave was identical in every respect to the one that George Thomson, the

Labour minister in charge of the preparations for the negotiations, would have given had he still been in office. The identification of the major problems on our side – transitional arrangements for the move towards the European Community's Customs Union and Common Agricultural Policy, Commonwealth sugar, New Zealand butter, the budgetary arrangements, fisheries – were just as they would have been had the government not changed. And the matching speech from the European Community side, long on warm words and short on substance, with emphasis on acceptance of the 'acquis communautaire' and on agreeing transitional measures rather than changes of substance in Community policies, set a pattern for all the subsequent negotiations for enlargement (in 1961, when we had last tried to join there had been very little 'acquis communautaire' and very few common policies to accept) thus reminding us, if we needed it, of the opportunities Britain had missed by not joining earlier, or indeed at the outset.

The negotiating team, of which I was a member, was partly (the smaller part) based in Brussels and partly in London. I was allocated to cover trade policy issues, for which Roy Denman, of the Department of Trade and formerly Kennedy Round negotiator, was responsible; and policies such as capital movements and the budget, which fell under Raymond Bell of the Treasury. My two First Secretary colleagues in Brussels covered respectively agriculture and fisheries, and Britain's adoption of and adaptation to the 'acquis communautaire'. In truth our role did not involve much negotiation as such; that task being controlled from the London end and tightly coordinated by Con O'Neill who was head of the negotiating team at the official level and John Robinson. The London team were in Brussels every fortnight for the regular meetings with the European Community at ambassadorial level; and every six weeks or so for the meetings at ministerial level; and they fitted in many negotiating contacts in the margins of those visits or between them. The main part of my work at this stage was to find out and report what was going on at meetings of the Six as they began laboriously to hammer out their joint responses to the problems we were raising, and also within the Commission where the technical analysis of these problems was undertaken. The network of contacts I had built up over my years in Brussels, both with the national delegations of the Six and with the key Commission officials who made up their negotiating team – Edmund Wellenstein, who headed it at the official level, his two deputies Roland de Kergorlay and Manfred Caspari, and the members of the cabinet of Jean-François Deniau, who was in charge at the political level – was to prove invaluable. Above all it was a crash course learning process for someone who had hitherto been on the periphery of policy formulation, learning not only about the techniques of multilateral negotiation but also about the labyrinthine intrigues in Whitehall and the dark arts of press handling. I enjoyed every minute of it, but there were not many minutes of my day which were not filled by it.

A detailed, authoritative, contemporary account of these negotiations from the British point of view is contained in Britain's Entry into the European Community: Report by Sir Con O'Neill on the negotiations of 1970–1972 *edited and with a foreword by the present author, Frank Cass Publishers (2000).*

So far as I was concerned, the early months of the negotiations were dominated by three issues. The first was thrashing out special arrangements for the few industrial products where we were not happy with the impact of the move of Britain's external tariff towards the Community's Common External Tariff that would result from agreement on a general transitional period (in every case these were products which we traditionally imported from Commonwealth countries at a nil rate of duty). This was an eclectic list including phosphorus, alumina, plywood, newsprint, wood pulp and something known as wattle extract (which came from South Africa and Argentina and was used in Britain to dye shoe leather while continental shoemakers used domestically produced chestnut extract to which they had adapted during the years of wartime blockade). The first step was to get Commission officials to understand why a rapid move from a nil tariff towards the Common External Tariff would damage British industry; the second to identify measures to soften the blow. Both steps took many wearisome hours of exposition and negotiation, at which Roy Denman was a past master. Our efforts were assisted by the fact that, when they had originally set up their customs union, the Six had negotiated amongst themselves similar special arrangements for a limited number of sensitive products. Gradually we and the Commission identified acceptable solutions, mainly involving transitional exceptions allowing Britain to continue to import limited quantities based on traditional import levels at a nil tariff rate beyond the date of the early general moves towards the Community's tariff; and the Commission set about selling these solutions to the Six member states, with external pressure applied by us. The whole process brought home the extent to which we depended on the goodwill and professionalism of Commission officials. In Britain's earlier accession negotiations (1961–3), when the Community had few common policies, the Commission had played a relatively minor role, but now they were much more prominent, although still less prominent than they were to become in later enlargement negotiations. By the late autumn of 1970 we had reached agreement on solutions to our list of sensitive products and thus cleared the decks for the negotiation of general transitional arrangements for trade on which our aim was to have the most rapid transition possible for industrial products and the slowest transition possible for agricultural products. In this we were only partly successful, the Six having exactly the opposite aim to us. I had learned the invaluable lesson that multilateral negotiation was not just a matter of grand strategy and political manoeuvre, but that it also required infinite attention to detail and a willingness to get down into the weeds of hitherto unknown problems.

The second focus of my activity was what to do about Hong Kong which, like others of our remaining colonial territories, was in a duty free relationship with us and which would be damaged if the Community's external tariff were in future to be applied to its exports. The straightforward solution, which would have been to have treated it in a similar way to our other overseas dependencies and to those of the Six by regarding it effectively as a part of the Community was not practicable for a number of reasons. For one thing, only the island of Hong Kong and a very small part of the mainland territory was in fact a British colony, the rest of the territory being leased from China until 1997; we could not therefore treat it like our other colonies. But in any case the Six, and the French in particular who had a tendency to refer to Hong Kong as an offshore factory in the South China Sea, were not going to agree to a solution which would have given Hong Kong unlimited duty free access for all of its exports to the enlarged Community. No solution had been found to the problem by the time negotiations were broken off in 1963 following de Gaulle's first veto. On this too the Commission came to the rescue, but in a quite different way. One of my regular trade policy contacts within the Commission, Paul Tran van Thinh, a Frenchman of Vietnamese origin, was responsible for the Community's contribution to the Generalised System of Preferences, an OECD scheme under which the industrialised countries gave limited duty free access to imports from the developing countries. Hong Kong was not a beneficiary under the Community's existing contribution to the scheme, but Tran began to hint that he thought it could be so included so long as some limits could be put on the quantity of Hong Kong's exports to be covered, and that this could settle the issue of Hong Kong in our accession negotiations. I reported all this and was encouraged by London to continue my contacts. Gradually the detail of this solution took shape; was endorsed by the Six; and was accepted by us. The government of Hong Kong was not particularly enthusiastic since the quantities covered by duty free access were not generous, but it was certainly better than the nothing that was on offer to the industrialised and the Asian members of the Commonwealth. So a small, but tricky, problem on our list was ticked off.

The third issue of those early months was both quantitatively and qualitatively of a quite different order. The arrangements for financing the Community budget which the Six had agreed for themselves only a few months before the negotiations opened were certain to impact disproportionately heavily on Britain. The problems lay on both the revenue and the expenditure side of the budget. The first two revenue slices, known as 'own resources', were derived from customs duties and from levies on agricultural imports. As a country which traded more with the world outside the Community than did the Six, and as one which imported a much higher proportion of its food, and that too from outside the Community, than they did, Britain was bound to contribute disproportionately to the Community's revenue, even if the third slice, provided by up to 1 per cent of VAT was not slanted as the other two were. The revenue problem was compounded on the expenditure side by the fact that a massive part of the Community's spending at this time went on the Common Agricultural Policy. Britain, with a relatively small agricultural sector, was certain to qualify for a much smaller share of the Community's expenditure than the relative size of its economy. No one on either side contested the existence of a problem, although on the Community side there was extreme doctrinal resistance to putting the two sides of the equation together and coming up with a figure for Britain's net contribution to the Community budget. It was argued that this would legitimise the concept of 'juste retour' – that is, that a country should get back as much as it put in – and thus be contrary to the whole concept of financing the Community budget from 'own resources', a concept which incidentally provided France and the Netherlands in particular with a handsome net benefit at the expense, mainly, of Germany. But the arithmetic of putting the revenue and expenditure sides of the equation together was not difficult, and the logic was hard to resist. For some months the number-crunchers on both sides struggled to project agreed calculations of the scale of the problem out into the future, well beyond the putative date when Britain might join and first become liable to contribute to the Community budget. But they came nowhere near to agreeing. On the Community side the argument was advanced that we were heavily underestimating the pace at which Britain's trade in both industrial and agricultural goods would be reoriented towards the members of the Community as tariffs came down (and went up against third countries). Thus, we predicated much too high British contributions to the budget from import duties and agricultural levies; and, more controversially, they argued that we were underestimating the capacity and determination of the Community to develop new policies – for example, for subsidising regional development and for research – which would reduce the proportion of the budget that went to agriculture and which would be of substantial net benefit to Britain. Our calculations took a more conservative view on both points. The trouble was that neither side could prove the other wrong since both were arguing about the impact of a budget of unknown and unknowable size an unknown number of years ahead when whatever transitional arrangements were agreed to phase in Britain's budget contributions had expired (the length of these transitional arrangements having not yet been settled). Suffice it to say that when these transitional arrangements did in fact expire (in 1980), the more pessimistic British calculations proved a great deal closer to the mark than the more optimistic Community ones.

By the end of the autumn of 1970 this dialogue of the deaf had reached a point from which it could not usefully go any further. The Community had, however, made to us one extremely important statement to the effect that 'should unacceptable situations arise within the present Community, or an enlarged Community, the very survival of the Community would demand that the institutions find equitable solutions'. This statement was made to us very formally on behalf of the Six even if they were subsequently not prepared to put it into the Treaty of Accession. When I queried its value at the time, John Robinson said to me, 'Don't worry. If we are forced to use it, and we surely will be, it will detonate a major upheaval'. How right he was! In the negotiating process itself Britain now faced a major quandary. Did we propose actual changes in the Community's financial arrangements or did we table proposals which were confined to transitional provisions and rely thereafter on the somewhat Delphic statement we had received? We opted for the latter, and I never doubted then or since that we made the right decision, even though the consequences of that choice subsequently consumed some five years of my professional life. Had we tried to change the financial arrangements we would have run a considerable risk that the French would not have agreed and that the negotiations for our accession would have failed. Alternatively we would have been fobbed off with something like the corrective mechanism to the revenue side of the equation only, which emerged from the 1974–5 renegotiation and which in the event proved to be of no practical value.

Through the winter months of 1971 the negotiations moved slowly. The Six began gradually to get to grips with the principal issues which we had raised – the transitional periods for industrial and agricultural trade, the phasing in of our budgetary payments, the treatment of preferential imports of sugar from the developing countries of the Commonwealth, New Zealand's exports of butter and cheese and the many problems in the fisheries sector. We had largely exhausted the scope for exploratory contacts and explanations the previous autumn. My main task during this period was to provide rapid and comprehensive reporting on the discussions going on between the Six at ambassadorial level in the Committee of Permanent Representatives and in the working groups preparing their meetings. Of course I was not the only source of information as the Six hammered out their negotiating responses to us – reports flowed in from our Embassies in the capitals of the Six and the senior London-based members of the negotiating team were in continuous contact with their opposite members. But the Commission's input to these preparations was increasingly important, and the synthesis amongst the views of the Six reached in Brussels was what really mattered to us in negotiating terms. So my network of contacts was put to full and constant use. This flow of information was all the more important because we were applying a negotiating technique which involved ensuring that the issues remained bottled up within the Six until they were ready to put proposals forward that were broadly acceptable to us or which were close enough to being acceptable to be shaped into an agreement without being fundamentally changed. The reasons for this approach were twofold. Given the leakiness of the negotiating machinery in Brussels, it was inevitable that anything that the Six put to us as an agreed position would immediately end up in the public domain. If such a position was seriously unacceptable to us, we would have to contest it and there would be an immediate rise in the press and parliamentary temperature at home. Moreover, once the Six had agreed to a position and put it to us, it was far more difficult to get it changed than when it remained under discussion within the Six; there was always a risk that one member state (with the French the obvious suspects), would refuse to change the Community position, and then we would be stuck. This negotiating technique served us well throughout the negotiations.

Then in mid-March 1971 the one, so far submerged, issue in the negotiations, the status of sterling as a reserve currency, surfaced with a vengeance. Late one evening I was telephoned after the weekly meeting of the Ambassadors of the Six by my most reliable informant to say that the French Permanent Representative, a man renowned for his sarcastic wit and adamantine determination, had raised the issue in aggressive and rather threatening terms, listing a whole number of aspects that would need to be negotiated with us. The other five ambassadors had reacted negatively to this onslaught, but it would clearly soon become public knowledge (it did, within hours). I spoke immediately to John Robinson in London who reacted, as usual, with admirable calmness. We should avoid any impression of alarm or crisis. The issue, after all, had not as yet been raised with us. Action would be taken in the capitals of the Six; and we should do nothing to make it easier for Raymond Barre, the Vice-President of the Commission responsible for economic and monetary matters, to get into the centre of the action. This latter point was particularly relevant in the light of the damage which Barre had inflicted on our application in 1967. In the end the sterling issue turned out to be more like the smile of the Cheshire cat, hanging over the negotiations for the next two months but never actually put to us, and then, after Edward Heath's successful visit to Paris in May to see President Pompidou, virtually disappearing, so that when a purely procedural outcome was agreed in June, Barre described it to the press as 'zero plus zero plus zero'. It had been an anxious moment. But in truth the sterling issue could only have been pushed to its logical conclusion if the French had wanted to torpedo the whole negotiation; and this, it was gradually becoming clearer, they did not wish to do.

It was during those spring months of 1971 too that the key tactical decisions were taken on how, in our parlance, to 'break the back' of the negotiations. For a number of reasons related more to domestic than to foreign policy the government could not just let the negotiations determine their own time frame. It was crucially important that the ratification of the terms of any deal we struck for our accession should take place in the early part of the Parliament which had been elected in June 1970; and that meant bringing matters to a head in Brussels in the summer of 1971. The question was how best this was to be done and in what negotiating format. Should we be aiming for a summit meeting ourselves with the Six, or a summit meeting involving all four applicants and the Six; or should we go for a preliminary summit between ourselves and the French alone, with the object of clearing the way for a subsequent multilateral deal? The choice, which eventually fell on the latter formula, was made easier by the fact that, during the first half of 1971 the French held the Presidency of the European Community and also by the accumulating evidence that it was France that held the key to success or failure and that, if we could reach a broad understanding with them, none of the problems in the negotiations would prove insoluble. The preparations for Heath's visit to Paris in late May were conducted in great secrecy and well away from the infinitely porous negotiating machinery in Brussels. The visit proved a triumphant success and, when President Pompidou and the Prime Minister emerged to brief the press at its conclusion, we all knew that the basic political decision to enlarge the European Community had been taken. Our problem thereafter in Brussels was to convince the delegations of the five other member states of the reality, namely that every single detail had not been stitched up between us and the French, and that much hard negotiating lay ahead.

Meanwhile, in the run up to the Heath visit to Paris and as an important contribution to its success we had begun to strike deals on some of the key issues. Early in May we reached agreement on the basic architecture of the transitional periods for trade in both industrial and agricultural products. Within an overall transitional period of five years we managed to secure significant front-loading of the tariff cuts on industrial goods and an even spread of the moves towards the Community's agricultural prices and tariffs. To secure this we had to accept a switch, from the outset of the transitional period, to the Community's system of agricultural support. The outcome to the negotiations over Britain's imports of sugar from the developing countries of the Commonwealth, which was also settled in early May, was less clear-cut and thus less easy to defend. It had been clear for some weeks before a deal was struck that, if we continued to insist on a quantitative guarantee of the amount of Commonwealth sugar which could continue to be imported by Britain after accession at prices well above the world market level, the figure which would be put to us by the Six would be a long way short of the amounts currently covered by the Commonwealth Sugar Agreement. The influence of the French and Belgian beet-sugar producers was weighing heavily on the negotiations. A low figure of the sort being bandied around among the Six would have been very damaging to the many small Commonwealth countries which depended heavily on their sugar exports to Britain; and there would have been a major row in Parliament. But there was an alternative which gradually took shape. Both the Commonwealth Sugar Agreement and the Six's own trade arrangements with their former colonies (known at the time as the Yaoundé Convention) had two more years to run after the most likely date for British accession (1 January 1973). Why not therefore simply leave the current arrangements of both sides in place for those two years and give a general, but unquantified, commitment by the enlarged Community to sort matters out equitably thereafter? That was eventually the basis on which a deal was struck. Its credibility as what the British negotiators described as a 'bankable assurance' was not greatly helped by the rather peculiar formulation of the French text of the commitment, 'La Communauté aura à coeur de sauvegarder les intérêts de l'ensemble des pays visés [au présent protocol] dont l'économie dépend dans une mesure considérable de l'exportation de produits de base, et notamment de sucre'. But John Robinson took care, at the time of the deal, that the English language text of what was agreed was also explicitly accepted by the Six, and that read, 'The Community will have as its firm purpose the safeguarding of the interests of all the countries...' Another lesson in the importance of nailing down every detail of a complex negotiation. That English text carried us through all the ribaldry which the British press threw at the formulation in French. And, when the negotiations of the new Lomé Convention took place in 1974–5, we were able to secure a quantitative guarantee for 1.2 million tons which compared respectably with the 1.373 million tons covered by the Commonwealth Sugar Agreement and massively exceeded the kind of figures of 500,000–700,000 tons which had been being discussed among the Six before the direction of the negotiations was switched.

So the negotiations moved towards what both sides intended to be their effective denouement at a ministerial meeting in Luxembourg at the end of June. The possible problems over the role of sterling as a reserve currency were dissipated, not without some frantic last minute bilateral Anglo-French confabulation, at a ministerial meeting earlier in the month. That effectively left only three major issues to be settled, the transitional arrangements for Britain's budgetary payments, imports of New Zealand butter and cheese, and fisheries. Of the three, it gradually became clear that fisheries would not be ready for settlement in June. This was partly because settling fisheries required a major negotiation with one of the other applicant countries, Norway, while the end-June ministerial meeting was inevitably going to be preponderantly a bilateral negotiation between Britain and the Six. It was also due to the fact that Britain only very belatedly came to realise that its principal interest lay in protecting its inshore fishermen (whose votes weighed in the balance of a number of coastal constituencies) rather than in using the Community's Common Fisheries Policy to gain access for its deep sea fishing fleet to Norwegian waters. This late switch of emphasis helped to push the fisheries negotiations into the second half of the year. The other two issues – New Zealand dairy products and budgetary payments – became umbilically linked, not least because the French were determined to toughen the terms on the latter in return for any additional concessions on the former but also because the reaction of the New Zealand government to any deal on their dairy exports was likely to be a crucial factor in the acceptability of the overall terms of accession to the government's supporters in the House of Commons. So the stage was set for us having to pay on the budget terms in order to achieve a settlement on dairy products which the New Zealand government would welcome.

The meeting in Luxembourg lasted the better part of three days, and was exhausting for all concerned, but most particularly for the ministers and delegations of the Six who spent far more time negotiating with each other than they did with us. We were all locked for the duration in what was at that time the only Community building on the Kirchberg hill looking across a deep ravine to the medieval city of Luxembourg (the whole area is now covered with the headquarters buildings of the European Investment Bank, the European Court of Justice, the Statistical Office and other European institutions). From time to time the New Zealand delegation, headed by their Deputy Prime Minister, Jack Marshall, was smuggled into the back of the building (a not very effective attempt to avoid the attentions of the press) to confer with Geoffrey Rippon about the terms which were gradually emerging from the Six's discussions. For much of the time, while the Six were locked in conclave we had nothing to do but kick our heels in our pretty cramped delegation offices; on the second night, when the Six were in permanent session, we settled down to play bridge as a means of whiling the time away and perhaps also as a mild form of psychological pressure on our friends in the Six who would drop by before returning to their discussions. Every so often too the Six would despatch emissaries, usually Jean-François Deniau, a member of the Commission and the head of their delegation, and Edmund Wellenstein, his Director General, to sound out our reaction to the various formulas that they were shaping up to put to us. So, long periods of tedium were interspersed by frantic bursts of negotiation; and, throughout, telephone calls from anxious government departments in London and from No 10 and the Foreign Office flowed in without our being able to provide much enlightenment. Finally, at dawn on the third day, with the rays of the rising sun streaming in through the windows of the main Council chamber, our delegation filed into a smoke-filled room full of exhausted Community ministers and officials to listen to the terms of the agreements reached between us in the preceding hours being read into the record. Then, following innumerable press briefings, the despatch of lengthy reporting telegrams to London, a certain amount of celebration with Luxembourg sparkling wine (by then it was in fact breakfast-time but no one cared about that), we dragged our way across the road to the Holiday Inn, where most of us were meant to have been staying if we had ever got to bed at all, picked up our belongings, and dashed to the airport, whence the ministerial plane delivered the Brussels end of the negotiating team to that city and went on to London with the rest of the team preparing the statement which would be made to Parliament. To me it not only *was*, but it actually *felt like*, a historic occasion; but not one I would wish to repeat too often.

✻ ✻ ✻

The following few months brought a brief but welcome reduction in the negotiating tempo, with fisheries, in which I was not directly involved, coming to the centre of the stage. Then, in September, it was decided by the negotiating conference to set up a treaty drafting group composed of representatives of the Six and the Commission and of the four applicant countries to draw up in legal form all the results of the negotiations, ready for signature in due course, but at a date still not determined, by all ten governments. Completely out of the blue, since I had no legal expertise, I was appointed to assist Ian Sinclair, the negotiating team's Legal Adviser, to handle this work, the rationale being that I made up in knowledge of the substance of the negotiations what I lacked in legal experience. Quite apart from providing me with four months of the hardest work I ever had to undertake, it gave me a crash course in the drafting of complex legal texts, and at the feet of a master of the art, which was to stand me in good stead for the future. Day after day we sat around a large, hollow-square conference table hammering out the texts of the accession treaty (quite short), the transitional provisions (lengthy and complex), the adaptations to the Community's secondary legislation – now usually known as the acquis communautaire – needed to fit in the four new member states (even more lengthy) and the numerous protocols (with full legal force) and declarations that would be appended to the Treaty. As the Commission delegation, which produced the first drafts of each document, disgorged the texts, these had to be sent to London, the comments of various Whitehall departments received and coordinated, and the process of negotiating changes to the Commission drafts undertaken in the treaty drafting group. Much of this process was purely technical, but, every now and again, we would stumble across an issue where the outcome of the earlier negotiations had left an ambiguity or indeed an unresolved difference of opinion between the Six, or some of them, and ourselves. This we would try to resolve at the treaty drafting group level and, if we could not resolve it at that level, we would refer it up to the negotiating conference of Ambassadors, and, potentially, to the Ministerial conference. About a dozen matters were referred up in this way, including such sensitive issues as whether the commitment to the Commonwealth sugar producers should be included in the relevant protocol and thus given legal force (it was) and the decision-making process within the enlarged Community for determining the provisions on the import of New Zealand dairy products once the five-year period for which precise quantities had been determined expired. We made no attempt to give legal force to the commitment by the Six to reopen the budget arrangements if they proved to be inequitable. And sterling was dealt with in an exchange of letters between Britain and the Six that remained a unilateral British statement of political intention, not a legally binding one. All the outstanding issues were in fact cleared up by a meeting at the ambassadorial level in January 1972, a few days before the Treaty was signed. Just over two months into the treaty drafting exercise, in early December, Ian Sinclair and I were consulted by London as to whether we saw any objection or inconvenience to setting a firm, and pretty early, date for signing the Treaty. It was clear that the timetable for parliamentary approval if our accession was to take effect as intended on 1 January 1973 was beginning to weigh heavily in the scales. Our response was that we would actually welcome the setting of a date for signature, so long as it was not ridiculously early, the process of drafting treaty instruments being subject, like many other bureaucratic exercises, to Parkinson's Law that work fills the time available for its completion. So the date of 22 January 1972 was chosen for the signature ceremony. From that experience I learned the value to negotiators of being compelled to reach a conclusion within a pre-determined time frame. Of course that puts pressure on both sides but, on that occasion, when the broad political outcome was not in doubt, it worked to our advantage.

*   *   *

Britain's Treaty of Accession was duly signed in Brussels on 22 January, not in one of those ugly, brutalist modern buildings that the European Community tends to occupy, but in the baroque splendour of the Palais d'Egmont in the old quarter of the city, recently refurbished by the Belgian government as a conference centre. The subsidiary documents were so voluminous that they had to be wheeled in on a trolley; but in truth the pile of paper on the trolley, as was often the case on such occasions, consisted mainly of blank sheets of paper, the task of printing up all the agreed documents having not yet been completed. I had failed to qualify for one of the limited number of seats in the main conference hall and so had wangled an invitation to squeeze into a corner of BBC Television's porta-cabin studio which was located in a cramped courtyard behind the palace, on the off chance that my experience of the negotiations might be of use in briefing the commentators. It was there that the news reached us that a spectator who had managed to get past the very lax security had deluged Edward Heath with printers ink as he went up the main staircase of the palace and that the ceremony was therefore being postponed for an indefinite period while the Prime Minister cleaned up and was found a new suit (in the end borrowed from Michael Palliser, the British Permanent Representative). The BBC was already broadcasting background material on the Accession Treaty, but they did not have an infinite quantity of this; they resisted, however, the temptation, yielded to by most of their continental counterparts – to switch to broadcasting solemn music, for all the world like a state funeral – and instead decided to continue a background commentary, for which I was required to provide frantically scribbled notes. I doubt if the viewing public has ever had, before or since, such an extended seminar on the European Community and its various institutions; and there was heartfelt relief when, after what seemed an eternity but was in fact only a couple of hours, Heath appeared in the conference hall and the signature ceremony went ahead. My hopes of thereafter getting away to one of the celebration parties were at that point frustrated by a frantic telephone call from the Stationery Office in London. They had been instructed to issue the Accession Treaty as a government White Paper the following morning. They had no problem over the text which was already set up in type. But they needed the precise wording of each of the signatories of the treaty. Could I please get this for them? I wrongly assumed that this would be relatively simple, and that the signed copy of the treaty would by now be safely in the archives of the Council Secretariat. But, when I finally ran the Council Secretariat's registrar of treaty documents to earth, no easy task since he had gone home, I discovered that he had taken the Treaty off with him to his house in the Brussels suburbs. So I trekked there, duly copied out the wording of each signature, and telephoned it through to the Stationery Office. Even later that night I was telephoned by a different official in the Council Secretariat, this time someone in the Publication Office. His instructions were to start publishing official Community documents for the first time in English from the following morning. Each language version had a colour code (blue for French, green for Italian and so on); what colour code did we want for English? By this time it was far too late to contact anyone in London so I asked him what was on offer. He ran through a series of fairly unappealing colours and eventually I chose purple, which was at least distinctive and for which I have always had a weakness. And so it was in purple that the first of millions of pages of documents in English were so coloured; but I thought it wisest to draw a veil of discretion over how this came about, and fortunately no one at the London end ever enquired or complained.

*　　*　　*

The account I have given of Britain's accession negotiations is, of course, a view from the coal-face and a fragmented view, largely of those parts of the negotiations with which I was directly concerned. But in the 40 years which have followed, and of course with the benefit of hindsight, I have sought to reach some sort of judgement on the terms that were negotiated. The first broad point that has to be made is that no one involved in those negotiations ever underestimated the massive burden imposed on the negotiators by the failure of our predecessors in the 1950s to have joined the Community at the outset. That fatal misjudgement, both of the likelihood that the three European Communities would succeed and of Britain's interest to be part of the venture, weighed on all our shoulders, from the Prime Minister downwards. It imposed the need, in Con O'Neill's vivid phrase 'to swallow the lot, and swallow it now' if we were now to join, as the leaders of all Britain's political parties had come to the conclusion that we should. Any other choice, to attempt to renegotiate the founding treaties or the decisions developed under them, would have condemned us to another failure. Within those clear constraints I would argue that the outcome was, with one exception, as good as we could have hoped for and in some cases better. The transitional arrangements on Community finance proved inadequate as we always feared they would do. But the commitment to reopen that issue if the outcome proved to be inequitable was accepted when the time came; and the idea that we could, in 1970–1, have negotiated something akin to the Fontainebleau mechanism, which was agreed in 1984, is totally fanciful. The terms on trade, sugar and New Zealand dairy products stood the test of time pretty well. Only on fisheries does my conscience tell me that we did less well than we should have done; and the fault there lay not so much in the terms we negotiated as with our failure to exert ourselves sufficiently in the run up to the opening of negotiations in June 1970 to block the key decisions on the Common Fisheries Policy, which were only taken by the Six just days before. Admittedly Britain was in the midst of a general election campaign at the time, but if we had been more alert to the signs that the Six were moving rapidly towards agreement and if we had pulled out all the stops, we might have stopped it in its tracks. In particular the Italians had no national interest in the matter (since the CFP under negotiation did not apply to the Mediterranean). Thus, we could have ensured that the CFP that was subsequently agreed took proper account of the interests of the major fishing nations which had applied to join.

6

BRUSSELS (COMMISSION) 1973–1976

CHEF DE CABINET

The year 1972 was much quieter both for the European Community and for me than its predecessors had been. The European institutions basically marked time, preparing for the appointment of a new Commission for the newly enlarged Community, with a substantial exodus of officials from the six original member states matched by an influx of newcomers; and not taking decisions of any major significance in order to avoid upsetting the complex national processes for ratifying the accession of the new members. Those ratification processes took various forms and produced varying results. There were no problems in the existing member states, although France, rather unexpectedly, decided to put the matter to a referendum. The outcome of Norway's referendum was negative, resulting in the withdrawal of its candidature. In Britain a battle royal in Parliament led to splits in both main parties, by far the largest and most significant being the split in the Parliamentary Labour Party, with a substantial number of its pro-European members voting with the government. Thus were sown the seeds of the renegotiation strategy, the 1975 referendum and the later breaking away from the Labour party of the 'Gang of Four' who in 1981 founded the Social Democratic Party. In Brussels one was no more than a fascinated spectator of these events. Activity there was focussed on the negotiation of free trade area agreements between the about-to-be enlarged Community and the EFTA countries that were not joining (Sweden, Finland, Austria, Switzerland, Portugal and Iceland, with

Norway added to the list when its referendum went wrong). Oddly enough, given the visceral opposition that the idea of Europe-wide free trade arrangements had provoked in the Six original members of the Community when first mooted by Britain in the 1950s, these negotiations were handled as largely technical affairs with no crises and little drama. The main difference was that the earlier proposals had envisaged a free trade area as an alternative to the Community's customs union and that Britain, by far EFTA's largest member, was now about to move inside the Community.

My own future remained for some time shrouded in obscurity. Having been in Brussels more than seven years by then, the assumption was that we would soon be moving either to another overseas posting or back to London. But in the spring I was asked whether I would be happy for my name to be included on a list of possible chef de cabinet candidates which the Foreign and Commonwealth Office (FCO) was putting together for submission to the two British Commissioners once they were nominated. I agreed to that, albeit with little expectation that I would get one of the jobs since I was considerably junior to and had less experience than, most of the other names on the list. The British Commissioners were duly appointed – Sir Christopher Soames, who had been Minister of Agriculture during the 1961–3 negotiations and who was currently Ambassador in Paris, and George Thomson who would have handled the accession negotiations if Labour had not lost the 1970 election. It gradually became evident that I was in with a better chance than I had thought. My lack of wider experience was balanced by the indisputable fact that I knew more about the workings of the Commission and had a wider network of contacts within it than any of the other candidates; and the two people to whom Soames turned for advice on the appointment, Michael Palliser, his former No 2 in Paris and my boss as British Permanent Representative in Brussels, and Christopher Ewart-Biggs, his current No 2 in Paris (subsequently assassinated by the IRA), both knew me well and were good friends. So, in due course, I was summoned down to the palatial grandeur of the Ambassador's residence in Paris and found myself on a superb summer evening dining on the terrace and being put through my paces on European politics by the brightest and the best of the members of the Embassy staff under the watchful eye of the Ambassador. The next morning

Soames offered me the job; and I signed on for four and a half years of gilded slavery which I enjoyed as much as anything I ever did in my professional life.

The title of chef de cabinet is not really translatable into English and no function like it existed or exists in Whitehall. It is surrounded by some mystery and much misunderstanding. Moreover, a chef de cabinet in the Commission operated rather differently than someone with the same title in Paris or one of the other continental European capitals. Part of the job was identical to being the Principal Private Secretary of a British cabinet minister, running the minister's Private Office, taking notes of meetings, drafting speeches, accompanying the Minister when he travelled officially and acting as a kind of guidance mechanism and transmission belt between the Minister and the officials in his department. Another part of the job was acting as what would now be called a Political Adviser, a source of advice separate from and more politicised than that coming from the department. But a chef de cabinet in the Commission had an additional collective function which would certainly not have been found in any national capital. The chefs de cabinet of the Commissioners (at that time 13 of them) met together every Monday afternoon for several hours, under the chairmanship of the President's chef de cabinet and the tutelage of the Secretary-General of the Commission, Émile Noël, to prepare the Commission's own weekly meeting on Wednesday. The Commission agenda for each week was carefully sifted and reviewed, some items were discarded or delayed and major differences between Commissioners were identified. A good deal of negotiation was undertaken to remove minor differences and to clarify major ones. Woe betide a chef de cabinet who arrived at a meeting ill-prepared on any issue which his Commissioner was putting to the College. Noël, the avuncular but encyclopaedically knowledgeable French Socialist, who had been Secretary-General of the Commission since the Community was first established in 1957, would grill you rigorously, and, if ever he prefaced a sentence with 'mais, cher ami...', you knew that you were in serious trouble. These collective meetings of chefs de cabinet were the basis on which Commissioners were briefed to enable them to intervene in policy areas for which they were not personally responsible – for example, agriculture or transport policy – the Commission being a much more collegiate body than any national cabinet. To handle this pretty considerable workload, each Commissioner had a staff allocation for his cabinet not too different from the Private Office of a major Whitehall ministry. At that time most, if not all, members of cabinets, apart from the President's cabinet which had always been multinational, tended to be of the same nationality as their Commissioner.

✻   ✻   ✻

From my appointment in the summer of 1972 until the summer of the next year my time was heavily absorbed in putting together the future Commissioner's personal staff (his cabinet in Commission parlance), in sifting the large number of British candidates for senior posts in the Community's institutions and then, once the new Commission had taken over at the beginning of 1973, in negotiating their placement in suitable jobs. Of these three tasks the first was the easiest and the last by far the most complex and difficult.

Christopher Soames himself played an important part in recruiting for the cabinet, bringing with him from the Paris Embassy Adrian Fortescue who had been his Private Secretary there and three out of the four secretaries we needed. He also enlisted Uwe Kitzinger, an academic who had worked at the Council of Europe and who had written a well-researched book on the accession negotiations, as Political Adviser. (He was succeeded in late 1974 by Robert Jackson who was to go on to be an MP and Minister for Higher Education.) To them we added two brilliant young civil servants, Richard Hay from the Treasury and Graham Avery from the Ministry of Agriculture (all three of the civil servants eventually rose to the top ranks in the Commission). It was a strong team and one that worked together as such. The challenge was to move fairly rapidly from a situation where there were literally no British nationals at policymaking level in any of the institutions (there were of course translators, interpreters and members of the Commission's London information office) to one where British nationals were occupying a share of posts at all levels which was roughly similar to that held by nationals of the three existing large member states, France, Germany and Italy. Clearly this could not be done simply by the sort of entry grade competitive examinations which are the standing practice in modern bureaucracies, although such procedures were needed for the longer term future and were in fact put in hand as soon as we joined. But finding candidates at the Director-General, Deputy Director-General, Director and Head of Division level (a span roughly equivalent to Whitehall's grades between Permanent Secretary and Principal) had to be done by careful scrutiny of CVs and by interview. In this process we were helped by the Civil Service Commission in London; and the Commissioners themselves interviewed all candidates for posts at the top two levels. While the prospect of a career in Brussels at a time when enthusiasm for Britain joining the Community was running high attracted many candidates of excellent quality, we had to be on our guard against a well-known tendency of senior management in such circumstances to unload people with whom they wished to dispense; and the Prime Minister's wise commitment to President Pompidou to ensure that British officials being sent to Brussels would have a reasonable working knowledge of French acted as another constraint. Anyway, we duly arrived in Brussels with a large portfolio of candidates but no very clear picture of precisely which jobs would be available for them to fill. At the Commission end a kind of mirror-image exercise had been getting under way. It had been agreed from the outset between all member states that simply adding new member state nationals on to the existing complement of Community officials would lead to an excessively inflated bureaucracy with substantially increased budgetary costs. So a 'golden handshake' scheme was set up to persuade nationals from the Six to leave, with Émile Noël firmly in charge of this difficult and at times painful process. His interest was to get the less good officials out and to avoid the best ones leaving; and he had to ensure roughly proportionate impact between the different nationalities. Thereafter we had to fit our candidates into the slots vacated, or alternatively to juggle those slots until a suitable match between available candidate and available job could be achieved. It was rather like a game of three-dimensional chess and it was every bit as frustrating and time consuming. I would not claim that the results were in every case satisfactory but, six months after we joined, the process was more or less complete; and I was able to ensure that recruitment below Head of Division level was de-politicised and placed firmly in the hands of the different departmental heads in the Commission (Director-Generals) thus frustrating the prevalent tendency among chefs de cabinet each to

try to run their own national patronage system down to the lowest
level of appointment.

✳   ✳   ✳

The arrival of the two British Commissioners in Brussels in January
1973 to take up their new posts was closer to farce than to pomp.
The night before there had been a big banquet at Hampton Court,
hosted by the Prime Minister, to celebrate Britain's accession.
A somewhat jaded party of Commissioners and their staff
congregated at Northolt the following morning to board the plane
which, at Christopher Soames' insistence, the British government
had provided to get us to Brussels. This was no sleek, executive
jet but rather an elderly aircraft belonging to the Civil Aviation
Authority and crammed full of calibrating equipment. There was
standing room only for most of us. And then it transpired that every
single airport on the continent was closed due to fog. It really was a
case of the well-worn joke 'fog in the Channel, Continent isolated'.
Finally, after several hours of waiting, the fog cleared sufficiently
to allow access to the small, provincial airport at Rotterdam; and
from there we were able to catch a train to Brussels. Late that
evening the Soames' baggage train, no small affair, was dumped
unceremoniously on the platform of the Gare du Nord. Next
morning we began work in the Berlaymont building, in a fine suite
of offices on the thirteenth floor which had everything by way of
office equipment and not a single document or background paper.
We really were starting from scratch.

Christopher Soames was a Vice-President of the Commission (a
purely honorific title given to the senior of the two Commissioners
from each of the four large member states) and, in the allocation of
portfolios that took place in the first week of the new Commission,
became responsible for external relations. The earmarking for him of
this portfolio was the result of an Anglo-French inter-governmental
deal which the new (French) President of the Commission, François-
Xavier Ortoli, scrupulously honoured despite the strenuous efforts
of the incumbent in the previous Commission, Ralf Dahrendorf, to
hang on to it. In the absence at that time of even the first vestiges
of a Common Foreign and Security Policy, external relations meant
effectively external trade policy where the Commission's powers

were clearly established in the founding treaty. What Soames lacked in detailed knowledge of the instruments of trade policy – the General Agreement on Tariffs and Trade (GATT), the Generalised System of Preferences (GSP), and all the paraphernalia of rules of origin and bound and unbound tariffs – he more than made up for with his political flair, the warmth and persuasiveness of his powerful personality and his capacity to absorb complicated issues and to cut through them to the essential points. He rapidly built up good working relationships with almost all his fellow Commissioners, the notable exception being the (Dutch) Commissioner for Agriculture, Pierre Lardinois, who intensely resented Soames' ability, as a former Minister of Agriculture himself, to challenge him in the many discussions of the Common Agricultural Policy (CAP). Soames' qualities of leadership, and of loyalty to those who worked for him, together with his ebullient sense of humour, also stood him in good stead with the generally highly talented group of officials in the Commission's department of external relations (then called DGI). As a steady flow of the records of his conversations with ministers and ambassadors from third countries began to percolate around the department – a British practice hitherto unknown in the Commission – a genuine team effort to fashion the external policies of the enlarged Community, a very different entity to the Community of Six with more extensive worldwide interests and greater weight in trade policy negotiations, began to take shape.

*   *   *

There was no questioning that the top trade policy priority when Soames took over was the relationship with the United States, the Community's biggest trading and investment partner, with whom dealings had become decidedly scratchy in the second half of 1972. There were two major issues of contention. The first was the negotiations under the rules of Article XXIV: 6 of the GATT which the Community was obliged to undertake to compensate its main trading partners for any tariff increases which resulted from the acceding countries' move to the tariff rates in the Community's Common External Tariff. Under these rules the United States was undoubtedly owed compensation, although the scale and nature of that compensation was hotly disputed. The second problem was the spread of the Community's preferential trading area following enlargement. A large number of countries in Africa, the Caribbean and the Pacific were set to move into that area, as were the Arab countries on the southern shore of the Mediterranean and Israel. The USA saw this shift as likely to damage its own trading position. Their concerns in this respect had already been raised during the accession negotiations, but the British government had managed to stifle them at that time by deploying the broader arguments for the USA to favour enlargement, which the Nixon administration accepted. Now US concerns surfaced again, fed by the anxiety that there seemed to be virtually no limit to the Community's ambitions to extend its preferential trading area.

The Article XXIV: 6 negotiations were a problem from hell so far as the new Commission was concerned since the American requests for tariff compensation had targeted products which were sensitive to the Six and there was no question of any balancing concession by the USA as there would have been in a classical trade negotiation; moreover, the Commissioner's nationality did not help since Britain was not so targeted. The negotiations were grinding on in an atmosphere of acrimony orchestrated by American threats of retaliation if adequate compensation was not forthcoming. But Soames managed quickly to establish a good working relationship with Bill Eberle, the US Special Trade Representative – even if he did resent Eberle's tendency to telephone him from the poolside in California at some unearthly hour in the European morning – and an agreement was struck by the summer of 1973. As to the second problem, Soames pursued a two-pronged approach. During his first official visit to Washington he managed, helped no doubt by his friendship with Henry Kissinger, the President's Secretary of State and National Security Adviser, to get to see President Nixon. He explained to Nixon that the extension of the Community's partnership with countries around the world went far beyond mere trading arrangements, including also substantial aid programmes and schemes to stabilise these countries' export receipts from primary commodities. The Community was thus playing a crucial role in helping to bring stability to a whole range of Third World countries whose poverty and fragility was obvious, and was thereby making a real contribution to overall Western interests. Of course if the USA wanted to share or take over that role in Africa and elsewhere that would be fine – an offer that Nixon had no hesitation in declining. In parallel with this direct approach, and having cleared his lines with the Commission in advance, Soames made a public speech in Brussels saying that the Commission had no intention of proposing any extension of the Community's preferential trading arrangements beyond the African, Caribbean and Pacific countries listed in the Treaty of Accession and the countries on the southern shore of the Mediterranean. This self-denying ordinance was in fact pretty well cost free since no one in the enlarged Community was at that time prepared to contemplate such trade arrangements with Asian countries. It did, however, cause some trouble with Iran, which fell on the wrong side of the line. And there was some audible sucking of teeth by the member states as to whether it was really the Commission's business to pronounce so trenchantly on policy matters in an area of responsibility shared with the Council. Nevertheless, it did the trick so far as the Americans were concerned and no more was heard of that particular grievance. While relations with the United States over the next four years were never entirely devoid of disputes they remained very much on an even keel, and even weathered the tensions aroused by Kissinger's call for 1973 to be 'the year of Europe', a misguided initiative which soon petered out. Soames' private reaction was far from relaxed and he said to Kissinger at one of their meetings for which he used to slip down to Paris (where Kissinger was conducting secret negotiations with the North Vietnamese), 'How would you like it, Henry, if I were to announce that next year was the year of America?' The Soames approach demonstrated that blend of robustness in defence of Europe's interests combined with a willingness to pay attention to American concerns, which often seemed to elude British foreign policy over the decades ahead.

The other main trade policy task in 1973 was to prepare for the launching of a new global round of negotiations for multilateral trade liberalisation. The Kennedy Round had been successfully completed in 1967 and was now being implemented; the results were proving strongly positive, with the growth of world trade consistently outstripping and stimulating economic growth. There was a developing consensus that the time had come for a further such round. A necessary condition for its launch was agreement between the three main players in world trade, the USA, Japan and the European Community. There was no doubt about the positive attitude of the first two, and Japan had indeed set up a ministerial meeting in Tokyo in September to decide on the launch of a new round. The situation in the European Community was a bit less straightforward. The Commission was in no doubt about the case for a new round of multilateral trade negotiations and, armed with that support, Soames made this the centrepiece of his first visits to the capitals of the member states. In most of them the reaction was strongly in favour; but there were traces of doubt in Rome and Dublin, and in Paris something close to outright opposition – in all cases the main concern was fear that the Community's system of agricultural protection and the subsidisation of its agricultural exports would come under threat. The visit to Paris included a rather bizarre encounter with Jacques Chirac, a rising star in the Gaullist party and recently appointed Minister of Agriculture, who, perhaps misled by the large Cuban cigar which Soames habitually smoked, seemed to believe that he was American and not British; and a more nuanced discussion with the Finance Minister, Valéry Giscard d'Estaing, who hinted at an attempt to link trade negotiations with the issue of exchange rates and the allegedly unfair parity of the dollar against other currencies. However, French grumbling never amounted to outright opposition, and so the Community was able to head for Tokyo supporting the launch of the new round. Soames and his team went there via Bangkok where we had a meeting with the ministers of the recently established Association of South East Asian Nations (ASEAN) and laid the foundation for a constructive relationship which was to develop steadily in the years ahead. The greater outreach of the recently enlarged community was already making itself felt. In Tokyo there was a good deal of confused toing and froing and some sharp skirmishing between Giscard d'Estaing and the US Secretary of the Treasury, George Shultz, over exchange rates; but none of this prevented the launch of what came to be known as the Tokyo Round. Those negotiations then disappeared, as is the wont of such major multilateral trade negotiations, into the long grass of technicalities and did not make decisive progress during the period covered by the present account. But they subsequently reached a successful conclusion that marked a further important step along the road of trade liberalisation and the rolling back of the protectionist surge of the 1930s.

✳   ✳   ✳

Then, in the autumn of 1973, the wheel of fortune took a sharp turn
for the worse, both for the European Community and for Britain in
Europe. The Yom Kippur War, the Arab boycott of oil exports and
the Shah of Iran's opportunistic move on the back of the boycott
to get OPEC to more than quadruple the price of oil, threw the
Community into disarray. The Community had no energy policy to
speak of, and even if it had had one, it would have been hard put
to it to decide what to do. There was a marked lack of solidarity
with the only member state under boycott, the Netherlands; and
one of the, in those days rather infrequent, meetings of Heads of
State and Government in the European Council that December was
hijacked by a group of Arab leaders and only reached a minimalist
decision on a regional policy which had been intended to contribute
to a reduction in the British budgetary imbalance. A number of
member states, with Britain in the lead, sought bilateral deals with
oil producers to guarantee their future supplies; the sight of British
ministers, rather incongruously dressed in dark suits and ties, visiting
the Shah's chalet in St Moritz caught the flavour. Soames spoke out
publicly against this dash to bilateralism and was soundly berated by
his former Conservative colleagues in government, who were sliding
towards an early general election and could have done without
such criticism. At this point Kissinger summoned the US's Western
partners to an energy conference in Washington. The object was to set
up international arrangements to encourage concerted programmes
of energy conservation, the development of energy resources other
than oil and a system to build up and to share oil stocks in the event
of a future crisis. But this conference divided the Community too,
the French being determined to avoid any such Western caucus
on energy policy and above all one led by the Americans and to
depend on a pro-Arab foreign policy to ensure their oil supplies.
For three days the assembled Community's Foreign, Finance and
Energy Ministers, cooped up in a claustrophobic conference room
in the State Department, struggled to reach a common view; and
failed. In the end, eight member states, with Commission support,
decided to join the newly founded International Energy Agency
(IEA), which was to be loosely attached to the Organisation for

Economic Cooperation and Development (OECD), while the French stayed out. Some years later they quietly crept in. The only people in Washington who were more distressed than the Community were the Japanese whose instructions were to go along with whatever the Europeans agreed to, but who had no line to take if the Europeans could not agree on anything. They too joined the IEA. Returning from this humiliating experience we stopped off in New York to meet Hushang Ansary, the Shah's Minister of the Economy. Ansary gloated lengthily over Western disarray and gave us a hard time on the Community's refusal to contemplate negotiating a preferential trade agreement with Iran. It was a fitting end to a miserable few days, and a salutary reminder of the fact that the Community still had a long way to go before it could hope to handle major upheavals in the world around it with any sort of unity.

The February 1974 general election in Britain brought to power, in place of the Conservative government led by a Prime Minister who wished to make the Community the main focus of Britain's foreign policy, a Labour government which lacked an overall majority and was deeply divided (three ways) over European issues. A group of pro-Europeans led by Roy Jenkins had voted for the terms of accession and were strongly opposed to the holding of a referendum on British membership; Harold Wilson and James Callaghan, Prime Minister and Foreign Secretary respectively, wanted to renegotiate the terms of accession and put the issue to a referendum; and another group of ministers, led by Tony Benn and Peter Shore, wanted to use the referendum to take Britain out of the Community. It was hardly a recipe for an effective British input to Community policymaking in Brussels. And, if anyone had nurtured any hopes that the matter could easily be fudged, they would not have survived Callaghan's first appearance at the Council, in Luxembourg in early April, where he laid it on the line with some brutality that renegotiation had been a manifesto commitment which would need to be honoured. The shock of this statement would probably have been greater had it not been followed within hours, just as the Council was breaking up, by the news of President Pompidou's death and thus a hiatus too in French policymaking. At this stage I wrote a paper for the two British Commissioners which I entitled 'Renegotiation without tears'. The main thrust of this was that the Commission should avoid taking too prominent a position on renegotiation and in particular should avoid pronouncing on whether the renegotiation of a treaty that had been solemnly ratified was either legally or politically acceptable to Britain's other partners and to the Commission. We should wait and see what issues the British themselves raised as part of their renegotiation strategy and thus whether these could be accommodated without actual changes being made to the terms of the Accession Treaty. And we should not be too pernickety if Britain chose to put a renegotiation label on decisions taken during the normal course of Community business. Although some in the Commission would rather have taken a tougher line, and the word 'renegotiation' was never allowed to enter the Commission's lexicon, Soames and Thomson were able to persuade their colleagues to follow those policy prescriptions. In the event the two main issues covered in the renegotiation, agreement on the quantities of New Zealand butter Britain could import in the years immediately following the end of the transitional period (a process provided for in the Accession Treaty) and a financial mechanism designed to prevent some parts of Britain's gross (but not its net) contribution from deviating too far from what had been projected at the time of its accession, did not require any changes to the Treaty (the financial mechanism in fact proving inoperable when the main budgetary crisis actually broke in 1979). In addition, some changes to the Community's GSP which were of benefit to Asian Commonwealth countries (and incidentally to the budding relationship with ASEAN) appeared in the British White Paper among the fruits of renegotiation. The Commission limited itself to providing low-key technical support as the member states hammered out these agreements. When the British government duly announced that it was ready to put these terms to a referendum, a difficult corner had been turned, even if in a rather inelegant manner.

The referendum that followed also required some careful navigation by the Commission. Soames and Thomson advised their colleagues that it would be better if no non-British Commissioners were to participate in the campaign, and that rule was respected by all except the junior German Commissioner, Guido Brunner, who did appear once on a liberal platform. The two British Commissioners undertook many speaking engagements, mainly on cross-party platforms involving Conservative, Liberal and pro-European Labour speakers. Both were surprised by how well the three different elements got on together; and that was to have implications for British politics at a later stage. We were careful too to ensure that no campaigning rules were broken, Soames being accompanied only by his Political Adviser, Robert Jackson, on engagements in the UK while the campaign was on. We did put a lot of time and effort into answering a flood of European Parliamentary Questions tabled by British parliamentarians which enabled us to showcase some of the Community's achievements and to dispel some of the myths spread by the 'no' campaign. Broadly speaking the media, and in particular the written press, favoured the 'yes' campaign, press attitudes then being as different as could possibly be from what they have become in recent years. The outcome, a two to one majority for the 'yes' campaign, was greatly welcomed by everyone in Brussels, partly, in the unfortunately mistaken belief that that would settle the matter of Britain's membership once and for all. Those of us who doubted that were simply relieved and elated.

*　　*　　*

Nothing was further from the minds of the new Commission that took office in 1973 and from those of the nine member states of the enlarged Community than the question of further enlargement. For one thing there were no very obvious candidates; the EFTA countries which at that time did not wish to become full members (together with Norway which did, but which had been frustrated by its 1972 negative referendum result) had successfully negotiated free trade agreements with the Community; the countries of Central and Eastern Europe were firmly locked in the embrace of Comecon and the Warsaw Pact, and the Soviet intervention in Czechoslovakia in 1968 had shown that there was no easy escape from that; Yugoslavia, while certainly qualifying for stronger economic ties with the Community, could not possibly be considered as a potential member without crossing several red lines which both sides in the Cold War had been careful to respect; and three southern European countries, Greece, Portugal and Spain, remained under authoritarian dictatorships whose contempt for democracy and human rights disqualified them from the outset, while Turkey drifted in and out of military rule. So the new Commission disbanded the remarkable team which had helped to negotiate the first enlargement, most of whose members found homes in the external relations department under Christopher Soames; and no provision was made in the distribution of portfolios for any Commissioner to have responsibility for new applications for membership, although all the relevant countries were covered by the external relations remit. As so often happens, events belied the best laid plans and, from the spring of 1974, the southern European dictatorships began to go down like ninepins. The first to go was Portugal in a bloodless coup which brought to power a group of young left-wing officers who had fought in the colonial wars in Portugal's possessions in Africa; then in July 1974 the regime of the colonels in Greece collapsed after having engineered a coup in Cyprus against President Makarios and thus triggered the Turkish intervention; and General Franco, while a long time a-dying was clearly soon going to leave Spain without any very obvious successor to his 40 years of authoritarian rule.

The new military-dominated regime in Portugal was undecided as to the direction in which to take the country and whether or not to hand over power to a democratically elected government; and it was therefore at the outset in no shape to define its future relationship with the rest of Europe. There were concerns that the country might slide towards a kind of Euro-Communism, undermining Portugal's membership of NATO, and these concerns were particularly strongly felt in and orchestrated from Washington. Elsewhere in Europe a more benign view was taken and the emphasis was on strengthening the hand of the democratic forces in Portugal, which had a foothold in the new government in the form of Mário Soares, a firmly democratic socialist who had long lived in exile and who was Foreign Minister; but Soares exercised no real power which was still firmly in the hands of the military members of the government. Soames decided to visit Lisbon to try to form a view as to which of the two schools of thought, the pessimistic or the optimistic, was closer to reality and to bring some encouragement to the democrats. Our visit certainly provided a good picture of what was a remarkably confused scene. Ensconced in the baroque splendour of the Foreign Ministry, Soares was warmly welcoming and wanted to encourage the strongest possible economic links between Portugal and the Community going far beyond the existing free trade area. It was clear that Soares' own final objective was membership. But he readily admitted that he exercised no authority in the government and that the political situation was very fragile. Our call on the Prime Minister, Brigadier Gonçalves, who was the leader of the military group which exercised power, was pretty weird. Barely waiting for the ritual exchange of pleasantries he launched into a diatribe against the European Community. Portugal had not rid itself of the shackles of the Salazar/Caetano dictatorship in order to submit to the neo-colonial rule of Europe. Portugal had no need of economic assistance; it could look after itself and choose its own path. All this was interlarded with much rather ill-digested Marxist rhetoric. I could see Soames becoming restive and he did not mince his words in reply. The Prime Minister seemed to have entirely misunderstood the situation. He was in Lisbon to offer such help as the new Portuguese regime might want, precisely in order to enable the Portuguese to choose their own future democratically. If they wanted nothing, that was it; and no doubt the Finance Ministers of the Community would be delighted. This riposte brought a rather calmer atmosphere to the discussion. And, as we left the Prime Minister's office, the young, technocratic Minister of Economic Affairs thanked Soames, his eyes shining, and said no one had ever spoken to Gonçalves like that before; other European visitors just loaded him with praise for having overthrown the dictatorship. Later that evening we saw another aspect of the scene when we dined with Melo Antunes, a more junior officer but part of the ruling group. He spoke much more positively, if vaguely, about a fully democratic future for Portugal and spared us the Marxist rhetoric. Soames' view, which he passed on to Kissinger and to Community Foreign Ministers was that the risks of Portugal going the wrong way were real but that it was all to play for and we should not give up hope of a positive outcome. In fact it took some considerable time for the complex power play, of which we had glimpsed a small part, to be resolved, and for a fully democratic situation to emerge. So the next phase of Portugal's future as an eventual member of the Community falls outside the time frame of this account.

Everything moved much faster in Greece and proved much more challenging for the Commission. For one thing the regime of the colonels collapsed and was swept away more rapidly and comprehensively than anyone had expected. Within a short time a democratically elected government, with Constantine Karamanlis, a former centre-right Prime Minister who had been living in exile in Paris at its head, was installed; and it had one major objective, to apply for and to become a member of the Community as quickly as possible. In this objective the Greeks had a powerful friend at court in the form of the new President of France, Valéry Giscard d'Estaing, who from the outset pulled out all the stops to help them in their endeavour. So the Greek application was duly received and passed to the Commission for it to provide its 'opinion', the first step towards the opening of negotiations for accession. It was quite clear that the political conditions for Greece's membership were met by its rapid transition to democracy, but whether it made sense in economic terms to move equally rapidly to early accession was less obvious. The Greek negotiating technique, deployed on this occasion, for the first, but by no means for the last time, was to accept everything they were asked to do by the Community without hesitation; no exceptions, no elaborate transitional measures, they would sign as many blank cheques as were needed to remove obstacles to their accession. Whether they would implement these commitments was, of course, another matter but not one easily susceptible of proof one way or the other. What was clear to the Commission officials whose job it was to assess all this, and to their political masters who would have to put their names to the 'opinion', was that the Greek economy, which had been weak before the colonels took over and which had suffered from the relative isolation to which they were subjected, was in poor shape to accept the responsibilities of membership; and that the gap between Greek per capita income and competitivity and that of the rest of the Community was a massive one, far greater than anything which had been contemplated in the case of the first enlargement. The question for the Commission therefore was whether to yield to Greek pressure for early membership or whether to contemplate first a period of preparation during which the Community would help Greece with substantial amounts of pre-accession aid and advice. And, while Soames, and, somewhat more surprisingly given the attitude of the French government, Ortoli, favoured the second approach, the Commissioners were sharply divided on the issue. The case for early membership was put forcefully and in highly emotional terms by Altiero Spinelli, the junior Italian member who had suffered much at the hands of Mussolini and who believed that anything less than an unambiguous and immediate green light would be a betrayal of the cause of democracy in Greece. In the end, after a lengthy debate, the Commission's 'opinion' in the sense proposed by Soames was agreed, but only by the slimmest of majorities, seven votes to six. And the public presentation was hijacked by Spinelli who dashed to the press briefing room and denounced his colleagues in flamboyant terms, thus demonstrating that his support for democracy did not extend to accepting collective responsibility for decisions reached democratically.

Even without Spinelli's onslaught we knew that the 'opinion' would not go down particularly well with the member states. The Commission had tried to sound out their opinion and to prepare the ground by raising the matter at an informal foreign ministers' weekend meeting that had already become a biannual feature of Community life. However, the French Foreign Minister had cut Ortoli off before he had said anything much, arguing that it was improper for the Commission to share its views with the Council before it presented them formally – a staggeringly specious argument, but it served the purpose of preventing any debate. Moreover, we had added to the 'opinion' a warning that early Greek accession would be certain to complicate, perhaps irretrievably, the Community's relationship with Turkey (which had not yet applied for membership but was in one of its periods of grace of having a democratically elected government), a consideration that was entirely valid but not popular in all quarters in the aftermath of the Turkish intervention in Cyprus. In the event, the reception of the 'opinion' by the Council was even worse than we had expected, thanks in part to Karamanlis having convoked the Community Ambassadors in Athens on the eve of the Council meeting and threatened that Greece would withdraw from NATO if the Council did not immediately authorise the opening of accession negotiations. And that was what the Council did the following day, unanimously, having been treated to a further denunciation of the Commission by the French Foreign Minister for having had the effrontery to express a view on a matter of foreign policy which was none of its business. It had been a bruising affair; but whether historians will judge that the Commission had more right on its side than wrong is another matter. Certainly the problems we raised are still with the Community today.

The third of the southern trio, Spain, was held back by the continuing, if increasingly tenuous, grip on power of General Franco. But signs of impending change there too reached us through the Spanish Ambassador to the Community, Alberto Ullastres, who had been one of the first technocrat ministers brought in by Franco to try to reform Spain's faltering economy and who dearly wanted to see a modern Spain anchored in Europe. When Franco died in November 1975 there had to be a delicate diplomatic minuet. Two ceremonies were scheduled: one Franco's funeral and the other to mark the emergence of King Juan Carlos onto the international stage. The Commission were invited to both, it being understood that attendance at the former could be at a lower rank than the latter. Even that proved a stretch for the Commission, hatred of Franco's regime and all it stood for in European history being deeply embedded. After much toing and froing, Edmund Wellenstein, the Director-General for External Relations went to the funeral, not because he felt any less strongly about Franco but because his sense of public service prevented him from flatly refusing as the Secretary-General, Émile Noël, had done. Finn Gundelach, the Danish member of the Commission, who was standing in for Soames away on sick leave, attended the second occasion where he had a long tête-à-tête audience with the king. Juan Carlos made it clear that his ambition was to see Spain join the Community. This would take time but he hoped for patience and support. The message could not have been clearer. And, although it was to take until 1986 for all three countries to join the Community, it was, for the first but not the last time, demonstrated what a powerful geopolitical tool accession to the Community could be. A similar process of transition to democratic institutions and market economies was achieved in the case of the countries of Central and Eastern Europe after the end of the Cold War and is under way now in the Balkans following the wars of the Yugoslav succession.

✻   ✻   ✻

From the moment of his arrival in Brussels in 1973 Christopher Soames' personal project was to find some way to open up relations with China. In this he was given no encouragement and little help by his officials, none of whom had any knowledge of or expertise on China and China having up to then emulated the Soviet Union in treating the Community as part of a capitalist conspiracy, to be shunned. But he persevered, encouraged by the US rapprochement with China which by then had taken place. The first contact occurred, rather bizarrely, at Britain's Royal Agricultural Show that Soames was presiding over in 1973 in his capacity as a former Minister of Agriculture. He spoke there to the Chinese Ambassador and said how much he would like to visit China. After a fairly lengthy interval a message came back via the same channel that he would be very welcome to come to China in a personal and private capacity. It was all I could do to prevent him taking the next flight out; but I explained that, as a Vice-President of the Commission responsible for external relations, he could not possibly travel on a personal and private basis. So a message was sent back that, while it was well understood on the European side that the visit could not be an official one, since China had no relations of any sort with the Community, Soames would have to travel in his capacity as a Vice-President of the Commission and would need to be assured that he would be received as such and would meet senior Chinese representatives. As a further test of Chinese intentions he asked that future contacts be put in the hands of the Chinese Ambassador to Belgium. In due course the Chinese accepted both points; and I found myself smuggling a rather large Commissioner in my little red Mini in and out of the Chinese Embassy for successive sessions over tea and cakes to plan the visit. Everything proceeded smoothly except that the Chinese flatly refused to say in detail whom Soames would meet, sticking to a mantra that he would be received at an appropriate level. They suggested delicately that May (1975) would enable him to see Beijing at its best (neither we, nor they I imagine, being unaware that this was immediately before the date set for the British referendum on membership). Miraculously this whole process was conducted without a single leak; and the member states were told what was afoot only a week ahead of the visit.

We arrived in Beijing from Tehran, where we had had another, slightly less scratchy, meeting with Ansary, although the issue of a preferential trade agreement remained a bone of contention. As the Chinese plane in which we were travelling (a Boeing) began its descent into Beijing, Soames asked, yet again, whom he would be seeing and I replied that I was sure the Chinese would do things properly. 'You had better be right', was the response (my confidence was not purely Micawberish since the Belgian Prime Minister, Leo Tindemans, who had been on an official visit to China shortly before we went, had been assured that we would be well received and that our visit was welcome at the highest political level). Anyway all concerns on that front were dissipated from the moment we touched down and were treated for all intents and purposes, apart from pure formalities, as official visitors. We immediately began a series of meetings at the Great Hall of the People with the Foreign Minister, Qiao Guanhua, and the Trade Minister, interspersed with banquets and copious libations of maotai. On the first day Soames was invited to set out in detail the Community's relations with other countries worldwide which he did for several hours with great elan and eloquence. The next day Qiao said he would respond by giving us China's view of the Community and how it fitted into their foreign policy. On balance they regarded the Community as a force for good and a barrier against Soviet hegemonic policies. They wanted to establish diplomatic relations and to negotiate a non-preferential trade agreement. After that Soames was whisked off to meet Chou En-lai, the Prime Minister (already ill and in a clinic); but there was no meeting with Mao whose health was given as the reason. At this point, as everything was going smoothly, we hit a rock. The Chinese, who had established, or rather re-established, diplomatic relations with a whole range of European and other countries, had always sought and obtained formal texts recognising China as a single country and renouncing any relations with Taiwan. They wanted a similar declaration from us. We explained in excruciating detail and any number of times that the Community as such was not itself a state and that it was not therefore competent to recognise or not to recognise other states and that the same was even more true of the Commission. We could say on behalf of the Commission that we had no contractual relations with Taiwan and did not contemplate having any; but we could not get into the recognition business. We even resorted to explaining this again to the chandelier in our hotel suite. For whatever reason, the Chinese finally got the point; and the decision to establish diplomatic relations and to negotiate a trade agreement was announced at the end of the visit. When we briefed the Community Ambassadors they were surprised and slightly miffed that a process which had taken some of then many months of hard work had been so rapidly and satisfactorily accomplished. Looking back now from a period when Europe is trying, laboriously and not always successfully, to build up a Common Foreign and Security Policy, it is hard to believe that the European Union of the present day could or would attempt to pull off such a daring diplomatic coup. It remained something of a one-off in an otherwise heavily bureaucratic landscape.

✻   ✻   ✻

The second half of the Ortoli Commission (1973-6) was a depressing period, when holding the line often seemed more important than making any further progress towards the lofty objectives which the Heads of State and Government had set out when they met in Paris in the autumn of 1972, just before enlargement took place. For one thing there was a leadership vacuum, with the departure from the scene of Heath, Pompidou and Brandt in rapid succession; the next leadership duo of Helmut Schmidt and Giscard d'Estaing took some time to make itself felt. The economic turmoil following the rise in the price of oil presented governments with a toxic combination of low growth and rising inflation and unemployment. The Werner Plan for achieving economic and monetary union over a ten-year period sank without a trace. The Belgian Prime Minister, Leo Tindemans, made an attempt to devise a new concept which he named European Union. This provoked a flurry of activity in the Commission, which could not afford to be sidelined in such an exercise, even if most believed, as they did, that it was premature.

Noël convened a meeting of an eclectic group of Commission officials, of whom I was one, to put together a paper on European Union; tasks were allocated as he went round the table; I kept quiet, having learned during my period of military service the old adage 'never volunteer'. It looked as if I was going to get away with it, all the obvious policy areas having been covered, but Noël was having none of it. So I offered to write a paper on what should not be included in any project for European Union. This I duly did, arguing that if the Community was at some stage to make a great leap forward to a European Union it would be necessary to set out the limits of the endeavour if fears were not to be raised that a federal United States of Europe was on the stocks. My attempt to inject a little realism into a highly futuristic exercise got nowhere, even if it did pre-figure by 25 years the debates that took place in the parliamentary convention set up to consider a constitutional treaty. The European Union idea got nowhere in the Council and rapidly fizzled out. In truth the most important achievement of those years, in which the Commission played a key role, was to demonstrate the resilience of the Community and its institutions as they weathered the first major world economic crisis since the end of the Second World War.

∗   ∗   ∗

I had escaped any close involvement with fisheries during the accession negotiations, but there was no escaping the gathering international pressure for major decisions to be taken on fisheries limits that came to a head in 1976. The pressure arose from a number of different quarters; from the overfishing of stocks in the waters around the British Isles which were outside any member state's 12 mile territorial and fisheries limits and thus outside governmental control; from the fact that overfishing was to a considerable extent due to the operations of factory ships from the Soviet Union and its East European satellites whose activities brought virtually no benefit to the member states; and from the worldwide move towards the extension of national fisheries limits and economic zones well beyond the current 12 miles, the most dramatic expression of which was the unilateral Icelandic decision to go out to 50 miles and to exclude the British deep sea trawlers which fished there for cod, leading to the so-called 'Cod War' between Britain and Iceland, which Britain was gradually but inexorably losing. As so often the Community had difficulty making up its mind what to do, and was far from being in the forefront of the move to 200 mile limits which was gradually becoming the international norm. The Commission, with Finn Gundelach, who was standing in for Soames, away on sick leave, in the lead, tried to nudge the member states towards a decision to go out to 200 miles which would then enable any member state that wanted to exclude the Soviet and East European factory ships. That summer I was asked to go to London to explain Commission thinking to an inter-departmental meeting and duly did so. I found a complete absence of coherent policy there; while the attractions of a policy which would enable the exclusion of the factory ships were evident, going out to 200 miles would massively increase the area to which the Community's Common Fisheries Policy would apply and, since fish had the inconvenient habit of swimming across any lines which humans might draw on maps, this would raise awkward questions about the protection of the livelihoods of British and Irish inshore fishermen to which so much time and effort had been devoted during the accession negotiations; and there remained the running sore of the dispute with Iceland which, of course, could no longer be sustained if the Community itself went out to 200 miles. Fortunately the Foreign Secretary, Tony Crosland, who knew all too much about these matters as the longstanding member of parliament for Grimsby, had the courage and clear-sightedness to cut through the confusion and indecision and to opt, broadly speaking, for the solution favoured by the Commission. At a long and difficult informal council meeting in The Hague that autumn the decision to go out to 200 mile limits was taken and at the same time it was agreed that the provisions for safeguarding the livelihoods of the inshore fishermen would be strengthened. As a gesture of support for the British government Gundelach agreed to try to persuade the Icelanders to admit a very small number of British deep sea vessels for a short period of time. So he and I found ourselves visiting Reykjavík twice, in November and December 1976, on one of the most forlorn hopes imaginable, trying to persuade Iceland to make a concession which would be very unpopular with their electorate in return for some pretty worthless tariff concessions on their own fish exports to the Community. Despite a few very faint early signs that a deal might be possible, we failed. It was something of a dying fall on which to end four tumultuous and fascinating years at the Commission. I got back from Reykjavík just in time to catch the last half hour of the farewell party we were giving for our friends in Brussels.

7

LONDON 1977–1979

OIL DIPLOMACY

From the middle of the four-year term of the Ortoli Commission thoughts and gossip in Brussels turned to its successor. A general assumption took root that the President of the next Commission should be British, the other three large member states having already held the post by then. And, for a time, it seemed as if the choice could well fall on Christopher Soames, his relationship with Harold Wilson being good ever since Wilson had sprung the surprise of appointing him to the Embassy in Paris. I rather suspected, although the matter was never put to me, that in those circumstances Soames would want me to stay with him; and both loyalty and inclination would have made refusing to do so unthinkable. But the unexpected resignation of Wilson early in 1976, the choice of James Callaghan, no admirer of Soames, as his successor, and the likelihood that Roy Jenkins, who had been one of those who lost out in the succession race, would be the British candidate for the Presidency of the Commission put paid to all that. I then had to make a career choice. I could either look for a senior, permanent post in the Commission (chef de cabinet posts were temporary appointments), and this would not in all probability have been too difficult to achieve, 'parachutage' by chefs de cabinet being all too customary in the Commission; or I could return to London and the Diplomatic Service. I did not hesitate for long. My heart was still set on a classical diplomatic career rather than the sort of Brussels-based civil service career that could have been on offer. And so I was appointed (no consultation as to preferences in those days) to be head of the Foreign and Commonwealth Office's Energy Department (later to become Energy, Science and Space department as some of the smaller, functional departments were amalgamated following the Berrill Report on the Diplomatic Service). I was less than enthralled by the prospect, since I had hoped for a geographical department and to get some greater experience of bilateral diplomacy, not another spell of multilateral economic work. But, when I bemoaned my fate to Roy Denman, by now head of the European Secretariat in the Cabinet Office, he gave me some sage advice. 'Just disappear for a bit. People around Whitehall have heard your name a bit too often in recent times'.

✻   ✻   ✻

As preparation for my new job I managed before leaving Brussels to wangle for myself what was called a young leaders invitation to spend a month in the United States (the Commission did the same thing in reverse, and one of the first beneficiaries was a young Richard Holbrooke, just out of the US Diplomatic Service in Vietnam, who proved a fascinating dinner companion with Soames for an evening in Strasbourg, the first of several occasions when our paths crossed). My American programme was naturally focussed on energy and the timing was perfect since the new President, Jimmy Carter, was inaugurated on the day we arrived in Washington and he had already made clear that reducing US dependence on imported oil, what he was to entitle 'the moral equivalent of war', was to be one of the main objectives of his term of office. By the time we had travelled widely around the USA and met a range of those who would be involved in this endeavour, people in the oil, gas and nuclear industries, environmentalists and staffers on the Hill, there was no doubt that he had taken on a formidable challenge, given that the simplest solution, a rise in the level of taxation on energy products was ruled out from the outset as politically unthinkable.

The second part of my familiarisation for the new job was to visit some of the main oil producers in the Gulf – Saudi Arabia, Iran, Kuwait and Abu Dhabi. I wish I could say that either I or anyone else I was in touch with anticipated the events which only one year later came to be known as the Iranian Revolution and which have constituted a major destabilising factor in a crucial region ever since;

or, for that matter, that anyone foresaw the outbreak of hostilities between Iran and Iraq. But I did not, and they did not. It was already clear that Iran's economy was in some trouble, with high rates of inflation following the Shah's breakneck investment splurge on the back of massively increased oil revenues, but these problems still looked like being no more than having too much of a good thing, not the precursor to disaster. And, while there was no doubt that Iran and Iraq were bitter rivals to become the dominant regional power, and were locked into an arms race of considerable dimensions (from which incidentally all major arms exporters from both sides of the Iron Curtain were profiting and which we were all encouraging), the Shah and President Saddam Hussein both had proven track records of successful brinkmanship; the expectation was that they would continue to avoid going to war. What did strike me as I visited some of the key installations – the Saudi export terminal at Ras Tanura, Kuwait like a pimple on Iraq's bottom, Kharg Island through which almost all of Iran's crude oil exports passed, the great export refinery at Abadan built by the Anglo-Iranian Oil Company between the two world wars and right on the frontier with Iraq – was their extraordinary vulnerability to either an outbreak of hostilities or to acts of terrorism. So that very much reinforced the case for the West to develop a whole spectrum of energy policies designed to reduce an ever-increasing dependence on Middle East oil.

Back in London I found myself working for a government that was in deep economic trouble, which was losing its overall majority in Parliament and which was very far from being a band of brothers. The cabinet was split three ways on Europe, and there were profound left-right tensions as well. Following the sudden death of Tony Crosland there was a new Foreign Secretary, David Owen, talented, forceful but not much of a team player and still low in the Labour Party pecking order. Almost every policy issue I had to deal with straddled these splits and involved complex inter-departmental manoeuvring, all the more so as the Secretary of State for Energy, Tony Benn, was at the Europhobe and left-wing end of the cabinet spectrum. Among the most interesting aspects of the job were the international implications of Britain itself becoming a substantial oil producing state as production of oil from the North Sea built up steadily and was set to make us, for a short time at least, a net exporter. Were we to become a kind of country member of OPEC? Should we be placing limits on which countries the exports of our oil might go to? Should we be trying to force the oil companies to refine a proportion of North Sea oil in Britain? Should we be pursuing a cautious depletion policy or be developing the North Sea fields as fast as we could? How did all this fit in with our European and IEA obligations? All those issues, and more, were pending, and all would need to be settled in the next few years.

Answering some of these questions did not prove too difficult, although hardly any were answered to the satisfaction of Tony Benn at the Department of Energy. But, with the contrary views of the Chancellor of the Exchequer (Denis Healey) and the Prime Minister (James Callaghan) against him, there was really no contest. For all the hyperbole in the press and elsewhere about Britain's burgeoning wealth from oil (known and studied in Whitehall under the acronym BONSO – the Benefits of North Sea Oil) the fact was that, even at its peak, oil and gas production was not going to account for more than a middle single figure percentage of our Gross National Product. We were not set to become a Saudi Arabia or a Kuwait; and that peak moment would not last for long. The rest of our economy would continue to be dependent on our manufacturing and service industries. We would remain one of the major industrialised economies, dependent for our prosperity on a steady growth in world trade and the reduction in barriers to that growth; and so we too would remain vulnerable to the negative economic consequences of volatile swings in energy prices and thus averse to contributing to them. The concept of distancing ourselves in economic and trade policy terms from our close allies in the industrialised world, with whom we were beginning to work together more closely in what would come to be known as the G7, therefore had little appeal. No more did the mercantilist policy of trying to force the oil companies who were producing in the North Sea to refine more of their production in Britain. There was, as a result of the economic turbulence following the quadrupling of the oil price in 1973, a massive surplus of refining capacity in Western Europe and most oil companies were losing money on their refining work. Trying to increase refining in Britain when it was a money-losing enterprise appealed neither to the industry nor to the wiser heads in government. On depletion policy David Owen was a lone voice (with which I strongly sympathised) in arguing for a conservative policy aimed at spreading the development of our North Sea resources over a longer time frame. The Treasury, even more desperate for additional revenue than usual and that as quickly as possible, were viscerally opposed and Benn gave no support. So the idea fizzled out.

Some other arguments for British exceptionalism as a result of our oil wealth proved less easy to handle, both within and outside government. One such was the preparation for a major conference, the Conference on International Economic Cooperation (CIEC), in Paris, designed to bring together the major oil consumers (the USA, Japan and the European Community) and the major producers (Saudi Arabia, in particular). The British government – and on this Callaghan, Owen and Benn were at one – believed that Britain, as an oil producer, needed to be separately represented on the Energy Commission of the conference, not be lumped together with the energy consuming countries of the European Community, which in any case had no common energy policy to represent. I was a heretic on this matter. The CIEC was clearly only going to be a one-off talking shop (as indeed it proved to be) and I did not believe that the gain from separate British representation was worth the candle of a prolonged row with our Community partners in Brussels. I made myself extremely unpopular by producing a series of papers in which the balance of the arguments for separate representation was less than compelling. And I had to watch helplessly as the government was reduced to pleading with the USA to argue our case in Brussels for separate representation, which they were predictably loath to do. Whatever the rights and wrongs of this dispute there was no doubt that it absorbed a quite disproportionate amount of ministerial time and energy; and it played its part in the shaping of a doctrine of 'British Gaullism' favoured by Owen which I found unconvincing at best and potentially dangerous. No wonder that Owen said to me at the time of the 1979 general election, when it was clear that, whatever the outcome, he would be leaving the Foreign Office, 'if we had not had to talk about Europe, we would have got along pretty well'. And so it proved when we were both dealing with Bosnia in the 1990s.

Deciding on policy about the destination of our oil once we became an oil exporter presented some genuinely difficult policy choices. We could, of course, have done nothing at all and just left it to the producing companies to decide, and there was something to be said for that. But there were two hard cases, South Africa and Israel, which raised tricky issues of foreign policy. There were no UN sanctions against exports of oil to South Africa, which was in fact at that time getting most of its supplies from Iran and Brunei (in which supply streams BP and Shell were involved). But direct exports from the North Sea to South Africa would clearly be quite another matter; and Benn was determined to prevent that. In the case of Israel the concern was that the attractions of North Sea oil, which would not need to pass through the Red Sea or the Suez Canal, would be overwhelming, and we could be locked into a supply situation which would prove very damaging if and when there was another round of Arab-Israeli hostilities (the Arab boycott of 1973 was, naturally, fresh in people's minds). With some reluctance Owen wanted that situation to be avoided, but Benn was no help. Eventually I came up with a solution which managed to avoid mentioning either South Africa or Israel by name. The government would issue a guideline to the companies producing North Sea oil recommending (that is to say it had no legal force) that they act in conformity with government policy and give preference to fellow members of the International Energy Agency and the European Community (the latter required to include France, which was not an IEA member). Neither South Africa nor Israel fell into either category. The companies were, in the event, happy with this Solomonic approach.

One day, quite out of the blue, I was telephoned by Owen's Principal Private Secretary, Ewen Fergusson, to say that I and my department were from that moment on to be in charge of the Foreign Office end of the enquiry already under way into allegations that British oil companies (BP and Shell) had been complicit in the evasion of UN sanctions against Rhodesia and that the British government of the day (Harold Wilson's 1966–70 government) had also been aware of this, and indeed might have turned a blind eye to it. The issue was given added spice by the fact that 'Tiny' Rowland, the Chairman of Lonrho (dubbed by Edward Heath in a different context 'the unacceptable face of capitalism'), was suing the British government for the losses he had incurred as a result of the closure of the pipeline his company owned between Beira in Mozambique and Rhodesia, alleging that there had been double standards applied to his sources of supply (blocked by the Royal Navy) and those reaching Rhodesia through South Africa (mainly from the BP-owned refinery in Durban). The Foreign Office's Rhodesia Department, which had over the years been responsible for the British implementation of these sanctions, were apparently out of their depth in the enquiry. Having found out, not to my surprise, that I was to be given no additional staff to take on what was to prove a pretty labour-intensive task, my first step was to contact Tom Bingham the brilliant young QC who was in charge of the enquiry (subsequently to be Lord Chief Justice) to make sure that he was satisfied with the cooperation he was getting over the provision of the relevant documents. He was. But any complacency on that front was dispelled a few days later when it transpired that, contrary to explicit instructions, Bingham had been sent by the Foreign Office copies of cabinet minutes about Rhodesia. This was, in Whitehall terms, high indeed on the Richter scale of misdemeanours, and that was brought home to me within minutes when the Secretary of the Cabinet, Sir John Hunt, came on the telephone to say that the Prime Minister was furious, and an official enquiry might be required. I asked if I could be given a little time to see if things could be sorted out; and this was conceded. There was no doubt at all about how this had all come about. The advent of the photocopier a few years earlier meant that the FCO Private Office had taken to sending copies (strictly forbidden) of the relevant excerpts of the Cabinet minutes to the departments concerned. They were then put on departmental files, and these particular ones thence found their way to Bingham. I decided to make a clean breast of all this to Bingham, who said he would reread the excerpts from the cabinet minutes which he had received; if, as he suspected, they added nothing to what he had already gleaned from other sources, he would return them to me and make no reference to the cabinet minutes in his report. A few days later a packet of the offending papers reached me. The Bingham Report, when it was published in early 1979, was a riveting piece of detective work which established beyond doubt that the oil companies had known that the Durban refinery was being used to evade sanctions (but the refinery was owned by a South African incorporated company and South Africa had never made any secret of its rejection of the relevant UN decision and of its refusal to comply with it); the extent of the Wilson government's knowledge of what was going on was less clearly established. Owen, without seeking or receiving any advice from me, immediately announced that he was referring the Bingham Report to the Director of Public Prosecutions (DPP). This was a politically astute move since it removed the whole issue from the arena of political debate during the 1979 election campaign; but in every other way it was a deplorable thing to have done since it left the oil companies with the Damoclean sword of a possible criminal prosecution hanging over them and their senior executives for an indefinite period of time. One of the first acts of the incoming Conservative government was to withdraw the referral to the DPP.

*   *   *

One part of my job was to stop the Secretary of State for Energy from breaking too much china in Brussels. This should not have been too difficult since not much was actually happening in Brussels on energy policy. But Benn's aim was to break as much china as possible as noisily as possible whether or not this was in any way justified. When visited in London by the Energy Commissioner, Guido Brunner, in my experience one of the least effective and least forceful commissioners I had, or have ever, met, Benn opined afterwards that he saw traces of Bismarck in him. None of this would have mattered very much if there had not been some parts of Community energy policy from which we stood to gain substantially. One such was the research programme into coal liquefaction. This we blocked for many long months because of the unacceptability in doctrinal terms of allowing the programme to be managed by the Commission. Another example was the JET project for nuclear fusion over which we were in contention with the French and, in particular, the Germans, about the site. Luckily most of the final stages of the negotiation to bring JET to Culham in Oxfordshire were handled by No 10 and not by the Department of Energy but, when the deal was about to be struck in the Council in Brussels in our favour, following the help we had given over the release of hostages from a Lufthansa plane hijacked to Mogadishu, Benn was horrified to discover that the Germans wanted there to be an expression of majority opinion in the Council before a unanimous legal decision was taken. Were they likely to cheat? Would this not set a disastrous precedent for taking other siting decisions by majority vote? I said the answer to both points was negative. This was just a politically necessary stage to be gone through to enable the Germans to concede gracefully. Which they duly did.

The quadrupling of the oil price following the Yom Kippur War in 1973, the subsequent establishment of the IEA, and the economic destabilisation and dislocation that dominated the world economy in the late 1970s were the backdrop to oil diplomacy during these years. A good deal was done in the IEA to establish a system of reserves of oil against the possibility of another disruption in supply, to encourage the development of alternative sources, coal and nuclear in particular, and to conserve energy, effectively to use less energy per unit of productive capacity and to waste less of it. But much of this was long-term stuff that would take decades to bring results; and we did not know how well these policies would stand up in another crisis. Meanwhile, the experience of 1973 had demonstrated that it was not the level of oil prices that mattered so much – trying to regulate that by international agreement was in any case beyond the bounds of possibility even if it was at all desirable – but the volatility of the price and the effect of rapid shifts on the wider economy. Having consulted the two major multinational oil companies headquartered in London, BP and Shell, whose presence and global outreach were an invaluable asset to policymaking, we gradually developed across Whitehall an approach that we described as 'smoothing' oil price movements, not trying to stop them happening. To achieve this would require a degree of concertation between producers and consumers. With Michael Butler, the Economic Deputy Under-Secretary in the FCO and my boss, in the lead we set about trying to develop support for such an approach, first with the other main Europeans, France and Germany, with whom we were reasonably successful, and then with the Americans with whom we were much less so. But all this was swept away by the onset of a new supply crisis resulting from the Iranian Revolution and the closing of most of Iran's production capacity in the autumn of 1978 for an indefinite period. I had a ringside seat at the West's increasingly desperate and unavailing attempts to manage the events of the revolution as they unrolled, and rather closer involvement in the totally inadequate response to the oil supply crisis and the spiralling price of oil. In the event the IEA reserve arrangements served no useful purpose at all, because the member states, confronted with an interruption in Iranian supply of indeterminate duration, could not bring themselves to take the risk of releasing some of the reserve supplies onto the market and thus reducing the size of the reserve cushion. I thought myself that was the wrong response but I was not the one who took the decisions. Whether it would have had much effect on the price rise we shall never know. As it was, the price rise triggered another global economic crisis which was to last well into the 1980s, by which time I had long since ceased to be involved in the diplomacy of oil.

8

LONDON 1979–1984

The European Budget Battle

By the time of the general election in May 1979 I had done more than two years in my energy job and was anxious, if at all possible, to spend the second part of my time in London as head of a geographical department. The first move proved a false start. I was asked if I would let my name go forward as a candidate for the post of the FCO Private Secretary at No 10 once the new Prime Minister was installed. I agreed to that; but my candidacy did not survive the preliminary sift and so I did not at that stage even meet the person who was to have a fairly important influence on my future career, Margaret Thatcher. My gloom over this setback was somewhat lightened by a meeting in the corridor of the FCO with Tony Parsons, recently returned from a gruelling time as Ambassador in Tehran during the downfall of the Shah, who said he too had suffered this fate some years before and 'I went straight to Westminster Abbey and dropped to my knees to offer thanks for being delivered from such an appalling fate'. A further boost to morale came with the news that I was in the autumn to become head of the Middle East Department (which by then covered the whole area between Afghanistan in the east and Iraq and the Arabian Peninsula in the west).

In the event, my time in the Middle East Department was cut to a few weeks due to an unexpected promotion that same December to the job of Assistant Under-Secretary of State supervising the work of the two European Community departments. But it was not a period without incident, including as it did the seizure of the Great Mosque in Mecca by a group of Islamic terrorists, the precursor, though few recognised it as such at the time, of later even more momentous developments, and also the occupation of our and the US Embassies in Tehran by groups of student protesters – in our case, fortunately and thanks to the calm skill of the Embassy staff, a brief episode, in the case of the Americans the beginning of a hostage crisis which had profoundly negative consequences for the West's relations with the new revolutionary regime in Iran. Add to those events an official visit from the Prime Minister of what was then called North Yemen, a first in several respects – most notably because the Prime Minister's plane had a court injunction slapped on it as it touched down in the UK, in pursuit of an unpaid debt to British Midland Airways, despite an assurance from the company's chairman that this would not happen. Finally, the somewhat belated discovery that I was responsible for a group of tiny islands in the Indian Ocean, Diego Garcia, and that no one the department had the slightest idea what that responsibility entailed and how it was to be discharged, it having been dropped in the FCO's lap a few years before on the disappearance of the Colonial Office. All very different from the far more predictable rhythm of the multilateral diplomacy on which I had spent much time already and to which I was now returning.

The European scene to which I was reverting was by this time dominated by the battle over Britain's contribution to the European budget. The last, transitional constraints on that contribution set out in our accession treaty were due to expire at the end of 1979 and so, from 1980 onwards we would be exposed to the full impact of the Community's financial arrangements. The trends in the Community's budget were turning out to be every bit as damaging for us as we had predicted during our accession negotiations and not as the rosy projections of the Commission had suggested, with agricultural spending racing ahead and largely out of control and with non-agricultural spending in no way matching or offsetting that; and the mechanism to moderate our gross contribution, agreed at the time of renegotiation, was proving inoperable. We were therefore on course to be the largest net contributor to the Community budget while we remained far from being one of the more prosperous members of the Community. This position was indefensible and unsustainable. So when Margaret Thatcher, in the summer of 1979, invoked the 'unacceptable situation' assurance we had been given by the Six during the accession negotiations, none of our partners tried to deny the validity of this move. The whole dispute, which was to drag on for five weary years, was over the quantity of the remedy and its nature. And the negotiations which had begun amicably enough in Strasbourg in the summer of 1979 had descended into acrimony by the time the Heads of State and Government met again in Dublin in December of that year. The iron law of European budgetary negotiations, that they are a zero-sum game in which less paid by Britain involves more paid by the other member states, was making itself felt. I took up my new job on the day after the Prime Minister had said she wanted her money back. The air was full of mutual recriminations and the Council chamber was metaphorically littered with broken china.

The budget negotiations that filled the next five years fell into three fairly distinct phases. The first, which was well under way when I came onto the scene in December 1979 culminated in May 1980 with agreement on a three-year, lump sum settlement; the second ran until the middle of 1982 when the negotiations for a long-term, systemic solution collapsed and Britain's attempt to exercise a veto on the agricultural part of the budget was brushed aside; the third lasted until agreement was reached on an abatement mechanism for Britain's net contribution at the European Council meeting in Fontainebleau in June 1984. Of course the budget battle was not the only important item of Community business; however, the negotiations for Spanish and Portuguese accession continued without yet getting close to a decisive breakthrough. A new Commission was appointed in 1980. Attempts to move forward from the customs union provided for in the founding treaty to a genuine internal market were mounted but tended to fail when confronted by the unanimity requirement laid down for most of the necessary decisions. But the budgetary issue was the item which we minded about most and which absorbed most of my time and attention. It was in any case a difficult period for the economies of all the member states, whose governments were distracted by their problems of high and rising unemployment, excessive budget deficits and inflation which followed on the second spike in oil prices. Some governments, as in Britain, opted for cuts in public expenditure and the privatisation of substantial parts of the economy; others, as in France, where François Mitterrand took over as President in 1981 from Valéry Giscard d'Estaing, made a dash for growth and took more of the economy into public ownership. There was not homogeneity of policy or effort and precious little political will to move forward collectively.

*　　*　　*

The first challenge Britain's European diplomacy faced at the beginning of 1980, in the aftermath of the Dublin confrontation, was to ensure that the negotiations over our budget contribution did not simply collapse or stagnate in deadlock. We were now in a budget year when our contribution was unconstrained. The clock was ticking. So Sir Ian Gilmour, at the time the second cabinet minister in the FCO and its spokesman in the House of Commons, was sent off on a tour of the other Community capitals; and I went with him. The task was a tricky one since we could not afford to indicate that there was any weakening in our position or any willingness to accept the thoroughly inadequate ideas which had been around at Dublin, but nor was it helpful to present an air of complete intransigence. Gilmour, a much underrated operator, carried out the task admirably. Although derided in the press at the time, the tour of capitals did what was needed and ensured that the Commission and the other member states understood that we were not going to be fobbed off with something completely inadequate; and they resumed the search for a solution. Lump sum figures for a rebate on our contribution for the next two years (1980 and 1981) of a genuinely substantial kind began to be bandied about. The prospects for the next Summit meeting in Luxembourg in April looked reasonably promising. But that meeting too broke up in discord and acrimony, with the German Chancellor, Helmut Schmidt, actually kicking the furniture in frustration. There were two main problems. One was a matter of personal chemistry. Heads of State and Government tend not to be good at negotiating face to face, each being accustomed to getting his or her own way in the domestic arena without too much ado. And Margaret Thatcher, invariably a master of the technical details and determined to get her way, sharpened up points of difference and riled her colleagues.

But there were substantive problems too. Two years of rebate, one of which was almost half expired, was very short; and the remit to the Council to look for a lasting solution beyond that period and not to nurture the hope that the problem would then just go away was inadequate. So the ball was kicked back to the Foreign Ministers in singularly unpromising circumstances. But the time factor instilled urgency. No one believed that it would be wise to take the issue back to summit level at the next meeting of the European Council in June; and Britain had invoked the Luxembourg compromise – the agreement to disagree reached amongst the Six in 1966 over whether or not to use majority voting when a vital national interest was at stake – to block the annual agricultural price fixing. So a make or break meeting of Foreign Ministers was scheduled for the end of May. The night before the meeting, Roy Jenkins, the President of the Commission, invited Gilmour and his team to an all-British dinner, from which he excluded the British Permanent Representative, Michael Butler, with whom he was at the time on very frosty terms. Since Jenkins and Gilmour were close friends and had just spent the weekend together in Tuscany playing tennis, I could see I was going to be put on the spot, as indeed proved to be the case. There was not much argument over the lump sum rebates for 1980 and 1981 which had been on the table at Luxembourg the month before and were broadly satisfactory. A third, non-quantified, year of rebate seemed now to be on offer; and the mandate to the Council to work on a longer term solution was shaping up. But the French were pressing, through the Commission, for a public undertaking from us never again to use a veto on the annual agricultural price fixing as a lever in budget negotiations. I said this seemed completely unreasonable – little better than a protection racket – given the central importance of the agricultural price fixing as a determinant of the size and shape of the budget and of our net contribution to it. I could not believe such an undertaking would be given. The temperature around the dinner table dropped very low. The next day the Council avoided any early collective discussion and moved into a series of what were called in the Brussels jargon 'confessionals' – meetings between, on the one hand, the President of the Council, the lively and skilful Italian Foreign Minister Emilio Colombo and the Commission, and, on the other hand, individual Foreign Ministers. This agonising process, which, of course, left most of the Foreign Ministers and their delegations for most of the time with nothing to do, lasted throughout the day and the following night. Finally a deal was struck in the early hours of the second morning – the figures for two years were agreed, with a further un-quantified third year to follow; a mandate was given to the Council to work for a lasting solution and no more was heard of the French try-on over agricultural prices. We went back to the Ambassador's residence for a very full English breakfast; and Peter Carrington and Ian Gilmour flew back to Britain to discuss the outcome with the Prime Minister and seek her agreement to it. This proved no simple matter, and they were given a torrid time; but, following some deployment of the black arts of press briefing over the weekend, the Cabinet approved the deal when it next met. It had indeed been a close run thing.

No one was in any hurry to grasp the nettle of negotiating a lasting solution to Britain's budget problem. In the Community, as elsewhere, when an issue is not urgent it is not addressed seriously. For a considerable time the discussion was held at Foreign Minister level and just went round in circles. This frustrating process was partly due to the unintended consequences of the May 1980 settlement. Because it was based on a lump sum rebate calculated for two years (1980 and 1981), the first of which was less than half elapsed and the second of which did not yet have a budget at all, there was never even the slightest chance that it would represent a scientific approach to establishing the appropriate level for Britain's net contribution to the Community budget. In the event the rebate proved to be far more generous to Britain than had ever been intended, leaving Britain with almost no net contribution at all for those years. The French Minister for Europe, André Chandernagor, missed no opportunity to describe this out-turn as a 'cadeau royal' some of which must now be clawed back in subsequent years. An alternative conclusion to be drawn, and the one we drew, was that this demonstrated the case for a systemic approach based on actual budget outcomes. Another unintended consequence was that our rebate used up quite a lot of the headroom between actual Community expenditure and the treaty-based revenue limits (the ceiling was the sum of customs duties, agricultural levies and 1 per cent of VAT) for such expenditure, which required unanimity to change; but this factor was not yet a critical or imminent one. Drawing on our bruising experience of the 1979–80 negotiations, which had continually pitted us against the other member states in a zero-sum confrontation, we set to work to devise a generally applicable approach to the whole question of net contributions and rebates which we hoped would appeal in particular to some other member states either already large net contributors themselves (Germany) or which were particularly negatively affected by a rebate limited to Britain alone (Netherlands, France). So the Treasury designed a system that would cap a member state's net contribution at a level that would take into account its size and Gross National Product per capita as part of a Community average. This scheme we put privately to the Germans, Dutch and French. Not one of them showed a flicker of interest, even though their Finance Ministers could easily work out the attractions for them; the resistance to any system based on net contributions remained solid. So we knew that, once again, we were on our own. By the early months of 1982 the matter really was urgent, since we were now again in a budgetary year for which no figure for a rebate had as yet been established. We were also in a year for which the Commission's agricultural price-fixing proposals were high and the majority tendency in the Council of Agriculture Ministers was to push them higher, with major negative implications for our net budget contribution. So, once again, as in 1980 we established a linkage between the two negotiations and invoked the Luxembourg Compromise to block the price-fixing negotiations. Our calculation was that the French, who had the largest political vested interest in the maintenance of that compromise (General de Gaulle having been its only begetter), would not be prepared to abandon the national veto; but they also on this occasion had the largest economic vested interest in overriding it to secure a generous agricultural price settlement. In the end Edith Cresson, the French Minister of Agriculture, was able to persuade President Mitterrand to brush aside the objections of the Quai d'Orsay, and we were duly voted down. A much smaller lump sum rebate for 1982 was agreed; and the negotiations for a lasting settlement were rolled forward. This miserable outcome from our point of view brought me about as close to despair as I ever got during the five years of the budget negotiation. I felt that I had failed professionally in not having warned Ministers that the roof might fall in – I had had some presentiment of it about a month before it happened, but I was unable to convince the Treasury or the Cabinet Office of the precariousness of our situation.

In any case there were no elements on the negotiating table either with respect to the 1982 rebate figure or the long-term solution which would have justified us demonstrating flexibility. However, the domestic political consequences of our humiliation were much less than might have been feared thanks in part to deft parliamentary handling by the Foreign Secretary, Francis Pym, and even more to the fact that it coincided with the conclusion of the campaign to regain the Falkland Islands. I sat down soon afterwards and wrote a paper for the Foreign Secretary arguing that, now that the agricultural price-fixing lever had been struck from our hands – and we certainly could not afford to try to use it again and to fail again – the only remaining trump we still had was the fact that Community spending was by now rapidly approaching the revenue ceiling. It was however the ace of trumps, so long as we were prepared to agree to the ceiling being raised as part of an overall package containing a lasting solution to our own budget problem. That became FCO policy, but not that of the Treasury or of the Prime Minister for some time to come.

The resumption of negotiations for a lasting solution to Britain's budget problem was, as in the previous phase, slow in coming and unpromising when it came. By the time of the Stuttgart European Council in June 1983, just after the Conservative government had been returned to power with a much increased majority, Margaret Thatcher was beginning to give very slight hints that she could be prepared to contemplate a wider budget package which would include steps to bring the rise in agricultural spending under better control, a modest increase in the Community's revenue ceiling and a systemic solution to Britain's net budget contribution. At Stuttgart she had agreed to a further, inadequate one-year lump sum deal and had, albeit through clenched teeth, accepted the Genscher-Colombo Declaration that mapped out an ambitious plan for the Community's future development. Thereafter negotiations got under way on that wider budget package. But the first attempt by the European Council to make progress on it, at a lengthy and appallingly badly chaired meeting in Athens at the end of the year, broke up in the, by now usual, acrimony. Only an inveterate optimist, which I tend to be, would have attributed the failure not just to Andreas Papandreou's chairmanship but to a well-known French tactic of pushing big and difficult decisions into their own Presidency (the first half of 1984). But so it was; and, very soon after the beginning of 1984, the signs of the breakthrough for which we had been working became apparent. The first straw in the wind was Mitterrand's appointment as his new Minister for Europe of Roland Dumas, a subtle and serpentine lawyer who had for many years been a confidant of the President. It rapidly became clear that Dumas held the reins of the French Presidency and that Claude Cheysson, the Foreign Minister, who had been a thorn in our flesh and who had never even begun to negotiate with us seriously, was being marginalised. Within weeks Dumas asked if he could come very discreetly to the UK to talk things over informally with the Foreign Secretary, Geoffrey Howe. That led to two successive weekend meetings at Chevening, the Foreign Secretary's country residence, just off the M25, at which I and my French opposite number in the French Foreign Ministry, Guy Legras, were the only officials present and which, by some miracle and by tightly limiting the circulation of the records, we managed to keep out of the public domain. It quickly became apparent that we were at last on the same wavelength. Gone was the verbal jousting over the wickedness of even thinking about net outcomes from the Community budget. The scheme that began to take shape was a relatively simple one involving a rebate of a percentage (as yet unspecified and undiscussed) of Britain's net contribution in any given year which would be an integral part of the Community's budgetary system. Following these two meetings we largely left it to the French Presidency to sell this new approach to the other member states, which they did with skill and determination, no doubt at least partly motivated by the need to avoid the dire political consequences for themselves if the money available within the Community's existing revenue ceiling, which in large part funded the Common Agricultural Policy, was to run out, a prospect which was no longer a distant one. The process did not proceed without a hitch, most notably at the Brussels European Council in April 1984, which had been intended to bring matters to a conclusion. After the Heads of State and Government dinner on the first evening, Michael Butler and I waited in the hall of the rather ersatz chateau of Valduchesse to debrief the Prime Minister. Margaret Thatcher, in a long blue evening dress with diamond earrings glittering, swept towards us crying out, 'They say it's their money and I say it's mine'. Our hearts sank. Then the next morning the German Chancellor, Helmut Kohl, dug in his heels and refused to accept a systemic solution, offering merely five more years of lump sum rebates at an inadequate level. Fortunately the French kept their nerve and continued to work on the basis of the scheme that Dumas and Howe had originally shaped up; and a deal was struck at the next European Council in June 1984 at Fontainebleau (by which time I had moved to the Embassy in Washington) on a two-thirds rebate of Britain's net contribution, the figure which we had indicated at the very outset of the negotiations would in our view be an equitable one. Over the months leading up to Fontainebleau it had become apparent to all those who followed the matter in detail that the total of the five years of lump sum rebates (two years – 1980, 1981 – of unintentionally generous figures and three years – 1982–4 – of intentionally ungenerous figures) came to a figure close to a two-thirds rebate. So the final outcome was not a great surprise.

A great deal has been written and said about the budget negotiations, about the performance of the British Prime Minister in them, and about the attitude of the FCO towards them. Much of it has been wide of the mark. My own view, which did not waver over the whole five-year period, was that getting a remedy to the budgetary injustice was an existential necessity if British membership was to be sustained, and that the remedy had to be a systemic one, which would last as long as the problem it was devised to address, and not just a series of ad hoc fixes. This was the tenor of the advice I offered to successive Foreign Secretaries (Peter Carrington, Francis Pym and Geoffrey Howe). So the widely promulgated suggestions that the FCO was at odds with the Prime Minister, whose views these also were, over our strategic objective, are simply untrue. Where we did have differences was over tactics and presentation. In particular it was clear to me from the outset that harping on populist phrases about getting our money back was actually making it more difficult to achieve our objective since it enabled the other member states to camouflage their reluctance to take on a heavier budgetary burden themselves behind a smokescreen of sanctimonious rhetoric about our not understanding the nature of the Community's 'own resources' system and seeking to achieve a 'juste retour', thus enabling them too to avoid engagement on the specifics of a systemic remedy. Moreover, exaggerating our periodic clashes with our Community partners over the budget negotiations, which frequently served the short-term domestic political interest of the Prime Minister, was militating against the British people arriving at a positive settled opinion on our membership of the Community. However, to avoid all misunderstanding, my view, at the time and since, was that no British Prime Minister for whom I worked would have got a better deal than Margaret Thatcher and several would probably have settled for something inferior.

The other main issue in those not very productive years for the Community was the accession of Spain and Portugal. Those accession negotiations bore little resemblance to our own, being spread wearisomely over a long period of years (Spain and Portugal actually joined in 1986). They did have one factor in common, however: the threat of a possible French veto, on this occasion due to the sensitivity of opening the French market to Spanish exports of fruit and vegetables. Britain throughout played a supportive role, much as the Five had done during our own negotiations for accession. But I was conscious of the fact that below the surface of the water there lurked an issue, Gibraltar, which could shipwreck the whole enterprise. When we joined the Community in 1973 Gibraltar, as a European territory for whose external relations we were responsible, became part of the Community. But, some years before, in a move designed to damage Gibraltar's economy and as part of the campaign to regain the territory, Franco had closed the border at La Linea; and thus it still was closed. Clearly this border closure was incompatible with any number of aspects of Community law, but the problem was that, in technical legal terms, this incompatibility could only be brought before a court (the European Court of Justice), once Spain had actually become a member of the Community, that is to say after our Parliament had been asked to ratify their accession treaty. The prospect of taking the Spanish accession treaty through Parliament with the border still closed was not an attractive one; but nor was the prospect of having to give the Spanish a public ultimatum to open the border if they wanted us to ratify their treaty, a course only too likely to lead to a major row with unpredictable consequences on both sides. So I duly put these considerations to Douglas Hurd, at that time Minister of State at the FCO, with the recommendation that we approach the Spanish privately, explain the problem to them frankly and suggest that the two governments engage a dialogue over Gibraltar which would enable Spain to lift its unilateral measures on the border well before the conclusion of the accession negotiations. This course of action was duly agreed; and I was sent off to explain what I had in mind to my opposite number in Madrid, Carlos Westendorp, who was in charge of their accession negotiations at the official level, and also to the Chief Minister of Gibraltar, Sir Joshua Hassan and the leader of the opposition there, Joe Bossano. My contacts in Madrid gradually bore fruit, although there was initially plenty of opposition from the political side of the Foreign Ministry, whose obsession with Gibraltar had led them to be known as 'the ministry for the foreign affair'. In Gibraltar, Hassan, an astute lawyer of Moroccan origin, was delighted that we had found a way of getting the border reopened, strongly supported the idea of giving Gibraltar Airport two points of access, one from Gibraltar and one from Spain, which was part of our approach, and was only mildly nervous about our engaging a dialogue with Spain over Gibraltar's long-term future. Bossano, the leader of the local branch of the Transport and General Workers Union, objected to everything, to dialogue with Spain, to joint access to the airport and even to reopening the border. When I asked him who he thought was going to pay the subsidy required to compensate Gibraltar for closure of the border he replied, 'You, of course'. Anyway, despite that, we proceeded as planned, a dialogue with Spain was engaged, the border was reopened and, although Bossano, when in due course he became Chief Minister, was able to frustrate the airport project, it too eventually came to fruition. The whole episode was a good example of how membership of the Community could help to resolve long standing disputes that had previously defied all attempts to deal with them bilaterally.

*　　*　　*

Looking back on these four and a half years of hard slog, dominated by the budget battle and bereft of many other positive achievements, it is hard to escape the conclusion that it could have been done better. If only our partners had put up less of a struggle over honouring the commitment they had given us to deal with an unacceptable budgetary situation should it arise, much bitterness on both sides could have been avoided. Part of the problem of those years was due to the appointment of a singularly ineffective Commission to succeed the Jenkins Commission in 1980. The obvious candidate to follow Jenkins as President of the Commission was Vicomte Étienne Davignon, a brilliant and infinitely imaginative Belgian diplomat, who had already been in the previous Commission. But his appointment was blocked by President Giscard d'Estaing, and the European Council, not for the last time, turned to a lowest common denominator candidate in the form of the Prime Minister of Luxembourg, Gaston Thorn. Tempted though the larger member states often are by the prospect of a malleable and unassertive President of the Commission, it was a formula which did not work well on this occasion and which has not worked well since. The next time they had to make a choice, at Fontainebleau in 1984, they appointed a high profile and forceful candidate, Jacques Delors, the French Finance Minister, and thus ushered in a period of achievement unparalleled in the history of the Community.

9

WASHINGTON 1984–1985

COMPANY TOWN

My family and I arrived in Washington to take up my new job as Minister at the Embassy in June 1984, the same month that Margaret Thatcher brought to a successful conclusion at Fontainebleau the negotiations over Britain's budget contribution which had dominated the previous four and a half years of my professional life. I was not a complete stranger to the city or to the United States, but I had never lived in either before for any substantial period of time. I had visited Washington first as an FCO desk officer for the CENTO alliance and had on that occasion seen something of the centres of United States military power; I had come several times to the city during my years at the Commission in Brussels with Christopher Soames when the focus of our visits were the issues of trade policy and the economy which both united the two sides of the Atlantic and also frequently plunged them into vigorous and quite vicious disputes. I had also spent a month in 1977 travelling round the country surveying the energy policy scene and marvelling at how dysfunctional the American approach to that policy area could be. So, while my frequently reiterated desire to broaden my diplomatic horizons had finally been granted – and nowhere in the world provided a broader canvas than being at the interface between British and US foreign policy – I had a lot to learn.

We soon settled into the large, sprawling but not particularly elegant or appealing house provided for the Embassy's No 2. Set on the heights above the Potomac River, close to the English Gothic splendours of the national cathedral and a ten minute drive from the Embassy, with ten minutes more required to reach the centre of the city, it could not have been more convenient. And it epitomised the nature of life in Washington which was essentially suburban, not urban. It was a city of the sharpest, and sometimes quite shocking, contrasts. The great federal buildings – the Capitol, the White House, the memorials to former Presidents, the national museums – oozed grandeur, power and wealth and were set in a park-like landscape which had been hugely improved even in the 20 years since I had first visited Washington. But go a block or two past the Congressional buildings on Capitol Hill down towards the Anacostia River or beyond the gleaming, white marble railway station and you were in malodorous slums where the incidence of violent crime meant that it was extremely unwise to stop your car and plain silly to walk around at night. It was a city, too, which lacked some of the normal attributes of urban civilisation. Apart from the recently built Kennedy Center and the museums it was almost completely lacking in cultural life, with few theatres and concert halls. Moreover, although it was populated by many of the brightest and most energetic citizens of a great country, it lacked variety because all their lives, whether they were politicians, civil servants, military personnel, journalists, diplomats or lobbyists, revolved around one thing: the US administration. It really was a company town. So to enjoy yourself there and to lead a fulfilling professional life you had to be passionately interested in the functioning of that administration. Luckily I was.

And then there was the climate, another source of contrasts, set as Washington is along the fault line, both climatically and politically, between the north and the south. Several months of hot, steamy weather in the summer, which even air-conditioning could not make more than barely tolerable; winter snow storms which brought the whole city to a standstill since it was too far south to be equipped to cope with such events in the way that Chicago or Boston were. In between the extremes, however, in spring and autumn, it was idyllic.

The British Embassy too was a place of contrasts. The porticoed splendour of Lutyens' great ambassadorial residence was set alongside a low, cramped and plain ugly set of office buildings which reflected much of what had been wrong with British architecture in the middle of the twentieth century. Into this office block was crammed a kind of mini-Whitehall in which pretty well every government department was represented. Each of these individual units tended to operate within a stove pipe, keeping itself to itself and fending off any attempt by outsiders to intrude; and those stove pipes stretched out to whichever part of the US administration was that particular department's opposite number and back to its parent department in Whitehall. So coordination was at a premium, particularly since very little of it took place in London; but it was not easy to achieve. The job of No 2 in the embassy was very much what the incumbent made of it; but even more it was what the Ambassador of the day allowed and encouraged them to make of it. In that respect I was remarkably lucky. The Ambassador in my time, Oliver Wright, who had been called back from retirement after serving for a number of years in Bonn, had decided to concentrate his efforts on the Hill and the cultivation of senators and congressmen; and on travelling widely around the United States promoting trade with, and investment in, Britain. He therefore left me to manage the relationship with the State Department and the National Security Council, effectively the interface between British and US foreign policy, as well as the overall coordination of the Embassy's work. And this, with the skilled and imaginative assistance of John Kerr, the head of the Embassy's political section, whose path was to cross mine many times in the future, I set about doing.

The political scene in the Washington to which we came in June 1984 was dominated, as it invariably is, by the personality of the President, in this case Ronald Reagan. Reagan, unopposed within his own Republican party, was running for re-election in 1984; and, through those early months of our time there, he was coasting towards the comfortable victory he achieved that November. The European view of Reagan, which I had to some extent shared, was not a positive one. He was seen as intellectually weak and often indecisive, and as a cold warrior, insensitive to the concerns of European countries which felt themselves to be in the front line of the Cold War. His administration's economic policies were the antithesis of those practised in the social market economies of the continental European countries. These downbeat views were not, however, shared by Margaret Thatcher who had already established a strong and effective working relationship with the President. Nor did my own views long survive a closer exposure to the realities of American politics. I took to listening to the weekly radio broadcasts which American Presidents from the time of Roosevelt habitually make, and this soon brought home to me how Reagan had earned the title of 'the great communicator'; he seemed to be almost effortlessly in tune with the views and emotions of middle America and had a knack of encapsulating those views in simple language and phrases, laced with anecdotes, which might have seemed corny to the foreign ear but which represented political leadership of a high order. I went in August to the Republican Convention in Dallas, which was in reality more of a coronation than a contest. The main events were held in a vast, hangar-like conference centre whose temperature had been driven down to polar figures in contrast to the 100° Fahrenheit outside; not surprisingly most participants were soon suffering from severe colds. Placards waved – my favourite one was 'Jesuits for Reagan' – banners from the different states were unfurled; huge nets full of red, white and blue balloons waited to be released at the moment the candidate was nominated. The proceedings were largely policy-free (indeed content-free) build-ups to the appearance of the candidate and his very much junior vice-presidential running mate, George H W Bush. Reagan's acceptance speech was a medley of the 'it's morning again in America' and 'a shining city on a hill' rhetoric that was to carry him successfully thorough the subsequent election campaign against his hapless Democratic rival, Walter Mondale. There was little doubt as to whose administration we would be dealing with for the next four years; and little clue as to the policies which it would follow.

The senior members of Reagan's cabinet, in particular those who dealt with national security issues and foreign policy, were by and large a talented group and the election brought only one major shift: the switch between James Baker (Chief of Staff) and Donald Regan (Treasury). George Shultz and Caspar Weinberger stayed put at State and Defence respectively; as did William Casey, Director of the CIA, whom I had known as a singularly unimpressive Under-Secretary for Economic Affairs at the State Department during the Nixon administration and in that capacity Christopher Soames' nominal opposite number. But these key figures were more rivals than part of an effective team, with clashing personalities and substantive differences over policy. Weinberger was a hawk on all matters to do with the Soviet Union, while Shultz, who was no dove, wanted to explore the scope for measures of arms control and to move away from the virtual state of non-communication with the Soviet leaders and regime which had followed the shooting down of a Korean civil airliner in September 1983. In sharp contrast, Shultz was proactive about the use of the military to meet challenges from terrorism and to project US power overseas, while Weinberger was intensely conservative about any such use, much influenced by the unhappy experience of such an intervention in Beirut in October 1983. Casey was a wild card who really did deserve the epithet of cowboy so often applied loosely to the President himself. These rivalries and tensions would have mattered less if it had not been for the weakest link in the administration, the lack of an effective National Security Adviser. None of the numerous incumbents in that job during the early and middle Reagan years filled satisfactorily either the role of coordinator and conciliator of conflicting views, for which the job had originally been established, nor were they the President's principal adviser on foreign policy issues as Kissinger and Brzezinski had been for Nixon, Ford and Carter respectively. So the performance of the Reagan administration in foreign policy was often less than the sum of its parts; and the battle for the President's ear was unceasing, with its outcome unpredictable. This was the quicksand through which foreign diplomats had to pick their way.

Like it or not the British Embassy in Washington often found itself cast in the role of the guardian of the sacred ark of 'the special relationship'. This hardy perennial of British media and political comment was liable to spring to life on occasions of state or official visits in either direction, or when there was some perceived snub or slight to a senior British visitor or, more justifiably, when US policy decisions were seen to be taking insufficient account of British interests. There was singularly little interest in the topic in American media and political circles, although the State Department could always be relied upon to crank out some formulaic reference to the specialness of the US/UK relationship on the occasion of state and official visits. That imbalance was in itself a telltale sign. In a sense the problem was at least partly a semantic one caused by the attachment of the definite article to the phrase 'special relationship'. It was that implied exclusivity to the relationship which made the concept so vulnerable and so unrealistic. It was clear to any objective observer that there were a whole range of countries which had a special relationship with the United States: Canada and Mexico, for example, plus Japan, Germany, Poland, Ireland and Italy, not to omit the most obvious case of all, Israel. No one could, however, reasonably contest that Britain had *a* special relationship with the USA based on trade, investment, culture, a common language and systems of law, the cooperation between the two intelligence communities and on nuclear matters, and our shared membership of a whole range of international organisations starting with permanent membership of the UN Security Council. But that same objective observer would note that the USA had often to juggle these special relationships when reaching decisions with foreign policy implications. Above all, the US administration of the day's assessment of the US national interest would invariably trump all other considerations. There had been a major outburst of breast beating over the state of the special relationship following the US invasion of Grenada in October 1983 which had taken place without any prior consultation with us, despite the fact that Grenada was a member of the Commonwealth and that the Queen was its titular Head of State; and the shockwaves from this episode were still being felt when I arrived the following year. A more insidious aspect of the problem was the belief in some parts of Westminster and Whitehall that the special relationship could somehow be prayed in aid when we wanted the Americans to do something which they would not otherwise have wished to do. The periodic outbreaks of soul searching by the British media and in Parliament could not simply be wished away and they certainly could not be ignored; they just had to be managed until they blew themselves out. But John Kerr and I did at least ensure that the phrase was never used in the Embassy's official communications with London or in our dealings with the US administration. What was required in both instances was a hard-headed analysis of the respective national interests of the two parties and careful consideration of how best they might be dovetailed to secure joint policies and approaches.

*　　*　　*

The Embassy's Chancery was staffed by a team of regional specialists who did their best to keep London abreast of all the main developments in US foreign policy, a tall order given its global outreach and the complexity and almost Byzantine nature of the bureaucratic machinery in Washington, including the close and influential involvement of Congress. Clearly we had our own foreign policy priorities and tended to focus particularly intensively on those, but we also needed to be aware of what US foreign policy was seeking to achieve in areas of lesser importance to us and to understand how this affected their overall approach. In particular it made sense for us to be cautious in those areas where we had no major interests at stake about offering advice or criticism; Harold Macmillan's idea that we should be Greeks in relation to the Romans in Washington was a flawed one in many respects. Two examples of these lower priority areas which were very active during this period were Central America and the Philippines. The Reagan administration's policies in Central America, which involved active support of the 'contra' rebels in Nicaragua who were aiming to overthrow the Sandinista regime there, seemed to us unlikely to succeed and to be of dubious international legality (as it later turned out they were also of dubious domestic legality in the United States), but our interests in the region were extremely modest, and prompting from us would neither have been welcome or heeded; so by and large we buttoned our lips. In the Philippines we were again largely spectators of the death throes of the Marcos regime which provoked much tension within the American body politic before a decision was taken to give support to its ousting while offering the Marcoses refuge in the United States.

Of the foreign policy areas where we were both actively involved, none was more important than the US/Soviet relationship. Here we were collectively on the side of those in Washington who wanted to see a renewed dialogue between the two superpowers and some serious discussion both of arms control measures and of regional sources of tension, particularly those in Africa. While the Reagan administration remained stymied by the succession of geriatric leaders in the Kremlin and by its own internal disagreements over resuming a wide-ranging US/Soviet dialogue, the Prime Minister, no soft touch when it came to dealing with the Soviet Union, became convinced by her meetings with Mikhail Gorbachev during his visit to Britain in the autumn of 1984 that he was the coming man (in which she was soon to be proved correct) and that he would turn out to be a serious and worthwhile interlocutor. When she visited Washington in December 1984 she pressed home these points with some effect, and certainly influenced American thinking at the highest level. Arms control issues were more difficult to handle since there were divisions at the London end as well as in Washington. Reagan's Strategic Defence Initiative, invariably known as 'Star Wars', aimed to develop an overall ballistic missile defence system. There were not only doubts in London about its practicability but also about the policy implications, the Foreign Secretary fearing a further consequential deterioration of East–West relations while the Prime Minister was relaxed about that aspect but deeply concerned that if and when the Soviet Union developed its own defensive system that would render Britain's nuclear deterrent ineffective. During her December 1984 visit to Washington Margaret Thatcher managed to straddle these two concerns by agreeing with President Reagan that the SDI programme would not at this stage proceed beyond research and that deployment would be a matter for negotiations in view of treaty obligations (a reference to the US/Soviet ABM Treaty). This was a notable outcome, and an instance of Britain being an effective spokesman for widely shared European concerns.

The main focus of British policy in Africa during this period, apart from a determination to avoid imposing mandatory economic sanctions on South Africa, over which we saw eye to eye with the Reagan administration but not with the majority of other countries, was the effort to remove Namibia from the control of South Africa and bring it to independence while in parallel getting Cuban troops withdrawn from Angola. Effective leadership was provided by Chester Crocker, the Assistant Secretary for Africa at the State Department, who devoted the whole of the rest of Reagan's two terms as President to this objective which was finally crowned with success long after the period covered by this account. We systematically pooled all our relevant information with Crocker and worked in close concert with him. Our biggest contribution was to fill the void caused by the fact that the USA did not have diplomatic relations with Angola. The British Ambassador in Angola, Marrack Goulding (who later became an Under-Secretary-General at the UN, first for Peacekeeping and then for Political Affairs) not only provided them with much reporting but also acted as a discreet channel of communication between the USA and Angola; and once a year Goulding came to Washington for several days to be debriefed by a whole range of US departments and agencies. Another focus of activity at this time was the negotiation over the future status of Hong Kong which was being conducted intensively by the Prime Minister and the Foreign Secretary. There was no lack of sniping about this in the US media and in Congress to the effect that we were selling out the people of Hong Kong and handing an uncovenanted benefit to a communist regime. The important thing, apart from countering this criticism, was to keep the administration on side and this we achieved by comprehensively briefing the relevant Assistant Secretary at the State Department, Paul Wolfowitz, at every stage of the process. But we were often a good deal less successful than in these two areas. Our hopes of persuading the administration to play a more active role in the Middle East Peace Process were continually frustrated, Shultz having burnt his fingers badly with the Syrians and as a result of the ill-fated US deployment of troops to Beirut and being unwilling to venture back into that arena.

There was also continuous tension over the arms embargo on Iran, with the USA nagging us over reports of British evasions of those sanctions, while we had our suspicions (well founded as it turned out) that their own record might not be blameless. We were concerned too that the Americans' lasting trauma from the saga of their embassy hostages in Tehran was distorting the formulation of policy towards Iran and leading to too strong a tilt towards Iraq in the Iran-Iraq war. And, even in cases where British interests were at stake, we could find ourselves brushed aside. Such was the case over the US reaction to the decision by the Labour government in New Zealand, an ally under the ANZUS pact, to deny access to US warships which might be carrying nuclear weapons and thus to reject the US long-standing policy of neither confirming nor denying the presence of such weapons. The Americans decided in retaliation to cut off the New Zealanders from the alliance's intelligence sharing arrangements and this had complex and negative implications for our own sharing of intelligence with New Zealand whom we had no wish to see ostracised in this way. A visit to Washington by my old mentor, Percy Cradock, now Chairman of the Joint Intelligence Committee and Diplomatic Adviser to the Prime Minister, failed to budge the Americans, who were determined to prevent any contagion from New Zealand's policy on ship visits to their other allies relationships in the region, in particular to Japan. And we had to fall into line.

Counterterrorism was at this point in time only just beginning to obtrude onto the diplomatic radar screen as a policy issue. Hitherto there had been a certain amount of fairly fragmentary exchange of information between intelligence agencies on the two sides of the Atlantic but no systematic drawing together of the various threads at the policy level. I set about trying to remedy that, at least so far as the Embassy was concerned; and that brought me into contact with a small, but growing, network of US officials, most particularly Vice Admiral John Poindexter, the Deputy National Security Adviser (and, from December 1984, on the departure of the incumbent Robert McFarlane, National Security Adviser) and Oliver North, the free-booting Marine Colonel who handled counterterrorism, as well as with Robert Oakley, the much more cautious Director of Counterterrorism at the State Department. Our own preoccupation was with Irish republican terrorism and its ramifications in terms of financial support and arms supplies from the USA; the American concerns were much more directed towards acts of terrorism by various Palestinian splinter groups and their governmental backers in the Middle East. But, following the IRA's attempt on the Prime Minister's life at Brighton in October 1984, we found ourselves getting much fuller US cooperation over the Irish threat than had ever been the case before. Previous US administrations had always trod carefully on Irish issues given the sensitivities in Congress where there were many influential Senators and Congressmen who, while they had no sympathy with acts of terrorism, gave much political support to the republican cause. Now a systematic effort was made to cut off IRA access to sources of funding in the USA; and intelligence cooperation led to the seizure of a shipment of arms going from Boston to Ireland. And, when a New York judge released a convicted IRA terrorist, who had escaped from our custody and whom we were trying to get extradited, on the grounds that he qualified for the political loophole in the US/UK Extradition Treaty because he had murdered a uniformed British soldier, there was an instant US reaction from the highest level that this was intolerable and that the loophole would need to be removed. I persuaded London to strike while the iron was hot and not wait for second thoughts to emerge about the probable problems with Congress over the ratification of any renegotiated treaty. A legal adviser from the FCO flew out and we managed to negotiate a new text removing the political loophole in a single day; the new treaty was subsequently signed in the presence of Vice-President Bush. Thereafter things went less smoothly, and two young members of the Senate Foreign Relations Committee, Joseph Biden and John Kerry, bottled up the new treaty and prevented its ratification. It was only finally released from the Senate's grip and ratified as a tribute to the UK's support for the US bombing of Tripoli in April 1986.

It was not many months after our arrival in Washington that I began to get intimations that our stay there might be shorter than we had expected. The trigger was the decision by Michael Butler, Permanent Representative to the European Community in Brussels, to retire unexpectedly early at the end of the summer of 1985 and take up a job in the City. I heard first that my name was on a list of possible successors, and then, by the usual whispering in the undergrowth, that the Prime Minister had approved and I was to get the job. It was quite some time later that the Ambassador actually told me I would be leaving Washington in August 1985. I had mixed feelings. I was enjoying Washington and had yet to realise the full potential of the job there. But the post I was going to in Brussels was the one I most coveted at the top level in the Diplomatic Service and the one for which I felt myself best suited. So any regrets were soon suppressed. I did learn a good deal from that short stay in Washington, about the complexity of the US system of governance, about the difficulties of accommodating US exceptionalism and about the limits of our influence even during a halcyon period in the UK/US relationship when the links between the Prime Minister and the President were at their strongest. Above all I concluded at that stage, and have never been shaken in that belief, that the idea that Britain had to choose between its relationship with the USA and its role in Europe was a fundamentally false choice. It was already clear, even then, that our influence in Washington could be greatly augmented if we were part of a European mainstream view on this or that policy issue. That had been the lesson of the successful campaign in 1982 to reverse a US decision to impose sanctions on European companies involved in the project to build a gas pipeline between the Soviet Union and Western Europe. Margaret Thatcher had fought as hard as anyone in that campaign, since a British company, John Brown, was under threat of sanctions. It had been the lesson too of her stance on SDI. In neither case would US policy have been influenced so effectively if there had not been a broad European consensus. But that did not mean that all foreign policy issues had to be handled on a European basis. None of the other large European countries actually practised that, although the speeches of their leaders sometimes suggested that they did. As to Britain's own relationship with the USA, experience showed that there was no such thing as a golden era when there had been no differences between us, not even during a period when the links at the highest level, between Margaret Thatcher and Ronald Reagan, were so strong. So the case for a robust and hard-headed assertion of our respective national interests remained as strong as ever. The key was to achieve a flexible and adaptable balance between the bilateral and the European dimensions of the relationship; and that, alas, has often proved elusive.

10

BRUSSELS (EUROPEAN COMMUNITY)
1985–1990

AT THE HEART OF EUROPE

My return to the European scene as Britain's Permanent Representative occurred, as it had done in 1979, in the midst of a crisis in Britain's always turbulent relationship with the other member states and the European institutions. With the debilitating trench warfare over Britain's budget contribution put behind them at the Fontainebleau European Council in June 1984 the thoughts of all member states, including Britain, had turned to ways of making their partnership more productive and effective. Their economies were emerging from the deep recession of the early 1980s, so the appetite for further trade liberalisation was picking up. At Fontainebleau they had appointed a new Commission which took office at the beginning of 1985 and they had chosen as its President Jacques Delors, previously the French Finance Minister, who had won his spurs even in the critical eyes of Margaret Thatcher by resisting President Mitterrand's early attempts to pursue an expansionary and internationally protectionist set of economic policies. Delors had a particularly warm relationship with Geoffrey Howe struck up during their time as fellow Finance Ministers in the ECOFIN Council. Working in close concert with the new senior British Commissioner, Arthur Cockfield, a former tax lawyer with a razor-sharp mind, Delors decided to put all the emphasis in his first term of office on the creation of a true single market. While the European Community had been a fully fledged customs union since the end of the transitional period in the 1960s, with internal tariff barriers and quantitative restrictions on trade removed and a common external tariff, it was by no stretch of the imagination a single market, many hundreds of what were known as technical barriers to trade remaining at national frontiers. The gradual removal of these barriers by Community legislation had proceeded at an agonisingly slow pace largely because of the requirement under the founding treaties to adopt such legislation by unanimity. Instead of simply issuing a classical Commission appeal to the member states in high flown language to summon up the political will to dismantle this logjam, Cockfield and Delors produced a White Paper which set out in meticulous detail what needed to be done to achieve a single market, and they buttressed the case with economic research demonstrating the benefits in terms of the higher rates of economic growth that could be achieved in such a market. They also made it clear that, in their view, progress required a treaty change from unanimity to Qualified Majority Voting (QMV), that is to say an amendment to the original treaty provisions. It was this last recommendation which set them at odds with the British government.

The Commission's White Paper immediately triggered an intensive debate among the member states. It was generally very positively received, not least by the British government which had been an ardent supporter of moves towards a single market since long before Delors and Cockfield came on the scene. But some member states, particularly those not traditionally much enamoured of trade liberalisation and those who wished to push European integration in a federalist direction, wanted treaty change to go much further than what was required to achieve a single market. So the division between minimalists and maximalists was there from the outset and remained throughout the subsequent negotiations. The British government set out its views in a paper, 'Europe: the future' which it circulated to its partners. This paper, which was by a rather long way the most positive and constructive policy document on Europe produced before or since by a British government, advocated making decisive progress towards a single market not through treaty change but by reaching a gentlemen's agreement between the member states that they would not insist on unanimity for single market legislation but would accept the expression of a majority view for such decisions. It also proposed a considerable strengthening of the system of foreign policy cooperation between the member states. In the last days before the Milan meeting of the European Council in June 1985 at which all these matters were due to be discussed, the Franco-German duo of Mitterrand and Kohl weighed in with firm support for treaty change and simply lifted, almost word-for-word and without attribution, the British proposal for increased foreign policy cooperation. This spectacular act of discourtesy did nothing to improve the atmosphere at the Milan meeting and merely ensured that the main discussion there would focus not on what everyone agreed about – the need for a single market and strengthened foreign policy cooperation – but on the institutional methods of obtaining these objectives. At the Milan meeting things went from bad to worse when the Italian Presidency ambushed the British government by announcing that, since the decision to set up an Inter-Governmental Conference (IGC) to consider treaty change was merely a procedural one, it could be taken by a simple majority; and then proceeding to take the decision, with only Britain and Greece voting against. The ensuing row was sulphurous, made worse by the way in which the British policy paper had been virtually ignored. The IGC thus began to meet under the worst possible auspices, with the British government reminding everyone of the simple truth that, while a majority vote could convene an IGC, only unanimity could bring about a positive outcome, and that it remained completely unconvinced of the case for treaty change. This was the stage onto which I stepped at the end of September.

By the time I did my rounds among senior ministers in London in the middle of September before setting off to Brussels, things had calmed down a bit but the wounds of Milan had not yet healed. My first meeting was with the Foreign Secretary, Geoffrey Howe, who I already knew well from his time first as Chancellor of the Exchequer and then as Foreign Secretary when we had worked as a team on the budget issue. I never could understand how he came to have a public image of a grey and boring politician when his humour, intellect and unremitting hard work, coupled with a powerful legal mind, made him a joy to work with and an impressive and determined leader. So far as the European Community was concerned, the principal formative influence on his views had been his experience as Solicitor General in the Heath government when he had piloted through the House of Commons the ratification of our terms of accession. This had left him convinced that Britain had made the right choice and that we needed to play a positive role in the Community's future development. It was clear from the outset that he wanted to see whether the treaty change route could be turned to our advantage. 'But', as he said pointing vaguely over my shoulder in a direction which I at first thought was towards Brussels but which I then realised was towards 10 Downing Street, 'your real job is over there'. Thus forewarned, a day or two later I called on the Prime Minister. Not surprisingly she had a good deal to say about the iniquitous way she had been treated at Milan. On the path ahead she stuck to generalities, while making clear her distaste for treaty change which risked becoming a Pandora's Box out of which a lot more than the single market might emerge. At one moment in the conversation I unwisely said that negotiation in Brussels was much like a game of snakes and ladders; my job was to find the ladders and avoid the snakes. 'Oh no, David, you are quite wrong there. In Brussels they are all snakes!', she responded. The conclusion I drew from these preliminary exchanges was that we needed at all costs to avoid a premature discussion in London of a theoretical kind on treaty change or no treaty change. Such a discussion would need to be based on a clear picture of the practicalities of what was involved, so that pragmatism as well as ideology could come into play. So, all through October and early November, I resisted the siren voices from various quarters, most insistently from our Embassies in other European capitals, pressing for a clarification of our position. In reality its very ambiguity was an asset to us in the negotiations in Brussels which were by then becoming intensive and practical. We were able to respond to the urgings of the maximalists by pointing out that the various additional areas they wished to bring within the Community's scope would make it even less likely that Britain would agree to treaty change; and we were able to use similar arguments to assist our own shaping of the provisions on the single market.

✳   ✳   ✳

My return to Brussels early one autumn morning in 1985 was not entirely typical of the life of a Permanent Representative to the European Community but it did reflect the overwhelming concentration that by then prevailed on the negotiation and drafting of the set of amendments to the Community's founding treaties which was to come to be known as the Single European Act. Catching the first flight out of London I went directly from the airport in Brussels to a, by then weekly, full day meeting of the IGC at ambassadorial level. I was certainly being thrown in at the deep end. Later in the week I actually got to meet my team in the Permanent Representation, many of whom I already knew from my earlier years working in Brussels and London on Community business. The IGC at ambassadorial level was the engine room of the negotiation. It reported up to the IGC at Foreign Minister level, which met on a roughly monthly basis, and they in turn reported to the Heads of State and Government due to meet in early December in Luxembourg. These structures were completely untried, since this was the first occasion on which there had been such a wide-ranging review and reform of the Community's institutional and operating procedures since its establishment in the 1950s (there had been some treaty changes agreed in 1967 when the executives, but not the treaties, of the three original Communities were merged, and in 1970 when the permanent arrangements for financing Community expenditure were put in place). The IGC at ambassadorial level was chaired by the Luxembourg Permanent Representative, Jean Dondelinger, a wily and cautious operator with decades of Community experience, whose objective from the outset was to deliver to his Prime Minister in early December a negotiable set of reforms, not to organise another confrontation such as had taken place at Milan.

The Commission was represented by Émile Noël, its Secretary-General ever since its establishment in 1957 and a person of encyclopaedic knowledge about the Community, whom I knew well from my time in the Commission; Noël too was a proven pragmatist who could be relied upon to keep in check some of the more ambitious and wilder ideas that poured forth from Delors and his cabinet, a group which came to be known as the 'ayatollahs'. This key duo of Dondelinger and Noël stood us in good stead. The other members of the conference were mostly serving Permanent Representatives, although the Italians were represented by an official from Rome. There were also representatives from Spain and Portugal which were due to join the Community at the beginning of 1986; but they were largely silent observers. We ourselves divided the task between myself and David Williamson (the Deputy

Secretary who headed up the European Secretariat in the Cabinet Office and who advised the Prime Minister on European affairs). This made good sense given my newness to the task; and the fact that we are still cooperating closely together on European matters in the House of Lords more than 25 years later is adequate testimony to our capacity to work together seamlessly. Those early weeks in the IGC were more hard slog than excitement, as the member states sussed out each others' positions and prepared the ground for the compromises that would be needed if agreement was to be reached. The division between maximalists (the majority) and minimalists (a shifting minority which invariably included us) was pretty clear. But some interesting changes in position did begin to show up. A few weeks into the process the French Permanent Representative, Luc de Nanteuil, asked me privately whether he had correctly perceived that we were negotiating for an agreed outcome which would include treaty change. I said I could not help him; he would have to draw his own conclusions; we were still not convinced of the need for treaty change. But from that point on the French began to take a more pragmatic and less ambitious line; and that, as usual, had its effect on the German position.

We soon settled in to our slightly strange but delightfully comfortable suburban house in Uccle that could have been designed for a family of our size (four mainly teenage boys spread between boarding schools and university in Britain). The 'slightly strange' epithet refers to the house's architectural style, which was more that of Marbella than northern Europe – a white stucco villa with wrought-iron grilles on the windows, it had been built in the 1930s for a member of the Solvay family of industrialists. It was blessed with an attractive garden which had been laid out by a well-known English landscape gardener and with a croquet lawn which encouraged playing techniques not entirely dissimilar to the practice of Community negotiation. It provided a wonderful base for what was an extraordinarily hectic professional life, quite apart from being well designed for entertaining, and for accommodating the steady flow of ministers who streamed through Brussels on their way to and from meetings of the Council. A typical week would include Monday and Tuesday meetings of the Council, either of the Foreign Affairs and General Council which brought the Foreign Secretary to Brussels each month or of the ECOFIN Council which brought over the Chancellor of the Exchequer, or of the Development or Energy Councils for all of which the Permanent Representative (as opposed to his Deputy who handled Internal Market, Budget, Fisheries and other Councils) was directly responsible. On Wednesday the Commission held its weekly meeting which often occasioned a fair amount of lobbying; and that tended to be the day too to visit Strasbourg to brief the different groups of British MEPs, a monthly practice which I reinstated and held to throughout my five years in the job. Thursday was taken up with the (normally full day) meetings of the Committee of Permanent Representatives (COREPER) preparing the various Council meetings for which they were responsible (the Deputies met on a separate day and effectively operated as a parallel system, which in itself put a premium on effective coordination). And then on Friday, invariably, I would catch the first flight to London for the weekly coordination meeting at the Cabinet Office which would take most of the morning. We would often spend the weekend on that side of the Channel seeing one or other of our boys, and returning to Brussels on Sunday evening. Into this schedule had to be fitted calls by members of the Shadow Cabinet, visits by Parliamentary Committees, meetings with businessmen, bankers and trade union leaders, weekly background briefings for the British press and calls on Commissioners. It was lucky indeed that the Community took a couple of weeks off at Christmas and Easter and a full month in August; without those breaks the timetable would have been intolerable.

It would be no exaggeration to say that those Friday coordination meetings at the Cabinet Office were the lynchpin of all the rest. It was there that we could take stock of what had happened at COREPER and at the Council meetings that week and could agree the lines to be followed at the Council meetings the following week. It was there too that we could set in hand lobbying of the Commission on matters coming up on their agenda; and could agree on representations to be made by our Embassies in the capitals of the other member states. Those Friday coordination meetings had begun under my predecessor, Michael Butler. At first they were so informal, cutting across as they did the formal structure of Cabinet and sub-Cabinet committees that not only was the discussion not minuted but even the conclusions reached were not recorded. I had at least managed during my time as Under-Secretary at the FCO between 1979 and 1984 to ensure that the conclusions were recorded and distributed to the Permanent Representation in Brussels and to the departments concerned; and I had no wish to change the practice of avoiding any minuting of the proceedings since that encouraged flexibility and frankness. The three fixtures at the meetings throughout their duration were the Deputy Secretary in the Cabinet Office who was head of the European Secretariat and who chaired the meeting, the Permanent Representative from Brussels and the Under-Secretary in the FCO responsible for Community affairs. Any of those three could ask for a subject to be raised and discussed and the department concerned was not allowed to cry off or to postpone it without good cause. The conclusions reached were largely procedural, and substantive disagreements were left to be resolved either through subsequent inter-departmental correspondence or through the formal structure of ministerial cabinet committees and sub-committees. It was a remarkably effective piece of machinery and, if Britain had the reputation, as it did, of being the best coordinated of all the member states, it was largely due to the existence of those Friday meetings.

As the autumn of 1985 wore on, all the focus turned to the preparation of the European Council in Luxembourg in early December, which everyone came to assume, encouraged to do so by the Luxembourg Presidency, would be a make-or-break meeting. This meant that, as the date approached, national positions firmed up and hardened and the search for compromises became more arduous. I argued throughout in Whitehall that the approach of the Luxembourg presidency suited us well as it would compel them in the end, in the interests of getting a result, to swing towards pragmatism and a more narrowly based set of reforms. We had more to fear from a long drawn out negotiation during which we could find ourselves in a minority of one on a whole range of issues, under pressure to choose between them or face the consequences of a major confrontation and resulting damage to our own main objective, decisive progress towards a genuine single market. This approach was agreed in

London, although our own ultimate destination remained veiled in mystery even to the main Ministerial players up to and including the Prime Minister herself. In advance of the meeting of the European Council the Luxembourgers summoned what they grandly named a 'conclave' of Foreign Ministers to prepare the ground for their bosses' meeting later in the week. This did not prove to be a good idea. Foreign Ministers were not prepared to concede points, often concerning matters for which they did not have Ministerial responsibility. So they spent two days of increasing frustration and mounting pessimism; and left the basic treaty amendment texts much as they had found them, festooned with square brackets marking points of disagreement.

It was against that background that Geoffrey Howe sent David Williamson and me back to London in the comfort of the Ministerial RAF executive jet to brief Margaret Thatcher. The briefing of the Prime Minister was, as was almost always the case with her, particularly when no other Ministers were involved, entirely business-like. We worked our way systematically through the 25 or so points on which officials believed we would need satisfaction before we could agree to treaty change. She took notes on her own carefully annotated negotiating brief and did not contest the overall analysis in any way. She only flared up once when I, perhaps unwisely, drew her attention to the fact that the European Parliament would now achieve that title in proper, treaty-based form and rid itself of the much-hated name of 'Assembly' which was in the original treaty and with which its critics (including Margaret Thatcher) used to taunt it. But neither then, nor subsequently in Luxembourg, did she contest that point. Later that day we returned with her to Luxembourg for the European Council meeting.

That December, Luxembourg European Council was a genuine marathon spread over three days (and much of the nights between) and ending late in the evening of the third day. For most of the time the Heads of State and Government and their Foreign Ministers, together with the President of the Commission, were locked in direct face to face negotiation without advisers, who were excluded quite deliberately, although they could follow the proceedings in a distinctly imperfect way through the notes emerging from the meeting courtesy of the Council Secretariat and the participants – the deciphering of Geoffrey Howe's handwritten notes being a considerable challenge turned over to his Private Secretary – and could feed in papers if asked for them. There were intermissions in this agonising process, sometimes for meals, sometimes quite impromptu as when the Italian Foreign Minister, Giulio Andreotti, at the end of a long objection by Margaret Thatcher to placing excessive regulatory burdens on small businesses in the process of constructing a Single Market, commented that he was glad never to have been employed in a business run by the British Prime Minister. This sally necessitated a lengthy break while tempers cooled off and apologies were offered. Throughout the proceedings Jacques Santer, the Luxembourg Prime Minister, presided calmly and phlegmatically, determined not to allow the proceedings to go off the rails or to run aground in deadlock. And throughout it too the Thatcher/Howe duo moved meticulously and remorselessly through the long list of amendments Britain was seeking. At the end of the second day very late in the evening, when a lot of progress had been made, although some tricky issues remained unresolved, David Williamson and I wound up our final briefing for the Prime Minister. Looking up she asked us whether we thought a deal could be struck the next day which would meet our requirements; and whether it was a deal worth doing. We answered yes to both questions and she nodded in agreement.

There was one unexpected twist on the final day that subsequently gave rise in London to considerable controversy and misunderstanding. Throughout the negotiations for the Single European Act the Belgians had ploughed a lonely furrow in demanding at least a symbolic reference to Economic and Monetary Union (EMU). EMU had been an agreed objective of the Community since the Paris Summit in 1972 and the first attempt at achieving it had foundered in the economic crisis following the Yom Kippur War in 1973. They received lukewarm support in this aim from the other maximalists, who saw little point in a purely symbolic reference with no operative conclusions to it; but any reference at all had been resolutely opposed by the British and German representatives at every level. Then, in a break during the last day's proceedings, Chancellor Helmut Kohl asked to see Margaret Thatcher. They closeted themselves in our delegation office together with their Foreign Ministers, Hans-Dietrich Genscher and Geoffrey Howe; only one official from each side, both Treasury representatives – Hans Tietmeyer and Geoffrey Littler – was allowed to participate.

And, to my considerable astonishment, they emerged to say that the two had agreed to accept the symbolic reference to EMU being promoted by the Belgians so long as it was accompanied by a binding provision requiring the negotiation of a new treaty (and thus separate national ratifications) before any progress towards implementing it could be made. Kohl and Genscher had argued that this would provide a stronger defence against the sort of incremental progress towards EMU which they suspected was the Commission's preferred route and which they strongly opposed. Was Margaret Thatcher deliberately misled by the Germans? I do not believe so. Their opposition to EMU was at that time (in 1985) genuine and strongly felt, when the tumultuous events in Eastern Europe that changed their attitude were still well below the horizon. In any case the symbolic reference to EMU in the Single European Act was never the fulcrum in the subsequent developments, which were driven more by high politics than by reference to legal texts. And so the Luxembourg European Council ended in agreement on a complete set of amendments to the founding treaties, focussed firmly on the creation of a Single Market and on the strengthening of foreign policy cooperation, and with only one issue, whether or not to move to Qualified Majority Voting on matters relating to health and safety in the workplace, left over for decision by the Foreign Ministers (with only the British opposing that).

There were three significant epilogues to the agreement on the Single European Act. The first came within weeks of the Luxembourg meeting when the Foreign Ministers met in Brussels for their last pre-Christmas Council. To general surprise and bafflement the President of the Commission asked for a highly restricted meeting with only Ministers and Permanent Representatives present. Once there, Delors launched into a lengthy, self-pitying and almost lachrymose critique of the Single European Act; too many compromises had been made, too many issues fudged, the essence of the Commission's Single Market White Paper had been betrayed; he feared that the mountain had laboured mightily and brought forth a mouse which would not have the stimulating effect on the European economy that all desired; it might be better to go back to the drawing board. The Foreign Ministers listened to this diatribe in appalled silence and then, one by one, and with no exceptions, they responded. An outsider who had not been familiar with the negotiations would have been unable to distinguish between them; the former leader of the maximalists, Andreotti, spoke in no different terms to Geoffrey Howe. It was sheer folly to denigrate the Single European Act before it had even been put to the test. The compromises had been hard fought but necessary, and there was no certainty that renegotiation of them would produce a different or a better result. The Community would make a damaging fool of itself if it resumed negotiations on an agreement which had been widely welcomed by public opinion and by European business. The Luxembourg Presidency wisely drew no conclusions after this humiliating rebuff; and no more was heard of Delors' doubts. It had been a fascinating confrontation between the pragmatic realism of the Foreign Ministers and the idealism of Delors. Why had he done it? Perhaps among other things he was answering his critics in the Commission who believed that he had been too accommodating at Luxembourg. For at least one observer he left some doubt as to whether he was really cut out for the rough and tumble of daily politics. In any case his prediction that the Single European Act would prove to be worthless was soon disproved.

The second epilogue came in January 1986. The incoming Dutch Presidency had scheduled a signature ceremony for the Single European Act towards the end of that month. Reasonably enough they needed to know what was to be done about the one issue left unresolved after Luxembourg, the shift to majority voting on health and safety at work. So I soon found myself in receipt of daily telephone calls from Charles Rutten, the Dutch chairman of COREPER, urging us to clarify our position. Obviously the Dutch wanted us to join a consensus to make the change, but their main concern was to get a definitive reply out of London. My own position was the same. I did not in fact believe this was a make-or-break issue for the whole Single European Act. Had our reply been to reject the change I doubted – although such negatives can never be proved – whether this would have put in jeopardy the signature ceremony at the end of January or the subsequent ratification of the package. So, while I was persistent with London about the need to make up our mind, I did not press one way or the other as to the content of our reply. Rather to my surprise it turned out to be positive; and the signature ceremony duly went ahead. I never did get to the bottom of what decision-making processes took place in London before I received my instructions – the Christmas break as usual produced a certain amount of confusion and dislocation. But, given the controversy that has subsequently surrounded this particular decision, it is perhaps useful to set the Brussels end of the record straight.

The third epilogue was a much longer, more drawn out affair, namely the implementation of the Single Market provisions agreed at Luxembourg. Although not everything was achieved by the target date of 1992 for the completion of a single market, a very great deal was by then on the Community statute book and was becoming a practical reality in the market place. Even in sectors which had lagged behind, such as transport and energy, the first moves towards creating a level European playing field were in the offing, although much, to this day, remains to be done. Most decisions were in fact achieved by consensus and not by voting down a recalcitrant minority and, when there was a vote – as, for example, there was on the main Banking Directive, on which Germany was in a minority of one – Britain was almost invariably in the majority and not the minority. The main effect of the shift to majority voting was not to create a kind of Brussels-dominated tyranny but instead to encourage some flexibility in the national negotiators and to encourage them to form alliances with like-minded member states, and thus to break away from the stasis induced by the unanimity requirement which had hitherto prevailed for Single Market legislation. This process, which served Britain well, is now pejoratively known as 'surrendering Britain's veto'.

The ink was hardly dry on the Single European Act when an entirely unexpected challenge arose not only to the putative single market that it was designed to facilitate but to the very customs union on which the Community was founded. In April 1986 a massive accident occurred at the Chernobyl nuclear power plant in the Soviet Union and rapidly thereafter a cloud of radioactive contamination began to spread across northern and western Europe; in particular wherever rainfall occurred this contamination affected the produce being grown and the livestock being raised. As luck would have it, the normal prevailing winds failed to carry the contamination eastwards, but rather it was spread in a large arc running through

Scandinavia, Britain and Germany. Naturally public and press concern arose immediately about the risk that foodstuffs would be contaminated and that doses of radioactive material well beyond the safe maximums would enter the food chain. Governments were under pressure to introduce measures to stop this happening and nowhere more than in Germany where the endemic opposition to civil nuclear energy linked with health concerns induced a reaction close to panic; and, since there were no Community standards setting the acceptable maximums for radioactive substances in foodstuffs, that pressure was soon translated into demands for national maximum acceptable levels to be set and implemented on all cross-border trade. The obvious solution was to take urgent action at the Community level to set such maximum acceptable levels and then for governments all to apply them without necessitating border controls. But that was easier said than done, although the necessary legal base existed in the EEC and Euratom treaties. Some member states like France, which depended heavily on nuclear power and which had been less affected by the contamination, wanted relatively high figures (the critics said absurdly and dangerously high) to be set at Community level. Others, with Germany in the lead, wanted extremely low figures to be set (at one point the critics from the other side of the argument pointed out that the figures put forward by Germany were below the normal background level of radiation and would thus, if implemented, have resulted rapidly in critical shortages of foodstuffs). The Dutch Presidency immediately set COREPER to work to find a Community solution, but for several lengthy and weary sessions no progress was made in reconciling the opposing points of view. Nor was the Commission, which desperately wanted such a Community solution, a great deal of help. Although technically well qualified to explain the scientific facts behind the crisis and thus able to controvert some of the wilder positions put forward on either side of the argument, their constantly repeated refrain that there were no generally recognised international norms to which to turn and that any maximum figure the Community embraced could only be validated after a great deal of lengthy research was not conducive to reaching an agreement. The Commission was not prepared to make any formal proposal.

A meeting of the Council only made matters worse as each Minister played to their nation's political gallery and thus accentuated rather than reduced the differences between member states and increased the pressure for separate national action. Eventually the Dutch Presidency took their life in their hands and put on the table a maximum limit of 1,000 becquerels (that rather esoteric unit of measurement of which I suspect no one in COREPER had heard before the crisis broke but which no one would forget once it was over). After a good deal of further dispute and manoeuvring it was generally accepted at COREPER level that, while this figure lacked any firm scientific validity, it represented the only one which had any chance of being agreed. And so the necessary Community legislation went through, and the fragmentation of the customs union into 12 separate national markets (Spain and Portugal having been members since the beginning of the year) was avoided. The whole episode could lead to somewhat cynical conclusions, but it did demonstrate both the potential fragility of what had so laboriously been achieved at Community level when confronted with an emergency situation but also the strong political will to avoid that fragility being allowed to spill over into fragmentation.

Chernobyl apart, 1986 was a relatively low-key period in Community business. The member states were engaged in ratifying the Single European Act, a process which, while not without controversy, aroused none of the major problems which occurred, both in Britain and elsewhere in Europe, when subsequent amending treaties, from Maastricht onwards, came to be endorsed. The Commission was principally occupied with consulting over and drafting the single market legislation for which it was hoped that the path for more rapid decision-making would have been cleared once the Single European Act entered into force in 1987. In the second half of 1986 Britain held the Presidency (for the second time since Margaret Thatcher became Prime Minister); so my life as chairman of COREPER was fully occupied in the transaction of routine Community business. Holding the Presidency always presented Britain with problems. We prided ourselves, with some justification, although less than we claimed, on the orderly and punctilious management of day-to-day affairs; but we were averse to 'grand ideas' for the future development of the Community, being more attached to an evolutionary approach. So there was never in our case some overarching theme around which to work. On this occasion that did not matter. And we were able, with the Home Secretary Douglas Hurd, very much to the fore, to follow up a commitment in the Single European Act to cooperate more closely over counterterrorism, international crime, drugs and illegal immigration – a series of subjects which were already at that time becoming of increasing concern to all member states but for which the traditional remedies of national action were proving increasingly inadequate – while not surrendering the prime responsibility of member states in these areas. So Ministerial and senior official meetings on these subjects were held outside the normal Community framework; and the foundations were laid for the cooperation on Justice and Home Affairs (JHA) which developed steadily in the coming years. Towards the end of our Presidency, however, at the time of the European Council in London, the relationship between the President of the Commission and the Prime Minister took a sharp turn for the worse and began the slide towards the open confrontation which characterised it – at least on Margaret Thatcher's side – by the end of the decade. Up to then one could describe the relationship as one of wary mutual respect. The Thatcher/Howe duo had played an important role in Delors' original appointment, when, at Fontainebleau in June 1984, they had blocked the appointment of Claude Cheysson, then French Foreign Minister and President Mitterrand's first choice for the job. The role that Delors had played in promoting the single market in close partnership with Arthur Cockfield had been warmly appreciated in London. But, when Delors called on the Prime Minister at No 10 in December 1986 on the day before the meeting of the European Council which Margaret Thatcher was due to chair, he dropped a bombshell. Despite the raising of the Community's revenue ceiling, agreed as recently as the Fontainebleau meeting a mere two and a half years before, the Community was once again on course to run out of money in a year or two's time. So he wanted to raise the matter now with Heads of State and Government and to initiate a new negotiation about lifting the ceiling again. Not only was it extremely unwise of Delors to have raised such a sensitive subject out of the blue and without fair warning; but it clearly confirmed him in the Prime Minister's eyes as yet another of those tax and spend socialists against whom she had been fighting all her political life. So, metaphorically, she swung her handbag. There could be no question of the matter being discussed at this European Council, the agenda for which had been set some days before. In any case the Community had to learn to live within its means; and above all it had to get the seemingly inexorable rise in agricultural spending under control. Delors' reaction could not have been worse. He lapsed into a sulky silence and made no attempt to explain the rationale behind his thinking, thus convincing the Prime Minister that, like so many of the people she had to deal with, he could be bullied into submission. The procedural issue was quickly sorted out. Delors would make a brief statement on the state of the Community's finances at the dinner for heads of delegation only on the first evening; and there would be no discussion at the Council itself. But the damage was done. At the end of the Council meeting there was a further incident. With some difficulty I had persuaded the Prime Minister that by tradition, the chair's press conference had to include the President of the Commission alongside her on the platform. She conceded grumpily, but alongside her he certainly was not; she sat centre stage under the arc lights while Delors was placed in the shadows to her right and several steps below her. She then proceeded to make a statement on the outcome of the meeting and to answer a whole string of questions without giving Delors a single chance to speak. Finally a journalist put a question explicitly to the President of the Commission, noting that he had hitherto played no part in the press conference. 'Ah', said the Prime Minister, 'Monsieur Delors is the strong, silent sort of person.' I cringed; and I felt pretty certain that there would be a price to pay for such a gratuitous insult.

❉   ❉   ❉

The negotiations on what came to be known as the 'Delors package' absorbed most of the time and political attention of the Commission and the member states for the next 18 months, from the beginning of 1987 to the middle of 1988. They were complex, tense and often bad-tempered (on one occasion Jacques Chirac, who had become Prime Minister in an uneasy coalition with President Mitterrand, said that Margaret Thatcher had spoken to him like a fishwife – what he was really complaining about was that she had stood in Chirac's way when he tried to exclude from the agricultural reform package some commodities of particular sensitivity to France).

They were, however, quite different from the negotiations over the British budget rebate which had pitted Britain against the rest. There were several different groups of member states in the Delors package negotiations, with different and often conflicting national interests. The new member states, Spain and Portugal, together with Greece, were determined to achieve a really substantial increase in expenditure on the regional and social funds (together known as the Structural Funds) and on a 'cohesion' fund which they saw as some compensation to them for accepting the rigours of the Single Market; they were not averse to some cutting back on expenditure on 'northern' agricultural commodities such as cereals, meat and sugar. There were member states like France and Ireland, which, while they paid lip-service to the need to reform the Common Agricultural Policy, fought like tigers to protect the benefits they received from that policy. And there was a small, but powerful group consisting of Britain, Germany and the Netherlands who were determined to bring the rise in agricultural spending under control and who realised from bitter experience in recent years that this could not be achieved simply by setting some overall guideline but that one had to drill down into the reform of the individual commodity regimes of which the overall agricultural spend was composed. The British, of course, were also determined to defend their hard-won two-thirds rebate, decided at Fontainebleau in 1984. The other member states were less clearly committed than these groups and would broadly accept whatever was agreed by those who were so committed. Moreover, unlike the negotiations over the British rebate, this was not a zero-sum game since it was clear from the outset that the overall expenditure ceiling would need to be raised. The negotiation spread over three successive Presidencies. The Belgians (the first half of 1987), determined to secure a Presidency 'success', mishandled their European Council by trying to reach agreement separately on one major component of the negotiations, the structural funds, before progress was made on the rest, which resulted in their getting agreement on nothing. The Danes (second half of 1987) came respectably close to getting an overall agreement, but were thwarted by French intransigence over agricultural reform and the refusal of the agricultural reform group, of which Britain was a leading member, to settle without something meaningful – also thwarted no doubt by the French calculation that they could get a better deal from the incoming German Presidency for the first half of 1988. The basic political deal was struck in February 1988 at a specially convened European Council when, as so often in the past, the Germans, by now by far the biggest net contributors to the Community budget, took the lion's share of the additional burden; after that all that remained was a great deal of complicated tidying up which was successfully completed by the end of June 1988.

This negotiation showed Margaret Thatcher at the height of her powers of advocacy and determination. She had just won a third general election victory by a substantial margin. She was by now a master of the intricacies of European budget procedures and practice. But she didn't know when to stop, and therein lay the risks. Moreover, she was falling steadily more out of sympathy with her Foreign Secretary, Geoffrey Howe (and he with her), which made for considerable tensions in the shaping of the British negotiating position and in its presentation, which Howe consistently found too shrill and too domineering. At an early stage of the negotiation I was summoned to No 10 to discuss our overall strategy with the Prime Minister, the Chancellor of the Exchequer and the Foreign Secretary, the last of whom had to leave the meeting early. Even the two hawks (Thatcher and Lawson) saw no point in refusing to contemplate any raising of the revenue ceiling. While it was true that much of the pressure came from the lack of control over agricultural spending, a substantial part came from the need to finance Britain's rebate (which was being systematically boosted by the rise in CAP expenditure) and the case for increasing structural fund spending in the new member states, which were a long way below the Community average in Gross National Income per capita, was pretty unanswerable. So the key question was how best to trade our willingness to raise the ceiling, which all other member states desperately wanted albeit for different reasons. Lawson said that our first priority must be to nail down our rebate. I argued that this would be a tactical mistake. If we insisted on discussing the rebate at an early stage of the negotiation we would split ourselves from our allies on CAP reform (Germany and the Netherlands) and weaken our leverage on that crucial subject, to which I suggested we should give full priority. Moreover, I could not see how we would be seriously at risk if we left discussion of the rebate right to the end. For one thing that fitted our own narrative, which was that the size of the rebate was merely a consequence of the decisions taken on the other budget headings. And in any case, with the rebate embedded since Fontainebleau in the Community's Own Resources Decision which could not be amended without our agreement, it would be remarkably foolhardy of anyone to try to tamper with it at the last moment just when we were being asked to accept a higher overall ceiling. The Prime Minister listened carefully to all this and finally concluded that she agreed with my reasoning. 'But you had better be right', she said; and I left No 10 with those ominous words ringing in my ears.

The denouement of the negotiation over the Delors package at an extraordinary European Council called by the German Presidency early in their term of office in February 1988, was a tense and unpleasant occasion. The CAP reform group of member states had from the outset of the meeting been deprived of its most important member, Germany, now compelled to play a reasonably objective role in the chair and clearly determined, under Helmut Kohl's powerful leadership, to achieve an agreed result where his two predecessors in the chair had failed – an intention which could not be in doubt once he had gambled by calling an unexpectedly early meeting. However, this did not prevent the remaining two members of the group, Britain and the Netherlands, from continuing to press hard and effectively for more specific commitments on CAP reform; and from making further ground, to the intense anger and dismay of the French Prime Minister, Jacques Chirac. Whenever I was summoned to the Council meeting room by either the Prime Minister or the Foreign Secretary the atmosphere was heavy with menace and the tone of debate acid. Only President Mitterrand seemed to be completely unperturbed, sitting quietly writing picture postcards – who knows to whom – while the debate raged around him. Finally late in the night Kohl summoned the British and Dutch Prime Ministers to his Presidency office alongside the Council chamber and told them he believed he had pushed the French and others who were resisting CAP reform as far as he could; it was now time for decisions to be taken. After considerable confused discussion, the Dutch Prime Minister Ruud Lubbers, said that he reluctantly agreed with Kohl and would be prepared to accept the package as it now was. Margaret Thatcher refused to follow suit, and said she would need to consider where things now stood before returning to the Council. So we (Geoffrey Howe, David Williamson and I) sat down with the Prime Minister in a small side room. All three of us argued for acceptance. We had made considerable progress on CAP reform (on paper, at least); we had completely protected the British rebate whose continuation was there for the plucking; the rise in the Community's spending ceiling – to 1.27 per cent of Gross National Income – was reasonable (it stands to this day, nearly 25 years later). Margaret Thatcher did not want to call it a day and was all for fighting on alone. But, eventually, having shed a tear or two – the only time I ever saw this happen, and they were tears of rage and not submission – she agreed to accept what was on offer. I was deeply relieved, not least because my own gamble of leaving the rebate out of the negotiation until the very end had paid off. In fact there was no real discussion at all of the rebate in the negotiation from beginning to end and only one feeble attempt by the German Presidency to get us to dilute it, when the German Permanent Representative, Werner Ungerer, approached me a couple of days before the European Council meeting and asked us to consider making 'a small gesture', to which I replied that, if the Chancellor really wanted an agreed outcome to the meeting he had called they should banish such ideas; and so they did. My relief would have been even greater had I then known what Nils Ersboell, the Danish Secretary-General of the Council, told me some weeks later: namely that Helmut Kohl had decided, in the event of Margaret Thatcher not agreeing to the package, to promulgate formally the agreement of the other eleven to what was on the table and to send us away to consider our position at more leisure. Ersboell indeed showed me the text of such a document that he had prepared for the Presidency but which, of course, was never used. So, by the skin of our teeth, we avoided a situation which would have been humiliating if, as was probable, in the end we had had to accept the outcome agreed by the others, or which alternatively would have led to an open confrontation with possibly unforeseen consequences including, very possibly as the money ran out, a challenge to our rebate.

The British are not particularly adept at lobbying for top level international appointments nor at securing them. Nor, even when our claim to such a post was not contestable, as was the case at the time for the two (now one) posts of Commissioner, were the choices generally well made. The reasons are complex. In general, the British political class are not well suited by professional experience for such appointments. They seldom have any serious knowledge of a language other than their own. The hard school of British parliamentary politics leaves little time or inclination to acquire the necessary international skills. The belief that there is no way back into British politics after a spell in Brussels (or elsewhere) acts as a deterrent. The disinclination of successive British Prime Ministers to make appointments from the House of Commons in order to avoid precipitating a by-election does not help. So the presence in Brussels when I returned in 1985 of two recently appointed and more than competent British Commissioners, Arthur Cockfield and Stanley Clinton Davis, was an uncovenanted benefit, even if the activities of the first of these in particular was to cause me plenty of headaches as his relationship with his former cabinet colleagues in London steadily deteriorated. Cockfield soon established complete control over the crucial Single Market programme, in which he was assisted by his unbreakable partnership with Delors, and he became greatly respected by his Commission colleagues precisely because of his willingness to stand up to criticism and pressure from the government in London. What he lacked in ability to handle the Council of Ministers he made up for in the clarity of his thinking and his skill at drafting effective legislation. However, when the time came in 1988 to appoint two British Commissioners for a new term, my attempts to plead for continuity and for the reappointment of the existing pair were of no avail. Margaret Thatcher was quite determined to get rid of Cockfield, whom she considered as having 'gone native' in Brussels; and she was not prepared to sacrifice a Conservative Commissioner while giving his Labour colleague a further term of office. So we ended up with one excellent new Commissioner in Leon Brittan, who, for all the difference in his personality, soon became as influential as Cockfield within the Commission, and a second appointee, Bruce Millan, who was neither effective within the Commission nor willing to pay attention to the advocacy of the British Permanent Representative when matters relating to British national interests were to the fore, on which he took a basically tribal approach. But Margaret Thatcher did, however reluctantly, lend her support to the appointment of Delors to a new term as President of the Commission. In roughly the same time frame as those appointments were being made, the long-serving French Secretary-General of the Commission, Émile Noël (over 30 years in the job and its sole holder up till then) decided to retire. For all his phenomenal skills, it was in reality time for a change as the Commission was becoming a much larger and more complex bureaucratic machine and could no longer be run like some kind of extended family business. It was decided in London that we should put forward David Williamson, the head of the European Secretariat of the Cabinet Office and the Prime Minister's principal adviser on European affairs, as a candidate for the post; and we were quickly able to secure the essential French support – essential both because the post had so far been 'theirs' and because of the nationality of Delors whose appointment this was. There were no strong alternative candidates. So, rather over-confidently, we assumed the matter was in the bag. And then nothing happened for many a long month; Delors showed no sign of making up his mind and was evasive whenever I raised the matter. Finally, on the basis of my by then reasonably extensive knowledge of Delors, I suggested a high risk gamble; I would simply suggest to Delors that he take advantage of one of Williamson's frequent visits to Brussels to have an informal meal with him and clear his mind about the succession to Noël. London agreed and Delors agreed; and, at the end of a dinner à deux, Delors offered Williamson the job. I never met anyone who regretted that decision.

*   *   *

I have had plenty of bright ideas during my professional life that have turned out to be not so bright after all, but none which I have regretted more bitterly than the initiative which led up to Margaret Thatcher's speech in Bruges in September 1988. The background was straightforward. Ever since Britain had joined the European Community in 1973 we had been on the back foot; first there had been the tensions over reconciling a split Labour party to our membership, with the charade of renegotiation and the 1975 referendum; then there had been the long, if justified, struggle over Britain's budget contribution; and then the negotiations over the Single European Act which had seen us cast in the role of minimalists. It was hardly surprising that those who were known in Brussels as the ayatollahs of the Community's institutional development regarded us with hostility and liked to caricature our approach as being purely negative. And yet, looked at reasonably objectively, all the Community causes which we championed – the single market on which much remained to be done, the further liberalisation of world trade with the Community in the lead, strengthened foreign policy cooperation, the further enlargement of the Community to include the remaining EFTA countries and those of Central and Eastern Europe, the reform of the CAP – made up a perfectly coherent, positive and defensible programme, much as some might dislike it or suspect it of being designed to weaken and dilute the Community's institutions. So was it not time for us to get off the back foot and set out our vision for the Community in a compelling and persuasive manner? This was after all what we had tried to do in 1985 with the paper pioneered by my predecessor, Michael Butler, 'Europe: The future'. So I argued; and my arguments were accepted in London, including by No 10. It required no great effort to persuade the Director of the College of Europe in Bruges, who was always on the lookout for opportunities to boost the reputation of his school, to provide the venue. And then I made a second mistake which was to take my eye off the ball as those broad ideas were turned into a speech for the Prime Minister to deliver immediately after the summer break. So, while John Kerr, the Under-Secretary for the European Community at the FCO, waged a lengthy war of attrition with Charles Powell, the Prime Minister's foreign policy adviser at No 10, over the content of the speech (in effect a proxy war over the differing views of their principals, Geoffrey Howe and Margaret Thatcher), I was on holiday; and by the time I returned, on the eve of the speech's delivery in Bruges, it was set in concrete.

In reality the struggle over the content was no contest, since Prime Ministers, even ones less dominant than Margaret Thatcher, tend to get their way over the speeches they themselves are going to deliver. Rereading the Bruges speech now, nearly 25 years after it was delivered, one can be struck with wonder that it caused such a fuss. Much of it was an eloquent and visionary appeal for the Community to open its doors to the countries of Central and Eastern Europe which were not yet free of the Soviet yoke but were already moving in that direction. But in truth it was not the content of the speech but the way it was spun by the Prime Minister's press spokesman,

Bernard Ingham, which caused all the trouble. He managed to give overriding emphasis to the passages which constituted a frontal assault on the Commission's aspirations for the future development of the Community. These were represented, with scant basis in fact, as designed to impose a socialist blueprint for Europe and thus to roll back everything that the Conservative government in Britain had achieved in the preceding ten years. And so I sat in the medieval splendour of Bruges' town hall, surrounded by a galaxy of Commissioners and Permanent Representatives, and watched my hopes of presenting Britain's European policies in a positive rather than a negative light going up in smoke.

✳   ✳   ✳

One set of issues, those relating to Britain's possible membership of the European Exchange Rate Mechanism (ERM) and, as the momentum built up within the Community for another attempt at reaching Economic and Monetary Union (EMU) following the foundering of the first effort in the economic and financial crises of the 1970s, those relating to Britain's attitude towards EMU, were never allowed by the Prime Minister to come anywhere near the formal inter-departmental coordinating machinery, either at official or at Ministerial level, no papers were circulated and no systematic cabinet discussions took place. Not only were the subjects sensitive but it was no secret that the government was split on all these issues, the Prime Minister being viscerally opposed to joining the ERM and to participating in any move towards EMU, the Chancellor of the Exchequer, Nigel Lawson, advocating joining the ERM but as opposed to EMU as the Prime Minister, and Geoffrey Howe, the Foreign Secretary, wanting Britain to join the ERM and taking a more accommodating view on EMU. The views of the Permanent Representative and his team in Brussels were neither sought nor proffered. So I was only vaguely aware of the first major attempt in 1985 by Nigel Lawson and Geoffrey Howe to persuade the Prime Minister to join the ERM and of its summary rejection. And, when it became clear during 1988 that Delors intended to lead a major push during his second term of office to get a precise commitment to EMU, including a timetable for establishing a European Central Bank (ECB) and a Single Currency, there was no proper preparation on these issues in Whitehall and no review of the options available to us. Matters first came to a head at a European Council meeting in Hanover in June 1988. At that meeting it became clear that the German position towards EMU was shifting away from the outright opposition expressed in Luxembourg in 1985, although they too were split, with Chancellor Helmut Kohl being far more positive than the President of the Bundesbank, Karl Otto Pöhl. Discussion at Hanover was largely procedural and, rather to my surprise, Margaret Thatcher allowed a committee composed of the central bank governors of the member states and chaired by Jacques Delors to be set up to look into EMU and to report back in a year's time. The Prime Minister appeared to believe that she could rely on the opposition within the committee of Pöhl and of Robin Leigh-Pemberton, the Governor of the Bank of England, to ensure that the committee did not come forward with a unanimous recommendation in favour of EMU, and that in any case the central bank governors were unlikely to vote for their own effective abolition. I expressed polite scepticism on both points, suggesting that the independence of central bank governors, even of the Bundesbank, would not suffice to put them in opposition to their governments when a matter of major political, rather than simply of economic and financial, importance was at issue; but this was brushed aside. The proceedings of the Delors Committee were followed in Whitehall by an inter-departmental committee chaired by the Treasury on which I sat. I argued throughout that, if we were to stand any chance of halting or at least of slowing down the EMU bandwagon, there would have to be a minority report from the Delors Committee setting out a coherent alternative approach to the fixed and binding timetable for passing through all three stages leading to EMU which it was by then becoming clear would be the main recommendation of the Delors Committee. But I got no support for this idea from the Bank of England representative on our committee; and the idea was never pressed on the Governor in the desultory contacts which went on between him, the Prime Minister, the Chancellor and the Foreign Secretary as Delors' report took shape. So we drifted towards the precipice without either a strategic or a tactical approach worthy of the name.

The report of Delors' Committee of central bank governors arrived on the Council's table in the late spring of 1989. It was predictably prescriptive and ambitious, aiming for the completion of EMU, the establishment of a European Central Bank (ECB), and the replacement of national currencies by a Single Currency (not yet known as the Euro) on a pre-arranged timetable. Although it was never intended that the report itself should be formally adopted or the sole basis for future action, it was clearly the precursor to a decision at one of the forthcoming European Councils to start negotiations in an Inter-Governmental Conference (IGC) on an EMU treaty, and that decision was one, as we had discovered to our cost in Milan in 1985, that could be taken by a simple majority of member states, being a procedural decision, even if agreement on any such treaty would require unanimity. So we were clearly going to be put on the spot, and, as the June 1989 European Council in Madrid approached, this prospect concentrated minds in London. Although the Chancellor and the Foreign Secretary had different views on EMU, they did both agree that it was now high time for Britain to join the ERM and they saw such a decision as likely to strengthen Britain's hand in the EMU negotiations, which were clearly about to start; in Nigel Lawson's case, although not in Geoffrey Howe's, the object being to derail the Delors Committee's report. So a process got under way in London, with John Kerr, the European Under-Secretary at the FCO, who had been Principal Private Secretary at the Treasury successively to Geoffrey Howe and Nigel Lawson, as the key coordinator, to try once again to persuade the Prime Minister to join the ERM. As in 1985, the circle of officials involved was extremely restricted and did not include the Permanent Representative and his mission in Brussels, although on this occasion I was aware of what was going on. The process culminated in a stormy meeting between Thatcher, Lawson and Howe on the very day that the Prime Minister and the Foreign Secretary were due to leave for the Madrid European Council. The Prime Minister dug in her heels; there were threats of resignations; and nothing was decided. When the Prime Minister arrived at the VIP suite at Heathrow she was looking like thunder, swept through without a word to anyone and shut herself away in a small, private room. The Foreign Secretary followed, looking shaken. On the plane to Madrid, the Prime Minister's section of the plane was curtained off and no attempt was made to hold the usual briefing session that preceded such meetings. Then, when we got to Madrid, the Prime Minister retired to her hotel suite and pulled out of the in-house dinner which the Ambassador had arranged for her. The next morning Charles Powell emerged from the suite with a piece of paper containing what the Prime Minister intended to say at the Council later that morning and asked me whether that would do. I said I would have to clear it with the Foreign Secretary and that was reluctantly conceded. The statement, which was entirely about the ERM, while relatively obscure did represent a real shift in the government's position, and, by setting out some fairly easy conditions to be fulfilled before we actually joined, pointed the way clearly towards the decision which was ultimately taken in September 1990, a little over a year later. After all this drama the Council session itself was rather uneventful, no one wishing at that stage to rush into the step of actually calling an IGC. Our own position aroused more interest because of the 'noises off' about the tensions within the government that were by now flooding the British press than because of what had actually been said. So far as the EMU process was concerned it was a case of too little and too late. But the ripples from Madrid continued to be felt in London at least. The following month the Prime Minister removed Geoffrey Howe from the FCO and gave him a quasi-sinecure as Deputy Prime Minister; and in the autumn Nigel Lawson resigned over what he regarded as the undue influence on exchange rate policy of the Prime Minister's adviser, Alan Walters, who was strongly opposed to both EMU and to Britain joining the ERM. European Council meetings were in general not life-enhancing occasions; and the Madrid Council certainly lived up to that epithet.

There were many more upheavals in 1989 than those associated with Britain's need to grapple with the issues posed by the ERM and EMU. Of most immediate impact on my daily life and work were the two changes in rapid succession at the head of the FCO. The removal of Geoffrey Howe, who had been Foreign Secretary for six years, was more of a shock than a surprise. His disenchantment with the Prime Minister's handling of a whole range of foreign policy issues, not just those relating to Europe, had been increasingly evident, as had their difficulty in working together in any sort of harmony. And, while his loyalty to her policy decisions remained intact, the same could not be said of her treatment of him. I deeply regretted his departure and the loss of someone with a remarkable grasp of the issues I had to deal with and a superb network of working relationships with his fellow foreign ministers. I continued to see him occasionally and to brief him in his role as Deputy Prime Minister; but in truth he was completely cut out of policymaking on European issues; and his mounting unhappiness with the direction of policy made his final departure from the government in the autumn of 1990 an accident waiting to happen. At the time of his dismissal from the FCO I wrote a personal note to Charles Powell at No 10 warning him of the risks I believed the Prime Minister was taking in treating Geoffrey Howe with such open contempt. There was no sign that this had any effect. The new Foreign Secretary, John Major, was ushered in on a tidal wave of press spin emanating from No 10 that he had been sent to the FCO to correct the department's endemic Europhilia. On the first Friday after his appointment I was plucked out of my regular weekly Cabinet Office coordination meeting to go and see him. We hardly knew each other, having only met a couple of times when he attended cabinet committee meetings on European budgetary matters in his capacity as Chief Secretary to the Treasury. We talked for nearly an hour, at the end of which it was clear that, while he might not know much about European policy in detail, he was going to be a quick learner and was likely to take a pragmatically sympathetic view. He made no secret of the fact that he regarded managing the relationship with No 10 on these issues as his biggest challenge and a daunting one. I concluded that (not for the last time) the Prime Minister had demonstrated a lack of feel for the personalities and basic political orientation of those around her. In the event John Major did not stay long enough at the FCO to put matters to the test since within three months he was whisked away to succeed Nigel Lawson as Chancellor of the Exchequer.

Douglas Hurd, who replaced Major, I knew well. We had first met when he left the Diplomatic Service to become Edward Heath's Political Secretary in opposition and they had come to Brussels to consult with Christopher Soames. Then our paths crossed again when he played a key role in the EU referendum campaign in 1975; and when he was Minister of State at the FCO in the early 1980s; and as Home Secretary he had been considerably involved in our EU Presidency in 1986. From the first day there was never any doubt of his mastery of the whole range of FCO business, nor of his capacity to give firm and well-focussed leadership. His cool detachment differed from Geoffrey Howe's passionate engagement, but it was more a difference of technique than of basic objectives. And he enjoyed a mutually respectful relationship with the Prime Minister which somehow managed to survive the troubled period which lay ahead.

*　　*　　*

By far the most significant of the 1989 upheavals had, however, nothing whatsoever to do with either ministerial shifts in London nor with the long approach march to the ERM and EMU; it was the fall of the Berlin Wall in October followed by the collapse of the East German state and the gradual dissolution of the Soviet empire in Central and Eastern Europe, including the disappearance of the Warsaw Pact and of Comecon. Even if the Community was not itself at the centre of the diplomatic manoeuvring and negotiations that flowed from this effective ending of the frozen certainties of the Cold War which had dominated the international landscape for so long, these momentous events had important implications for the European Community ranging from questions over how the former East German state was to be incorporated into it, through the knock-on effects of the German sovereign decision to exchange deutschmarks at 1:1 parity for the now worthless East German currency, to the prospect that the countries of Central and Eastern Europe would now apply to join the Community as the Prime Minister had looked forward to in her Bruges speech the year before. The first reactions in London were confused and confusing; and they were certainly not positive so far as Germany was concerned. There were clearly tensions between No 10 and the FCO, the former's views being dominated by foreboding about the consequences of the likely increase in the diplomatic weight and power of the enlarged German state and how best to constrain and circumscribe it. I was, frankly, appalled by this reaction, which not only flatly contradicted the policy objective of working for a reunified Germany firmly embedded in the Western Alliance, to which every British government in the post-war era had subscribed, but also seemed certain to put us on a collision course with the largest member state in the Community and quite possibly, to distance us from the other countries with special responsibilities

1   *With Max, a much-loved mongrel, in the author's garden in Kabul.*

2   *Author crossing a tributary of the Oxus River at the foot of the Wakhan corridor where Russia, China and Pakistan meet, during his time in Afghanistan in the early 1960s. The local chief of police was not pleased to be photographed in such an undignified pose; but he did not want to get his feet wet.*

3   *Author manoeuvring his Land Rover onto one of Afghanistan's more problematic ferries across the Kabul River, near Jalalabad.*

4   *Christopher Soames' larger than life personality is conveyed forcefully in his appearance before the European Parliament in Strasbourg in 1974, while his chef de cabinet (the author) is keeping a very straight face.*

5   *An historic moment as China and the European Community agree in
1975 to establish diplomatic relations and to negotiate a trade agreement.
No wonder both Christopher Soames and the Chinese Foreign Minister
(on his left with his hands clasped) look pleased.*

6   Margaret Thatcher, Geoffrey Howe (with Christopher Meyer, who was at that time head of the News Department at the FCO) and the author at a European Council meeting in the late 1980s. These were not life-enhancing occasions; and the press conferences given after them by the Prime Minister often produced fireworks. But sometimes tensions were not visible, as here.

7 *A vintage image of Margaret Thatcher, complete with handbag, and of Bernard Ingham impersonating a bulldog. The author's friends assumed he was praying that neither of them would do too much damage.*

8 *Margaret Thatcher signs the UN Convention on the Rights of the Child in 1990 with a bright-eyed Robin Raven under the beady eye of his father Martin (bearded). The Prime Minister gave the Mont Blanc pen, which the UN had provided for the signature, to Robin, who has it still. Within less than two months of this occasion she was to resign.*

9 *The Security Council resolute in December 1990. The US Ambassador's scowl denotes this was a resolution condemning Israel. 'It is wise not to look as if you are enjoying it' was Tom Pickering's explanation.*

10 *Douglas Hurd was always completely at home at the UN where he had served as a junior diplomat in the 1950s. He did not even find General Assembly debates like this one in 1991 particularly boring. The patient young man on the left is his Private Secretary John Sawers, later head of MI6.*

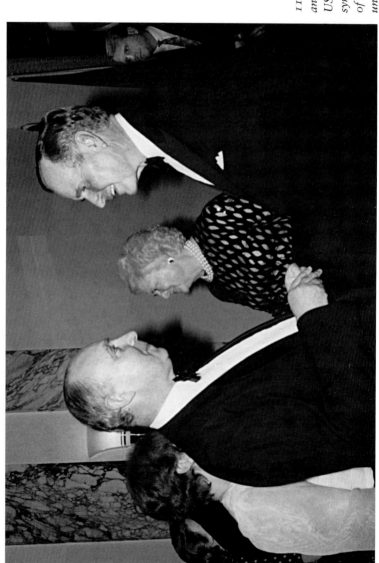

11 The author with Barbara and George H W Bush, the US President with the greatest sympathy for and knowledge of the UN. The US wore its unipolar mantle with grace.

12 All passions spent. The author and Margaret Thatcher in friendly and animated conversation, both ignoring her veto of his appointment as head of the Diplomatic Service earlier in 1990, attending a conference in Palm Springs a year after her resignation.

13 The author chairing the UN Security Council, January 1992, speaking to Secretary-General Boutros Boutros-Ghali, a subtle and incisive intellect.

14 John Major mastered the intricacies
of Security Council procedures just
before the January 1992 Security Council
Summit, over which he presided. Despite
his reasonably well-concealed nervousness,
no hitches occurred during the session.

15 The never before photographed Security Council informal consultation room, with Madeleine Albright in the chair; that was where the real negotiations took place and the formulaic diplomatic niceties of the official sessions were left at the door.

16   Discussions of the Cyprus Problem with President Glafcos Clerides tended to be tough
and detailed. But on his yacht he was all anecdotes and warm hospitality.

17 George Papandreou, a Foreign Minister with a genuine grasp of diplomacy, was the architect of Greco-Turkish rapprochement in 1999. He really wanted to find a solution to the Cyprus Problem and was unfailingly imaginative in his attempts.

18 *Author receiving insignia of Companion of Honour
in 2003 from the Her Majesty the Queen, finding out
how much she knows about his profession.*

19 *The UN Secretary-General meets the High Level Panel on Threats, Challenges and Change in Baden, near Vienna, in July 2004. It was very hot, but you would not guess it, and the apparent bonhomie masked the difficulties of grappling with the great white whale of international diplomacy, Security Council enlargement.*

for Germany, in particular France and the United States. But this was something outside my influence. What I could do was to throw some light on the process by which East Germany was likely to be brought into the Community. On that issue much wishful thinking was going on in London where it was initially assumed that East Germany would be brought into the Community like any other third country applying for accession, following a negotiation which would require the unanimous decision of the existing member states, thus providing us with a substantial degree of leverage. Probing in Brussels and Bonn showed just how wide of the mark this assumption was and, as the constitutional shape of the future Germany began to emerge from the mists, with the component regions of East Germany simply opting by democratic process to join the existing Federal Republic and to accept its constitution, it became clear that there would be no inter-governmental negotiations over accession at all. The Commission would have an important role to play in policing the Community's competition policy and in applying the technicalities of the Community's customs union and internal market legislation in what had formerly been East Germany; but that was all. It cannot be said that this clarification was particularly welcome to London but it was recognised that it was not contestable. This did not, however, resolve the wider issues about the future of Germany and on these the Prime Minister took an increasingly alarmist and strident line. When she met President Mitterrand in the margins of the Strasbourg European Council in December 1989 she devoted the whole of their tête-à-tête meeting not to the decision which was about to be taken on summoning an Inter-Governmental Conference to negotiate a treaty on EMU (which she had in any case decided not to contest, thus avoiding the problems which had followed the Milan Council in June 1985), but to the question of Germany. She returned from that meeting to the British delegation office in high spirits, reporting that Mitterrand shared all her doubts and fears and was far from reconciled to the prospect of a larger, more powerful Germany. The Foreign Secretary and I warned her there and then not to place any confidence in such expressions of opinion as presaging any practical hardening of the French position or any willingness to ally with us on courses of action which would bring them into a confrontation with Germany. Experience showed that the Franco-German alliance would continue to dominate French policymaking and that they would work out whatever concerns they might have over reunification bilaterally with the Germans, not by ganging up on them internationally. This advice (which was broadly born out by subsequent developments, with the EMU project, deeply desired by the French but feared by many Germans – although not by Chancellor Kohl – forming the basis for a Franco-German deal) was simply swatted aside. Thereafter the German question moved away from the Brussels arena; but it continued to damage the overall effectiveness of our diplomacy and our relationship with key allies; and it certainly also contributed to the rising unease among many of the Prime Minister's cabinet colleagues that she had become, in the words of one of them, 'reckless'.

With the decision now taken that an Inter-Governmental Conference on EMU should be set to work during 1990 (it actually met, in parallel with a similar conference on what was rather misleadingly called European Political Union [EPU] in July of that year and I attended its first, purely procedural meeting just before I left my post in Brussels and departed to the United Nations in New York), it was no longer possible to delay implementing in London a proper, systematic, inter-departmental analysis designed to underpin the work of the IGC when it began to meet and to draw up the outlines of the British positions on the many complex, technical issues that were sure to arise. A group, similar to the one earlier established to follow the work of the Delors Committee, under the chairmanship of Nigel Wicks from the Treasury, began this work early in the New Year. I had been cudgelling my brains for some months to try to discern some way through what looked all set to be a damaging and fruitless confrontation between Britain and its other European partners. At an early meeting of the group, and having achieved the sort of clarity in my thinking which seemed to come to me best when I was on the first Friday flight to London at about six in the morning, I posed a number of questions. Did anyone in the group think that, if Britain said 'no' to EMU or tried to confine any treaty simply to the first, rather anodyne stage of the process, this would be accepted by the others; or would they more likely press ahead on their own outside the formal Community treaty framework thus getting round our veto and leaving us cut off from a major area of European policymaking? All agreed that a flat 'no' would not be accepted and that progress outside the Community framework was the most likely outcome. I then asked if anyone in the group thought that this or any other probable British government could simply sign up to the full, three-stage prescription for EMU set out in the Delors Committee report, with dates fixed well in advance for the creation of a European Central Bank and the introduction of a single currency replacing existing national currencies; and could hope to get such a treaty ratified by Parliament. Again no one believed this was possible. So I then sketched out what at the time I called a 'fire-break' strategy, designed to square the circle (it later became known as 'Britain's opt-out', or more precisely its 'opt-in'). Under this, Britain would not be committed in advance to a fixed timetable but would make its decision, one way or the other, much nearer the time of entry into force of the key central bank and single currency provisions and only if and when the Parliament which would be sitting when these events took place had given its approval. Among other advantages this seemed to me the only way of proceeding that was consistent with British constitutional practice. Somewhat to my surprise there was rapid agreement to this approach and this was then built into the first report the group made to ministers.

Thereafter the Chancellor of the Exchequer (John Major) and the Foreign Secretary (Douglas Hurd) put it to the Prime Minister as their joint, preferred strategy. She would have none of it. The Foreign Secretary and I made one further attempt on a Ministerial flight to Dublin for a European Council there in April 1990 to persuade her of its advantages but to no avail. She was firmly set on the 'no, no, no' approach, which was to prove the proximate, although not the only, cause of her downfall following the Rome European Council in October 1990. Some months later, in July, when Jacques Delors and his wife gave us a farewell lunch, à quatre, at one of Brussels' better fish restaurants, I decided to brief him on the 'fire-break' strategy. Making it very clear that what I was outlining was in no sense the position of the British government, I took him through the arguments, emphasising that the probable preferred approach of the other member states had no realistic chance of being accepted by Britain or ratified by Parliament whoever was Prime Minister. He was immediately taken with the strategy, which he could see offered some chance of resolving a paradox that had been troubling him too. I left him with the advice that in no circumstances should he surface the idea prematurely or it would be torn to pieces in the rough and tumble of the IGC and that he should be quite sure that the British government could go along with it before he put it forward. I admitted all this to John Kerr, who was to succeed me in Brussels, but to no one else. Meanwhile, in parallel with the preparations going on within government for the EMU IGC, another idea had been put forward from outside that machine. Michael Butler, my predecessor as Permanent Representative in Brussels, who had since been working in the City put forward a plan for what was called a 'hard ECU'. Unlike the existing Community ECU which was simply a unit for accounting purposes in Brussels, the hard ECU would be established as a common currency circulating alongside the existing national currencies of the member states for an indeterminate period. This idea picked up support from the Bank of England and the Treasury and, finally, with much reluctance and after considerable delay, from the Prime Minister. But, when eventually it was launched with the other member states, Margaret Thatcher managed to kill it stone dead by making it clear that she was only prepared to support it if it was a full alternative to the creation of a single currency. For the hard ECU idea to have had any appeal to the other member states, I had warned in advance of its launch there had to be ambiguity about whether or not it was an alternative to a single currency or, as they were bound to insist, a transitional step towards one. With that ambiguity stripped away the idea was unfortunately too little too late once again, and was not given any serious consideration by the other member states.

✳   ✳   ✳

By the end of 1989 I had been more than four years in Brussels as Permanent Representative, and both the Foreign Office and I clearly thought it was time to be contemplating a further move. I was asked, earlier in that year (while Geoffrey Howe was still Foreign Secretary) whether I would like to be considered as a candidate for the post of Permanent Under-Secretary and head of the Diplomatic Service which was due to become vacant on the retirement of the incumbent, Patrick Wright, in the late summer of 1990. I said I would. I certainly felt it was time to break out of the almost exclusive concentration of my career on European matters and to avoid becoming just a well-worn flywheel in the complex machinery of Brussels. Moreover, with an IGC (two as it turned out) looming on the horizon, I did not want to be locked into an open-ended commitment of that sort. Of course there were plenty of aspects of leaving Brussels which I regretted, none more than the fact that the Community was at last showing signs of turning more purposefully towards the outside world which it had largely neglected during most of the 1980s. The single market negotiations with the EFTA countries to be soon followed by the negotiations for the accession of Austria, Finland and Sweden (with Norway too until yet another negative referendum result put an end to that prospect); the signs of life in the Uruguay Round of multilateral trade negotiations in which the Community inevitably played a leading role; and the daunting task of coordinating the Western economic response to the upheavals in Central and Eastern Europe and the Soviet Union so as to assist their transition to market economies and working democracies; these were all policy challenges in which I would have liked to participate.

For many months I heard no more of my candidature – the two changes of Foreign Secretary no doubt complicating matters – but it was clearly being taken seriously because I was not sounded out about any other job. Then early in 1990 it was announced that David Gilmore, the Deputy Under-Secretary at the FCO in charge of security policy and intelligence and a highly credible contestant for the top job, was to go to the United Nations in New York. That looked like a positive signal, but in fact it was a false dawn. Early in April I was told that I would be going to New York and that David Gilmore's appointment had been cancelled as he was to become head of the Diplomatic Service. It was not too difficult to read the runes. Margaret Thatcher had clearly intervened to block my appointment. Many years later one of her ministers told me that she had said, 'I did not want to be met by a burst of machine-gun fire from the FCO every time I came out of No 10'. I was naturally upset at this turn of events, as much by the implied criticism of my loyalty to a divided government which I had done my best to serve through some tricky moments; the job itself might anyway not have suited me, or rather I it, since I have always been more interested in policy than in administration and in recent years the Permanent Under-Secretary's job has tended to be more about the latter than the former. I took some wry satisfaction in the fact that David Gilmore's attitude to the Community was, if anything, even more enthusiastic than mine, although he had not been so involved in the detail; and that John Kerr who was to succeed me in Brussels, had been at the heart of the pre-Madrid manoeuvrings over the ERM and EMU while I had not. The Prime Minister's somewhat patchy assessment of character had let her down again. When I went to see Delors to give him advance warning of the announcement of my new appointment and thus of my impending departure, he looked unhappy and merely said, 'Oh, quelle gaffe', which was certainly the nicest compliment I ever had paid to me. In truth my dealings with him and with his formidable alter ego of a chef de cabinet, Pascal Lamy, while not invariably easy, had more often than not been fruitful. I did not share his highly integrationist view of the future of Europe nor his rather traditionally French scepticism about the United States, but he was always frank and straightforward in our discussions. Despite all the problems the British government gave him over the years, he never succumbed to the view that Europe would have been better off without us; for him we remained one of the key member states whose views must be taken seriously however much he disagreed with them and however aggressively they were being promoted at the highest level.

In those days it was still the custom for outgoing ambassadors to send the Foreign Secretary a valedictory despatch. Even though the system has sometimes been abused to provide a platform for eccentricity or even criticism and defiance of government policy, its passing is regrettable, a triumph of ministerial pique over the desirability for ambassadors occasionally to stand back from the day-to-day examination of the trees and to look instead at the wood in a wider perspective. As someone moving on to a new post I was not in any case much tempted by the wilder shores of obstreperous commentary. However, I did feel that, as this was likely to be the last occasion in my career when I would be addressing ministers on European affairs, in which I had personally been involved for almost all of the previous 25 years, I should try to distil my thinking on the main issues in more of a conceptual than an operational manner. During a long and fascinating holiday in southern Africa that summer I thought hard about what I was going to say and tried to achieve a bit of distance from the routine business of life in Brussels. The result of these reflections is set out in full at the end of this chapter. Looking back after a further 20 years on what I wrote then there is not much I regret except perhaps my dismissive comment about the possibility of Turkey joining the Community. I did pull one or two punches. In particular I said nothing about the 'fire-break' option for EMU mentioned earlier in this chapter since I had no desire to trigger prematurely yet another stand-off between the Prime Minister and her senior ministers. I never did get any real idea of how this despatch was received in London or indeed whether it had any influence on policymaking there. It did get a wide circulation; but by that time the state of discord within the government over Europe was too deeply embedded to have made putting together a substantive response at all easy and probably not worth the effort. In any event I was by that time in the midst of the existential crisis at the UN caused by Saddam Hussein's invasion and annexation of Kuwait.

28 August 1990

My valedictory despatch from Brussels

I am leaving Brussels almost 25 years to the day after first being posted here to the small delegation we maintained during the period between our first and our second applications for membership of the European Community and almost five years after being appointed Permanent Representative. Of the 25 years since I first came into contact with the European Community, 21 have been spent dealing with its affairs; if the Berrill Report recommendation that Diplomatic Service officers should spend up to one-third of their careers in a specialisation such as the European Community is taken as the norm, then I have rather comprehensively over-fulfilled it.

In these last five years I have prepared and attended a dozen European Councils, over 100 meetings of the Council in its other manifestations, and 200 or so meetings of COREPER; and UKRep has sent rather over 20,000 telegrams to the Department. These figures alone show how hard it is for any of the main participants in Community business to maintain a view of the wood as well as of the trees which crowd around them week in, week out. They also illustrate graphically how easy it is to become obsessed by issues of negotiating technique and procedure to the exclusion of a wider view of policy; and they highlight one of the besetting weaknesses of the Community, that it often seems to outsiders to be an organisation designed by bureaucrats for bureaucrats.

So a sense of perspective is an important attribute for handling Community business. The widest perspective sets it in the framework of European, and indeed world, history in the twentieth century, with the collapse, disintegration and destruction of so much, and so many of the inhabitants, of our continent in the first half of the century, contrasting vividly with the prosperity and security achieved within a framework of cooperative effort and the rule of law which has characterised the second half. A somewhat narrower perspective contrasts 1965, the year I came to Brussels, with the present day. In 1965 the Community of Six seemed set to stay that way, the UK having been on the receiving end of De Gaulle's veto and appearing to have no stomach for another attempt. The Community was in any case dead in the water, crippled by a French boycott of its meetings; no Council met, not even COREPER. As an external force it was negligible except in Africa and in the Kennedy Round of trade negotiations. Now we have a Community of Twelve which has come successfully through three successive enlargements, with another (to include the GDR) imminent, and further accessions before the end of the century more likely than not; a single market is being created not just in the meeting rooms of Brussels but by the economic operators, and it is transforming the economies of Europe; the Community is regarded as an important, if hesitant and unsure, actor from one end of the world to the other. To sharpen the focus still more one can contrast the first half of the 1980s with the second, the former characterised by stagnation and internecine quarrelling over the need to right the inequity of our budgetary contribution, the latter a period of unprecedented development both internally and externally. These exercises in perspective are not tricks but they do conceal much. There have been plenty of failures, there are plenty of weaknesses and there are tensions, some of them set up by the very speed of developments in recent years. Recent success has owed as much to the substantial economic growth following the hard decisions taken by the national governments earlier in the last decade, as to any Brussels alchemy.

The main landmarks 1985–90

My early months as Permanent Representative were entirely absorbed in negotiation of the Single European Act. This strange animal, whose name epitomises the Community's capacity to reduce even the most significant development to almost meaningless mumbo-jumbo, was denounced at the time as a minimalist mouse and subsequently as a federalist trap. In truth it is neither. It was a compromise between those who sought much more wide-ranging constitutional reforms and those, like ourselves, who, while sharing the main objectives of achieving the Single Market and strengthening Political Cooperation, saw no need to change the basic treaties to do so. Its substantive content fell a good deal closer to our end of the spectrum than to the other. That judgement need not be taken on trust; an analysis of the decisions taken since then on matters falling under treaty provisions switched from unanimity to qualified majority voting by the Single European Act, shows the UK voted down only very seldom, much less frequently than a number of other member states. But the episode demonstrated that our own strong preference for proceeding pragmatically and step by step, without too much thought about, or too much definition of, the final objective, was in conflict with the views of all other member states which felt the need to reflect substantial developments in Community policy in new treaty provisions.

Close on the heels of the Single European Act came the accession of Spain and Portugal. This third enlargement went more smoothly than the previous two. Fears at the time of a prolonged bout of indigestion proved misplaced. Spain, in particular, made its mark with a notably successful first Presidency. Contrary to much conventional wisdom, this enlargement tended to reinforce the Community's centripetal rather than its centrifugal tendencies, majority voting being more widely practised where it was provided for in the original treaties but had long been in disuse, it being generally recognised, even before the Single European Act came into force, that conducting the business of a twelve-member Community on the basis of consensus was going to be impossibly difficult.

1987 was the year the Community ran out of money and when even creative accounting could no longer conceal it. Profligate spending on the Common Agricultural Policy despite earlier attempts at reform, linked with the ambitions of the poorer member states, the Commission and the European Parliament to boost Structural Fund and other spending, dragged the member states back into another major <u>budgetary negotiation</u> only three years after they had wearily concluded the previous round at Fontainebleau. Like all such negotiations, this one was long, arduous and bad-tempered. But the final outcome was a clear advance from our point of view. Not only were we able, with the bare minimum of fracas, to carry over our two-thirds rebate provision into the new budgetary arrangements. But, for the first time, serious progress was made on CAP reform. Overall limits on agricultural expenditure were buttressed by individual product stabilisers. Since then, and thanks admittedly in part to the effects of two years of drought in the USA, agricultural spending has been well below the limits set and most of the main products in surplus have been subjected to effective penalties. A price had to be paid in the form of the doubling of Structural Funds; but, given the effect of the Fontainebleau mechanism on our own contribution and the support that was gained from the poorer member states for the Single Market programme, that could be considered an acceptable trade-off.

When the Milan European Council in 1985 set the 1992 deadline for achieving a <u>Single Market</u> and gave a broad blessing to Lord Cockfield's White Paper laying out what would be necessary to bring it about, few would have ventured much money on its fulfilment. After all, the history of the Community was littered with the whitening skeletons of such promises; the procedures for taking the decisions were laborious in the extreme and, although they were about to be facilitated by the introduction of Qualified Majority Voting, they were also about to be complicated by giving the European Parliament a greater say in the process. Most member states had not suddenly been transformed into fervent partisans of a liberal, economic approach but rather were being dragged reluctantly towards such policies. So the legislative programme which has ground its way remorselessly through innumerable Council meetings since then and which is now well past the two-thirds mark was certainly not condemned to succeed, as most historians will now, no doubt, say it was. It owes much to our own support, assisted by a scanty band of like-minded member states, and the effective determination and hard work of the Commission. Most important, we have together been able to ensure that the legislation reaching the statute book is generally of an open and deregulatory kind and to resist the attempts of a number of member states to make it no more than a further layer of regulation piled on top of existing ones. Fortress Europe has been comprehensively seen off.

As the Single Market programme took shape, the pressure began steadily to build up for progress towards economic and monetary union and now that issue dominates the Community's current agenda. It presents us with many problems. As a non-participant in the Exchange Rate Mechanism, I feel we have tended to underestimate the forces propelling our partners towards a treaty commitment to the final stages of EMU. Having committed themselves to maintaining a stable relationship with the strongest currency in the Community, the deutschmark, most dramatically in the case of the French who tore up their previous interventionist and expansionary policies to achieve this, they see little political or economic merit in fighting to retain a national autonomy of decision-making on monetary policies which is widely regarded as a mere façade. This analysis has, quite fortuitously, been reinforced in their eyes by the imminence of German unification. Acquiescence in the DM zone, as opposed to what they hope will be a system in which decision-making will be genuinely shared, becomes that much less acceptable as general concerns about excessive German strength lurk close to the surface.

The previous landmarks have all concerned the internal development of the Community and, in truth, these internal issues have dominated the agenda for much of the last five years. They have, however, influenced the <u>Community's external relationships</u> quite notably. The Single Market programme in particular has exerted a powerful external influence, at first arousing considerable alarm lest it be fundamentally protectionist and, more recently, as those fears receded and as the successful completion of the programme became more likely, acting as a kind of magnet. Thus the Community's responsibility for, and stake in, a successful outcome of the Uruguay Round has become more evident. And the EFTA countries seek a relationship amounting to a kind of country membership of the Single Market and going well beyond the simple industrial free trade arrangements they concluded when we joined the Community. Meanwhile, the United States has clearly re-appraised its view of the Community's significance and potential usefulness and, since President Bush took office, has sharply upgraded it.

But the external development which has wrought a sea-change in the Community and in its external policies has of course been the collapse of communism in <u>Eastern Europe</u>, bringing in its train the unification of Germany and thus the inclusion of the GDR in the Community, the emergence of democracies and putative market economies in the Soviet Union's former satellites, and the Soviet Union's own remarkable shift from outright hostility towards the Community to a somewhat bemused anticipation of its emergence as an exemplar and a source of much-needed material support. With the Commission propelled overnight at the Paris Economic Summit of July 1989 into the role of coordinator of all free world assistance to Eastern Europe, the Community has risen well to the challenge; emergency food aid, longer-term assistance and, in the case of Romania, firm political action when it was needed, has been forthcoming. But a long and expensive road lies ahead; and choices no doubt less clearly black and white than those of the past year will have to be made.

A glance to the future

Prediction of future developments in and of the Community is always a chancy business, especially when it is, as now, in a period of rapid evolution and lies close to the centre of upheavals, to its east in particular, which are bound to have an important influence on it. Some major issues, German unification, two Inter-Governmental Conferences on political union and economic and monetary union are likely to come to a head in the latter months of this year or in the course of 1991; others, such as further enlargement, the completion and dynamic effects of the Single Market and the budgetary review of 1992 lie further off, but certainly not over the horizon.

The Community dimension of German unification will come first. It looks like being a rather messy affair as a result of the date of unification being advanced from December to October. A more orderly and systematic process with a December timetable would have been preferable. But the outcome is not in doubt nor is the detailed content likely to be much altered; nor should it be unduly costly, though some net costs there will be. Neither the derogations needed from the immediate application of Community law in the GDR nor the costs are likely to be as substantial as would have been the case if the GDR had formally acceded to the Community, the former because so much of FRG law will simply apply in the GDR without more ado, the latter because the FRG seems itself to have set its face against expensive solutions.

None of this addresses the concerns that have arisen since the Berlin Wall came down about the economic, political and military strength of a united Germany and the purposes to which that strength might in the future be deployed. These concerns are felt throughout the Community and beyond, even if their articulation and the response to them differs widely. All suffered to some degree from the events of the first half of the century. Most see the problems of that period as lying not so much in the economic strength of Germany but in the combination of that strength with a footloose and erratic foreign policy and a willingness to apply Clausewitz's dictum about war being an extension of diplomacy by other means in a singularly irresponsible and destructive way. In this view the right response is to sustain and to strengthen the multilateral disciplines, constraints and capacity for collective action of the Community and NATO, with the former playing the central and most durable role, given its readier acceptability to all shades of political opinion in Germany itself. German economic strength cannot in any case be gainsaid, based as it is now on a pluralist democracy and a free market economy. I find this analysis convincing. The thesis that a unified Germany will come to dominate the Community and thus be able to bend it to its will, I find much less so. After all Germany has been the dominant economic force in the Community for a long time now; it bears by far the heaviest budgetary burden; and yet it still punches below its weight in the conduct of Community business. Nor does the Community, its processes and its institutions, lend itself to domination by one member state, as the French found to their cost in the 1960s. So I would argue firmly that we should treat the Community as part of the solution to this problem, not as an extension of the problem itself.

The Inter-Governmental Conference on Political Union is not something we would ever have gone out of our way to look for, but now that we are landed with it, I believe we can put it to purposes consistent with our own approach and can contain the pressures for the sort of changes we wish to resist. The perception that this negotiation is designed to produce a kind of Single European Act Mark II and not a futuristic charter for a federal Europe is now general, whatever the rhetoric of the maximalists to the contrary. Some extension of majority voting – on environmental issues, for example – may make sense; but we will need to resist it on social matters, where the pressure will be strong, and on fiscal matters, where it will be less so. The European Parliament and its chief protagonists among the member states will keep up a noisy clamour throughout the negotiation for more powers. Our own ideas for strengthening its control over the executive – that is, the Commission – may help to channel this pressure in a helpful direction. The awakening awareness of national Parliaments to the fact that the European Parliament is as much a rival as a partner may also prove useful. But we shall face some difficult choices at the end. The least predictable area is that covered by the Franco-German call for a common foreign and security policy. So far the two authors have failed to put flesh on the bare bones of their April initiative; it is hard to believe that either is really willing to accept the full implications of their rather opportunistic move. But other, smaller member states will have few qualms. It is all the more important therefore that we should ourselves come forward with a set of sensible and evolutionary changes to strengthen Political Cooperation; this would be the right move tactically, even if it were not also, in my view, the right approach in strategic terms given the trend of recent events, the shifting of international forces and the reinforcement of Germany's weight.

The outcome of the Inter-Governmental Conference on Economic and Monetary Union is a good deal less easy to foretell. The gap between the approach broadly favoured by the other eleven member states and the Commission and our own preferred approach has narrowed but it has not disappeared. It has narrowed because the original ideas in the Delors Report for elaborate, centralised decision-making on budgetary and fiscal policies have faded; and because our own recent proposals for a 'hard' ECU and a European Monetary Fund in the next stage are seen as a clear step forward. But it has not disappeared because the other member states appear determined to write into the treaty a commitment to a single currency and a central banking system to manage a single monetary policy, while we are equally determined to avoid any automaticity as to a move beyond the next stage and to ensure that any such shift, if it does eventually come about, results from an evolutionary process and is not pre-determined in advance. Can this gap be bridged? It is too soon to say. There are major advantages to all if it can be; and serious risks if it is not. Our partners are less keen to go it alone than they sometimes let the press suppose but they are determined to press ahead. We on our side need to weigh carefully the downside consequences – for the City and for inward investment to mention only the most direct ones – if it does go that way.

The further enlargement of the Community is not an issue for decision in 1991 but it is an issue for the 1990s. It is hard now, with four declared applicants and others speaking freely of their future applications, to see the Community reaching the turn of the century as a Community of Twelve. Our present policy of stating a general welcome to accessions by democratic European states which can assume the full obligations of membership while keeping clear of specific commitments on the timing and detail seems likely to serve well for some time to come. In particular it offers the East European countries the maximum incentive to stick to the stony path leading to stable democracy and a flourishing market economy. We are wise to be cautious about the specifics. There are plenty of snags. Enlargement could be expensive if it involved the East Europeans, all likely to be substantial beneficiaries from the CAP and the Structural Funds and modest contributors to the budget. We can certainly not afford to assume that enlargement will lead to looser, more flexible institutional links. Putting off the evil day when the Community has to explain to Turkey that there is no room at the inn must surely be a plus. All these tricky problems will be easier to handle tactically if we ourselves have not shown too much zeal in the cause of enlargement in the meantime; accession terms tend to be shaped more by those who hold back than by those who dash forward.

The Single Market will remain a constant and crucial theme through the 1990s. The process neither begins nor does it end on 1 January 1993. We still have a substantial amount of unfinished business, on financial services and transport in particular, on which we have to keep up the pressure. But things are moving the right way and the Commission are solid allies. In two difficult areas for us, taxation and frontier controls, we are not out of the wood yet, although our tactical position has considerably improved over the last year. A system which will permit the abolition of fiscal frontiers without the bureaucracy of Lord Cockfield's clearing-house approach and without elaborate measures of tax harmonisation should be agreed by the end of the year. But there will remain strong pressure from other member states to complement that system at the very least with a minimum VAT standard rate as a safety-net provision to avoid the risk of competitive ratcheting-down and we will have to decide whether we can live with that. The frontiers question remains a delicate one but there is now a better understanding that the different geographical characteristics of member states justify quite different solutions; and the rising political pressures generated by the domestic sensitivity of Third Country immigration in virtually every member state are beginning to cause them to take a more cautious view of the sweet simplicities of the Commission's 'Europe without frontiers' approach. If we play our cards well, it should be possible to achieve a substantial reduction in the present controls on business and individuals without sacrificing the essential checks needed to maintain our defences against drugs, terrorism and illegal immigration.

As the legislative thrust of the Single Market programme tapers off, so will the twin issues of implementation and enforcement come to the fore. The former is already moving sharply up the agenda as a result of the initiatives we have taken. Peer pressure is beginning to have some effect; the threat of Court action, particularly if new treaty provisions can be devised to give the Court more bite, should do the rest. Enforcement will be a slower, messier business but one in whose success we have just as great a vested interest. We will be sure to face some dilemmas in that, as with fraud, it is the Commission that will have to set the pace. In some instances that is bound to mean giving them powers and authority which will be criticised as intrusive. But the Commission is the only heavy roller available and, if we want a level wicket, then we will have to be ready to make use of them.

Some lessons learned

The European Community is no simple, tidy organisation, conforming to a recognisable pattern of multilateral international activity and proceeding towards clearly defined objectives. Nor is it any embryo of a sovereign state. It remains today and for the foreseeable future a construction sui generis, operating somewhere between these two extremes. Moreover, it is shot through with paradoxes and criss-crossed with historical fault lines which do much to explain the tensions which invariably surface when major decisions are imminent, as they are now.

A fault line which runs as deep as any is the different historical experience of its member states in the first half of this century. Broadly speaking one can classify them into two categories; the first consists of countries whose national institutions – government, Parliament, civil service and judiciary – foundered comprehensively in the maelstrom of that period; the second consists of countries whose national institutions survived that experience and indeed helped to carry them through intact. It is striking how often the instinctive reaction of each country to a further development of the Community runs along that fault line. In the first category the tendency, when a new problem arises or an old one gets out of control, is to look for a Community solution; the proposition that a national solution makes more sense gets short shrift, given the fundamental lack of confidence in national institutions. Countries like Italy and Belgium fall quite obviously into this category; but so, to some extent, do countries as inherently nationalistic as France, whose flirtation with a Gaullist approach to Europe is now receding into the past. In the second category the tendency is the opposite, to turn towards a national solution unless it can be shown very clearly that a wider approach will make more sense. The UK falls quite obviously into that category, as do the Netherlands and Denmark. The second category is much less numerous than the first. It is not difficult to categorise aspirants to membership, Austria and the East Europeans in the first, the other EFTAns in the second.

There are plenty of other paradoxes around. Some are almost semantic but they are none the less real. For a German federalism means decentralisation, the avoidance of a unitary state; for us it means almost the opposite. To most member states the word union is a gloriously loose and imprecise concept that can mean all things to all men; to us it contains very precise connotations, the Acts of Union with Scotland and Ireland being characterised by the abolition of the Parliaments of those two countries. Some paradoxes exist within our own policy. We recognise the crucial role of the Commission in bringing about the Single Market, in working to reform the CAP, in negotiating liberal solutions in the Uruguay Round; as a member state in a smallish minority on all these issues, we know we could get nowhere without them. But at the same time we resent and oppose the Commission's pretensions to greater power and are reluctant to give them a greater degree of democratic legitimacy.

It is quite clear that the Community cannot simply resolve these paradoxes or erase these fault lines. They are too deep-seated for that. But nor can it simply camp on them. So it has to try to soften them, to build bridges across the fault lines. In recent years it has been reasonably successful at that. The exercise requires a lot of pragmatism and a commitment to an evolutionary approach, two concepts which we hold dear but which I have sometimes felt we preach more actively than we practise.

The increase in majority voting following the 1986 enlargement and the Single European Act underlined, but did not create, the need to seek allies in Community negotiations. Although in some cases it is bearable, and indeed in the case of our budget contribution it was necessary, to be in a minority of one, this is something to be avoided if at all possible because it is not easy politically to sustain it and, if you cannot sustain it, you may end up failing to influence the outcome as well. Making allies in the Community is not simply a matter of seeking trade-offs; indeed that sort of crude horse-trading is not all that common and is certainly not desirable. It consists much more of identifying our important interests on any issue and then making common cause with other member states with similar interests or whose interests can be met with solutions similar to those we are seeking. We are rather better at identification than we are at making common cause. What is essential, however, is to pursue an active, alliance-building approach, and that requires the cultivation of a complex network of contacts between capitals.

There are, however, no permanent allies for us in the Community or permanent adversaries. We may make common cause with, for example, the Dutch over a wide range of issues – CAP reform, trade policy, budgetary questions – and very valuable that has been, but we will also differ on some such as EMU or the UK rebate. The only exception that appears to prove this rule is the Franco-German partnership, the handling of which presents us now with almost as many unsolved questions as when we first joined the Community. We can have no illusions that it is about to disintegrate, less still that we could bring that about, even if it was desirable to do so. We can also have no illusion but that it has from time to time a formidable, almost irresistible, influence on Community debates, limited, fortunately for us, by the difficulties the two have in agreeing on the details and substance of individual issues. In the future, with a more powerful Germany this influence can only be greater. So I draw the conclusion that we must redouble our efforts to strengthen our links with both of them at every level and on every aspect of Community business. Even that will probably not spare us a few nasty surprises. But it will keep them to the minimum. And there is no doubt that the quality of our relations with France and Germany crucially conditions the attitude towards us of the other member states and their willingness to cooperate with us.

Meetings of the European Council are not life-enhancing occasions, let alone pleasurable ones. They are poorly prepared, often chaotic and they are all set to become once again too frequent. But they are now an essential part of the governance of the Community. Past are the days when a bout of bad-tempered wrangling in the European Council could simply lead to the abandonment of any conclusions at all and the Community could more or less proceed as if nothing serious had happened. We need therefore to update constantly our techniques for handling these meetings and develop on each occasion a systematic tactical approach designed to maximise our influence at them.

It would be remiss, although perhaps prudent, to avoid a direct comment on Britain's role in Europe, contentious as that has been both within parties and between parties ever since I first began to deal with these matters. In my view we have in fact travelled a long way in the last decade towards a mature and successful role in the conduct of Community business. Of course you cannot have everything your own way in such a venture; but we are getting steadily better at furthering and securing our interest and at doing so in a way which is consistent with the overall Community interest. There remains, however, some way to go. Our caution, scepticism and rigorous analysis of Commission proposals are widely appreciated by those in the know, but more widely they are less so. We do need to be more selective about taking up the cudgels on particular issues and to ensure when we do so that our criticisms are directed principally at the policies we oppose and not in a blanket way at the institution, Commission or Parliament, or at the member state, which proposes them.

I have been struck and a little saddened by the number of people who have said to me in recent months 'you must have had a terribly difficult time defending our corner these last few years'. I do not in fact feel I have had a terribly difficult time of it. But it cannot be healthy that there should be so fundamentally negative and defensive a perception of what the British Permanent Representative is up to in Brussels. I am not among those who believe we should be trying to vie with the Italians or others in our Community rhetoric; if we did so, we would merely make fools of ourselves and convince nobody. The reality, it sometimes seems to me, is that, just as there is a large gap between the rhetoric and performance of a number of our partners to their considerable discredit, so there is in our own case a gap in the opposite sense, not to our discredit but to our disadvantage.

Envoi

UKRep is no ordinary Diplomatic Service post. With well over half its staff drawn from seven other departments, it is a mini-Whitehall. But it somehow manages to avoid, or at least to minimise, the departmental in-fighting which is such a feature of Whitehall life. For the unremitting hard work, for the loyalty, and for the negotiating skills of those who worked with me I have nothing but gratitude and admiration. Taken together with the superlative coordination machinery in Whitehall, these are major assets which we should do our best to nurture and to sustain. They are the envy of our Community partners.

The job of Permanent Representative to the European Community may be one of the more demanding in the

Diplomatic Service but it is also one of the more rewarding. I am grateful indeed for the confidence you and your cabinet colleagues showed. I am sure you will do no less for my successor, John Kerr, whose skill at the London end of the formulation of Community policy has been so notable over recent years.

Finally a word of dedication to my wife and to all those other UKRep wives who sat so often waiting for their husbands to return from this Council, that COREPER or the other Working Group and did so for many weary hours.

11

NEW YORK (UNITED NATIONS)
1990–1995

NEW WORLD: ORDER OR DISORDER?

The prospect of moving to New York and the UN had not made much impact on me in those last, hectic months in Brussels as preparations began for two Inter-Governmental Conferences on treaty change and as Britain's relationship within the Community moved into ever more troubled waters. The logistics were relatively simple. We would move directly from Brussels to New York early in September in good time for the annual gathering of Foreign Ministers later that month at the opening of the General Assembly. I would take a much-needed break during August as would my predecessor in New York, Crispin Tickell, leaving our two missions in the competent hands of our deputies. So much for the best laid plans. Of the UN and its workings I knew relatively little, having observed it from afar but never worked there or been much involved in the policy areas with which it dealt. Its long marginalisation during the Cold War had made more of an impression than had the relatively recent signs of life, in particular the successful UN peacekeeping mission in Namibia. As to the interface between the Community and the UN, the two organisations might as well at that stage have been living on different planets for all they knew, cared about or cooperated with each other. The atmosphere of ignorance and suspicion was mutual, each fearing the other might trespass on the other's turf and both being unwilling to adapt their often complex working procedures and methods, the result of many a messy compromise between their member states, to enable cooperation to take place.

If I had failed to appreciate the speed at which profound international developments were taking place outside the Brussels goldfish bowl that ignorant complacency did not survive the first few days of our holiday in South Africa. Within hours of Saddam Hussein's invasion of Kuwait at the beginning of August I was run to earth at a small game reserve close to the border with Lesotho by the FCO Under-Secretary responsible for the UN. Ministers had decided that either Tickell or I needed to be in New York to handle the consequences of the Iraqi aggression. Which was it to be? I did not volunteer; and common sense soon prevailed at the expense of Tickell's holiday plans rather than mine. We had not chosen South Africa as our holiday destination with any political purpose in mind, rather to achieve a complete break from Brussels and Europe and because my brother-in-law and his wife who lived there had finally persuaded us that we could not continue to neglect their pressing invitation to see a fascinating country at a remarkably interesting moment in its history. It certainly did not disappoint. Not only was much of it stunningly beautiful and a good deal of it (the Bantustans and the townships) quite horrifying examples of the consequences of misguided and immoral policy decisions by the apartheid regime; but the political transition which had begun with Nelson Mandela's release from prison in February 1990 was in full flood and was by now clearly irreversible. What was still quite unclear was whether the outcome of that transition would be a peaceful shift to a democratic South Africa or a bloody confrontation. Thanks to our nephew, William Rex, who was working at Capetown University and had good contacts with the African National Congress (ANC), we were able to visit the largest (and most dangerous) of the Capetown townships on Cape Flats, stretching for many miles east of the city. It was explained to us that there was no question of visiting the townships without an ANC minder; and so we bounced our way along rutted tracks, through miles of truly appalling scenes of human degradation, to be shown some of the projects such as schools and health clinics in upended shipping containers, which the ANC, with the help of many international Non-Governmental Organisations, were running. The atmosphere of determination and optimism was tangible but so too were the problems that would remain even if the political transition under way was successfully accomplished. The implications of all this for the UN, which had for decades been semi-paralysed by disputes between the African countries and the West (most particularly the USA and the UK) over how to handle the apartheid regime, were clearly going to be profound in whichever direction things moved. And then, to complete a trio of game-changing developments in those few weeks, just as Saddam Hussein's Iraq was seeking to wipe Kuwait from the map by force, the UN was witnessing the peaceful disappearance of another of its members, East Germany, following the formal reunification of Germany, this time by international agreement involving four of the Permanent Members of the Security Council. Clearly the UN I was actually going to was in the process of becoming a very different place to the UN I thought I was going to when my appointment was first announced.

* * *

To arrive in New York in the early stages of the first major post-Cold War international crisis and one in which the UN was close to the centre of the action was certainly to be thrown into the deep end; and to be told on arrival that I would in three weeks time be chairing the Security Council for the month of October was even more so. The water on this occasion was a good deal deeper than on the day five years before when I had driven straight from Brussels Airport to my first meeting of the IGC on the Single European Act, including as it did decisions on war and peace which would do much to determine the role the UN was to play in the new era which was dawning. At least the temperature of the water was made more tolerable by the truly first class team who were working at the UK Mission to the UN and by the splendid domestic staff we inherited from our predecessors. The Foreign Office has invariably sent the brightest and the best of its young diplomats to do a spell in New York, believing, rightly, that it provided a window on the world, practical experience of negotiation at an early stage in their careers and a range of contacts which would stand them in good stead wherever they subsequently served; and so it was when we arrived.

Our elegant duplex apartment was only a few blocks from both the UK Mission offices and the UN building itself, enabling me often to walk to either and thus to avoid the almost totally sedentary fate of many UN diplomats; it was small enough for an agreeable family life when one could find any time for that (we were accompanied by our third son, Jonathan, who had enrolled at Columbia University for a four-year course) and it was small enough too to avoid being used as a hotel by the many official visitors who passed through New York in any year and to discourage its use for the sort of large diplomatic receptions which I detest, while being quite big enough to entertain the wide range of New Yorkers and UN diplomats and officials we soon came to know. My life quickly settled into a frenetic, but just tolerable, pattern that lasted throughout the five years we were there. If anything it became more frenetic as time went on and the number and scope of the problems piled onto the UN's plate continued to grow. I would be up at seven; and escaping from the flat before the many impatient FCO officials (five hours ahead of us) could begin working the telephones I would go down in my dressing-gown to the pool in the basement of the building and, while swimming as many lengths as I could manage – and nothing is more boring that that form of activity – I would clear my mind and order my thoughts for the day ahead; then back for a shower and breakfast, most usefully listening to the feed the BBC World Service fixed up for me from their office at the UN, but more often than not, fielding telephone calls from London by officials briefing ministers for parliamentary business or meetings with visiting colleagues. I would then go round to the UK Mission office for the daily meeting with my staff at which the many tasks for action would be allocated and we would seek to ensure that we were operating in a coherent way – joined up government it would be called now, but the phrase had not been invented then; and thereafter there would be back-to-back meetings all day, of the Security Council in long, informal consultation meetings where policy was thrashed out and differences reconciled if they could be. There were also formal, carefully scripted sessions of the Council, and meetings of the Ambassadors of the Five Permanent Members of the Security Council (P5), a forum which had been largely created in the 1980s by one of my predecessors, John Thomson, and which was now reaching the apogee of its effectiveness. Add to that meetings with various groups in the General Assembly, regular press briefings and the briefing of visiting British ministers and members of parliament. One of the main contrasts with Brussels was the amount of public diplomacy involved. In Brussels, while I had briefed the British press corps assiduously and regularly on a background basis,

I was certainly not encouraged by London to speak on the record or to undertake public speaking engagements; European issues were just too sensitive domestically to permit that. But in New York press briefing to a bank of television cameras outside the Security Council's meeting rooms was a daily event (it was important to ensure that you did not place yourself where the charging bull in Picasso's great Guernica painting, an example of which adorned that particular wall of the UN building, appeared to be emerging from your own head); and the range of think-tanks, seminars and discussion groups looking for informal comment from people regarded as being on the inside track at the UN was almost infinite. Add to this that Security Council activity did not always stop at the weekend, and that European concepts such as the August break had no meaning at the UN, and one had a pretty demanding life.

My early months in New York were entirely dominated by the response to Saddam Hussein's aggression against Kuwait. Some big decisions – the mandatory call for him to withdraw, the annulment of all Iraqi decisions about the future status of Kuwait, the imposition of the most comprehensive set of economic and financial sanctions in the UN's history and the authorisation to use force if necessary to implement those sanctions – had all been taken in August before I reached New York. It was already clear that the response was not going to be of the slap on the wrist kind generally associated with the UN and that nor was the UN going to be paralysed by old Cold War alliances and rivalries, both miscalculations on which Saddam had relied. But a good deal remained to be done to tighten up the sanctions package, in particular cutting off all civil aviation links to Iraq, and overshadowing all that loomed the much more momentous decision on whether to use force to expel the Iraqi forces from Kuwait and, if so, whether to have that decision legitimised by a Security Council resolution or whether to rely on the provisions of the UN Charter (Article 51) which recognised the inherent right of member states (and by implication of their allies too) to act in self-defence. Most foreign ministers attending the General Assembly at the end of September tiptoed round the use of force issue while not ruling it out. But Eduard Shevardnadze, speaking for the Soviet

Union, did not, and clearly hinted at the fact that the use of force might be needed.

This crucial signal seemed to have eluded Saddam Hussein; but it was not overlooked by anyone else. So, when the US Secretary of State, James Baker and Douglas Hurd met privately, with only myself and my US colleague, Tom Pickering, present, in the margins of a Conference on Security and Cooperation in Europe ministerial meeting in the first days of October, the use of force dominated the conversation. In particular, Baker put Pickering and me through our paces on whether a Security Council resolution authorising the use of force was obtainable – that is, whether it was likely to attract nine votes and no vetoes. We both said we believed it was doable – the Soviet signal had been clear, the Chinese were prepared to look the other way and, apart from Cuba and perhaps Yemen, we doubted whether there would be any other negative votes or abstentions once the chips were down. But we warned that this outcome could not be achieved by the normal processes of negotiation and haggling in New York; UN ambassadors, often with views somewhat different from those of their governments, were well skilled at side-stepping their instructions, assuming they got any and that these were unambiguous; votes would have to be assured by contact at the political level in the capitals of the Security Council members. Baker took all this on board. He and President Bush were clearly leaning towards the UN authorisation option as a means of influencing positively the voting in Congress, which could not be avoided. Douglas Hurd said little, since he was well aware that Margaret Thatcher's views were opposed to going back to the UN. But just how violently opposed we only discovered when I (with Hurd's approval) reported the meeting by telegram, all copies of which were then withdrawn from circulation in Whitehall on No 10's instructions. So, if I had thought that by going to the UN I had escaped from the tensions within the government, I was now disillusioned. In the end our opposition to returning to the UN did not signify much because, once President Bush had made up his mind in the other sense and sent Baker out on his travels to garner votes, the Prime Minister just had to grin and bear it.

Before all that was put to the test in the Security Council at the end of November (and Pickering and my head count was broadly validated), the solidarity of the coalition against Saddam was

seriously threatened when the Israeli security forces killed a number
of unarmed Palestinian protesters in the precincts of the places
holy to both Muslims and Jews in Jerusalem. As I heard the news
of the killings coming through on the BBC World Service on the
morning of 8 October I realised that, as the current President of the
Security Council, I was in for a hard time. I was not wrong. Within
hours the Security Council was in session, tempers were running
high, and the Arab delegations, led by the PLO observer mission,
were demanding action. Under normal circumstances a resolution
condemning Israel, however justified, and these events certainly
justified condemnation, would have been vetoed by the United
States (the mid-term congressional elections were only a few weeks
away). But the circumstances were far from normal, and it became
clear at an early stage that the USA would go a long way to avoid a
veto which could well have put at risk the solidarity of the coalition
against Saddam. Just how far they would go and in what terms
remained to be established. The situation was greatly complicated
by the fact that the PLO had supported Saddam Hussein's invasion
of Kuwait and would far rather have provoked a US veto than have
had to compromise over the terms of the resolution. For five days
and much of three nights the Security Council struggled with this
Rubik's cube of diplomacy. I resorted to an old Brussels tactic of
holding separate bilateral meetings, known in the Brussels argot as
'confessionals', with each of the other 14 delegations. This helped
a bit, although the PLO delegation, which was naturally also
involved in these consultations, kept changing its position or was
unable to get instructions from Yasser Arafat in Tunis. Gradually we
edged our way towards a unanimous vote condemning the Israeli
action and asking the UN Secretary-General to send an emissary
to establish the facts. Given US reluctance to mention the occupied
status of East Jerusalem explicitly in the text of the resolution we
only got there by dint of my clarifying from the chair at the official
meeting of the Security Council that all references to the occupied
territories in the resolution covered East Jerusalem. This provoked a
furious Israeli response. It had been a close run thing; and I learned
a lot about the black arts of chairing the Council.

In the first week of 1991, when the UN was still becalmed in that
period somewhat hypocritically known as 'the pause of goodwill'
– the six week gap between adoption of the Security Council

resolution authorising the use of force to remove Iraq from Kuwait and to restore international peace and security to the region and its effective entry into force – and while everyone was still waiting to see the outcome of the US Secretary of State's meeting in Geneva with Tariq Aziz, the Deputy Prime Minister of Iraq, I sent the Foreign Secretary my first impressions of the UN, both retrospective and prospective. I make no apologies for including here a substantial proportion of what I wrote then because it manages to elude the heavy overlay of hindsight inherent in any book of memoirs and because it does convey quite a good flavour of what the UN at that particular point in time looked like to someone who was reasonably close to the centre of policymaking there but who had recently come to the UN from the outside:

The new arrival at the UN in 1990 could not fail to be told that here was an organisation undergoing a renaissance. Every speech even on the most informal occasions, and there are very many speeches at the UN and virtually no occasion is too informal to make one, proclaims the fact. The recent successes – the ending of the Iran/Iraq war, Namibia, Afghanistan, Nicaragua – are ticked off; the robust and effective response to Iraq's aggression against Kuwait is extolled; the future challenges – Cambodia, West Sahara, El Salvador – are noted with an optimistic assumption that they too will be successes; and the liberating effects of the end of the Cold War are given much of the credit for this happy state of affairs.

That is the conventional wisdom. Is it justified? I think largely it is, but there is a tendency to underestimate the fragility of the renaissance; to turn a blind eye to the fact that the extent of the renaissance is magnified by comparison with the extremely low straits into which the organisation sank in the 70s and early 80s; to forget that this heady new wine is being poured into some pretty cracked old bottles.

Moreover, the impact of the renaissance on the various parts of the UN system has been singularly disparate. The Security Council, for all the imperfections in its procedures, is quite evidently the jewel in the crown. The General Assembly has, both by contrast and in absolute terms, lost much ground. The Secretariat seems somehow bemused by the turn of events, not quite sure whether it heralds a threat to its vested interests or an opportunity to be seized with both hands. The outlying parts of the system, the specialised agencies and so on, seem to be proceeding much as before, hardly aware that anything very much has happened. This disparate impact is setting up many tensions which are only gradually beginning to surface. For every person or country which regards it as bliss to be alive in this particular dawn, I suspect there are several who doubt whether it is a dawn at all and others who would be not too unhappy if it turned out to be a false one.

The tensions in the system are really an inevitable function of the Charter itself, written as it was by the victors of the Second World War with one eye fixed on the awful lessons of the failure of the League of Nations and the other on the preservation of their own status and national advantage. I have been quite startled by the extent to which the UN is a caste-ridden society. First there are the five Permanent Members of the Security Council, then the non-permanent members and then the rest, all 140 plus of them (the numbers have been going up and down like a yo-yo this year, what with the unification of Yemen and Germany and the arrival of Liechtenstein and Namibia), jockeying for an occasional two-year spell on the Security Council or busying themselves with the more or less insubstantial activities of the General Assembly and its myriad subordinate bodies. Now that the Permanent Members are working closely together and the Security Council is actually taking decisions, in late November a decision on a matter of peace and war with potentially extremely far-reaching implications for the whole membership, the distance between the tables has widened and this is both felt and resented. General de Gaulle's concept of a directoire may remain anathema in Brussels but it is alive and well in New York. The next few years may see attempts to challenge it.

The workings of the Permanent Five were a real eye-opener for someone coming from Brussels where an exclusive caucus of this nature would have been completely taboo. During my first three months in New York the Ambassadors of the Five met more than 50 times, their Political Counsellors as often again. Most, but by no means all this activity, was occasioned by the Gulf crisis on which, so far, the Five have achieved a

*pretty monolithic front, it being tacitly understood that the
Chinese will look out of the window when things of which they
do not entirely approve are being mooted. The influence of the
Five currently considerably exceeds the sum of their collective
action partly because those outside an exclusive club of this sort
always tend to exaggerate its significance and partly because its
members go out of their way to avoid crossing swords in public.
But this unity is fairly precarious and it requires continuous
effort to sustain it. The Americans are clearly primus inter pares
and are set to remain so as their relative strength vis-à-vis the
others is on the increase, given the Soviet Union's accelerating
collapse as a superpower; but they will need to nurse the other
four along and take fuller account of their susceptibilities than
some in Washington would wish to do if they are to make the
most use of this instrument which has served them (and us) so
well over the Gulf crisis. We for our part will have a particular
role to play in ensuring that the Americans remain alive to
the advantage of action through the UN, as opposed to going
it alone or to bilateral dealings with the Soviet Union. The
Gorbachev/Shevardnadze commitment to the UN and within
it to the Permanent Five, seems to hold good as the need to
find a way of withdrawing from the Soviet Union's previously
over-stretched foreign policy commitments becomes if anything
more urgent; but Shevardnadze's resignation is a new element
of uncertainty and I suppose that isolationism could become
an alternative option to internationalism if the latter failed to
deliver the protection of Soviet interests. The Chinese remain
hesitant somewhere between their desire to be at the top table
and their conception of themselves as representing the interests
of the developing world. As to the two European members (UK
and France), they are both boxing a bit above their weight,
which demands a good deal of ingenuity and fleetness of foot if
it is to be done successfully.*

*Britain's own position at the UN, largely as a result of our
Permanent Membership of the Security Council, strikes me as
being a substantial national asset and one which we can actively
put to good use. For it is at the UN that our combined position
as a country which understands and influences the evolution of
US foreign policy and as one of the two Permanent Members*

from a European Community which is groping its way towards a more united approach to foreign and security policy, can be deployed and built upon.

1990 at the UN: International peace and security

The year divided, almost equally, into two parts, before the invasion of Kuwait and after it; and the distinction was very clear both in the extent to which the Gulf crisis dominated all other business in the Security Council and at the General Assembly and in the way the crisis and its handling accelerated and developed in practical terms a number of trends already apparent, most particularly the capacity of the United States and the Soviet Union to work at the UN in close and effective cooperation.

The first of the two periods saw a great deal of steady, and in some cases spectacular, progress in the implementation of a number of UN actions. The long saga of Namibia was brought to a successful conclusion despite the nasty hiccough which had occurred at the beginning of the transitional period and despite a good deal of fairly bad-tempered sparring between the Permanent Five on the one hand and the Africans on the other. To the extent that this involved the scale and thus the cost of the UN operation required, this is likely to be the precursor to several further such hassles (West Sahara and Cambodia are looming), it being more or less certain that the Secretariat will bid for more than they need for such operations and that the regional countries principally interested (but never the principal contributors) will support them. In Central America the holding of free and fair elections in Nicaragua, the subsequent transfer of power to Mrs Chamorro's government and the disarming of the Contras were evident successes in a region noted for the failure of innumerable previous peace-making efforts. The Iran/ Iraq peace process limped forward but managed to stay on the rails laid down for it by SCR 598; real progress had to wait for Saddam Hussein's remarkable volte-face and attempted rapprochement with Iran after his invasion of Kuwait. Afghanistan did not get noticeably nearer peace but it did drift further away from being a real threat to international security.

But it was not roses all the way. On two important issues, the Arab/Israel peace process and Cyprus there was no forward movement at all and matters, if anything slipped backward. During the first half of the year discussion of Arab/Israel issues was pervasive but deeply depressing. The gradual foundering of the Likud/Labour government in Israel and its eventual replacement by a more hard-line coalition gave the quietus to the peace proposals which the US Secretary of State had tried so hard to sell. Endless debates on the situation in the Occupied Territories, including an odyssey by the Security Council to Geneva to enable Arafat to appear, culminated in a US veto and a not particularly useful visit to the Occupied Territories by the Secretary-General's Representative, Aimé. The second half of the year, at least in damage limitation terms, was a little better. Three resolutions on the Occupied Territories passed through the Security Council unanimously, the United States being heavily influenced by the need to avoid a veto on this issue which could have caused serious strains in the alliance against Saddam Hussein. Just before Christmas they even signed up to a Presidential statement endorsing the calling of an international conference at the appropriate time. But Baker's extreme sensitivity on this issue, which was evident in discussion by the Foreign Ministers of the Permanent Five in New York in September, demonstrated how far the Americans still are from grasping the nettle of UN involvement in the peace process and of accepting an effective role for the Permanent Five. Indeed there were some indications that the evolution in Soviet policy under Shevardnadze was making the Americans think more kindly of US/Soviet cooperation on Middle East issues than of the full-blooded involvement of the UN and the Permanent Five. Our own gruelling experience in the chair of the Security Council at the time of the Jerusalem killings in October (five days and three nights to get a resolution with fairly modest content) and the 50 day ordeal that ran through the US Presidency in November and preceded the adoption of a further resolution on the Occupied Territories just before Christmas, should have served to dissipate any illusions that even a successful resolution of the Gulf crisis would make the handling of Arab/Israel issues at the UN much easier.

Cyprus was certainly a case of steps backward rather than forward, despite all the Secretary-General's continuing valiant efforts. Denktash was the main culprit and came close at the meetings organised in New York early in the year to derailing the whole process. Vassiliou continued to run tactical rings round Denktash and the Turks but the pursuit of his policy of internationalisation, including Cyprus' application for EC membership, made its own contribution to the backward steps on this issue. Only Turkey's enhanced standing with the alliance against Saddam Hussein prevented a General Assembly debate and further deterioration in the latter part of the year. There is no substitute for the Secretary-General's continuing efforts on this issue, but his reiterated determination as one with a long personal involvement with the problem to see it on the way to solution before his own retirement at the end of this year, looks ever more quixotic.

During 1990 two further longstanding regional conflicts, West Sahara and Cambodia, began to look ripe for the classic UN recipe of a ceasefire, UN supervised elections, transitional arrangements, both civil and military, under UN auspices and a good dollop of resettlement and reconstruction assistance; and a third with somewhat different characteristics, Salvador, began to look ripe for Nicaraguan treatment. In the case of Cambodia the Permanent Five held an unprecedented series of meetings between Asia Directors to hammer out a comprehensive peace plan. At the year's end neither the Cambodian nor the Western Sahara peace initiatives are home and dry; the former was suffering from a lack of harmony amongst the internal parties which perfectly matched the harmony amongst the Permanent Five; the latter lived under a real doubt as to whether King Hassan of Morocco was a signed-up supporter unless he was quite sure in advance that the outcome of the referendum would be incorporation into Morocco. But though it may take longer than anyone hopes to bring these two operations to fruition it seems unlikely that a viable alternative will emerge or that any of the parties will wish to throw over the processes entirely. By year's end the pace of negotiations over Salvador had quickened, and another major UN operation there in 1991 looked at least a possibility.

The General Assembly played no part in these developments. But on two issues of importance to us it ceased to be quite so obstructive. There were two consensus resolutions on South Africa; and while neither will directly affect the outcome of the negotiations there they do at least mark the erosion of the destructive influence of the Front Line States' missions and (as the ANC leaders recognise) a weakening of the sanctions regime. 1990 also saw a growing awareness that the Assembly's overblown activities on decolonisation were out of date.

This was a pretty formidable agenda for any one year but it was only an hors d'oeuvre for 1990. But, while the UN was an essential midwife in the search for peaceful solutions, it was hardly a prime mover in any of them. Peace came because the combatants were exhausted, because of Soviet bankruptcy and policy changes and the resultant ending of the Cold War or because of a complex mixture of these influences. The UN's role was essentially more reactive than proactive. The Gulf crisis marked a fundamental change in this, as in many other respects.

Saddam Hussein's invasion of Kuwait took the UN by surprise as it did everyone else, but any student of history would surely find the Security Council's unity of purpose in responding to it a great deal more surprising. A simple enumeration of the main milestones of that response is impressive enough:

2 August	*Iraqi invasion condemned (SCR 660)*
6 August	*Comprehensive economic sanctions imposed on Iraq (SCR 661)*
9 August	*Iraqi annexation of Kuwait declared null and void (SCR 662)*
18 August	*Release of hostages required (SCR 664)*
25 August	*Detailed application of sanctions to air traffic defined (SCR 670)*
29 October	*Provisions agreed on compensation for Iraqi invasion and for handling breaches of human rights (SCR 674)*
29 November	*Use of force authorised after 15 January (SCR 678)*

I doubt if anyone asked on 3 August to plot the course of the UN reaction to the crisis would have predicted half of this. Why did it materialise? Partly because this was such a black and white case; there had been plenty of cases of aggression in recent years but never before an attempt to wipe a whole country off the map, and its people and infrastructure along with it. Partly because Saddam Hussein could be relied upon at each stage to stiffen the determination of all but the most feeble of his critics; the whole episode of the hostages is an example of this factor, even though most of the Western press seemed to interpret it as evidence of his fiendish cunning. But the key determinant in UN terms was the attitude of the Soviet Union, for so long Iraq's international sponsor and supplier of arms. As the full meaning of the Soviet Union's rejection of Iraqi aggression, of the hints of support for military action in Shevardnadze's September speech to the General Assembly, of the support in November for the use of force, sank in, those countries which had for so long played happily in the interstices of US/Soviet rivalry were simply left gasping and were compelled to follow in their wake. At the year's end attention is temporarily off the UN stage. It will return soon enough, whether the outcome is a post-crisis negotiation preceded by hostilities or by a peaceful Iraqi withdrawal. It will not be so easy to maintain the same unity of purpose in the next phase...

The prospects for 1991

It is not easy to offer any very meaningful predictions for 1991 since the crystal ball is entirely dominated by the saturnine features of the ruler of Iraq. It is no exaggeration to say that the whole future development of the United Nations in the area of international peace and security depends to a great extent on the outcome of the Gulf crisis. If Saddam Hussein is successfully expelled from Kuwait, whether peacefully or by force, not only will the UN have a large amount of follow-up work to do on regional security and other matters, but it will receive a tremendous shot in the arm. Indeed a successful outcome may lead to an altogether excessive euphoria about the capacity of the UN to resolve regional issues in the post-Cold War era. Be that as it may, we will certainly in those circumstances find a major increase in the business flowing towards the UN and major increased demands on its resources. Angola and the Horn of Africa would be early examples.

If, on the contrary, the Gulf crisis and the UN's so far remarkably robust handling of it turn out to be a failure, whether because of dissension in the alliance, successful manoeuvring by Saddam Hussein or a loss of will by the United States, to name only three of the many ways in which matters might go wrong, then I fear that the UN renaissance may indeed turn out to be a false dawn. In such a perspective it would be hard to see the UN successfully playing the sort of proactive role it has over the Gulf in other disputes which are likely to be of a less clear cut nature and less susceptible to effective economic and military action. After all there can be few countries more vulnerable to economic sanctions than Iraq and few against which the marshalling of a multinational military force is geographically and politically so feasible.

So a very great deal rides on this issue. If all goes reasonably well, I think we will then need to give serious thought as to how we wish to see the UN operating, particularly in the field of peacekeeping and peacemaking in the post-Cold War era. With the United States unwilling, and in the long term unable, to carry the whole burden itself, with the Soviet Union ceasing to have a worldwide intervention capacity and throwing its weight behind a UN approach and with middle ranking powers including, the UK, France, Germany and Japan either unwilling or unable to sustain independent activity in the future, there is a great deal to be said for thinking imaginatively about an expansion of the UN's capabilities and activities in the field of collective security. The Soviet Union and the Secretary-General have put forward many ideas some of which could be worth pursuing in the wake of a Gulf crisis. In particular the future role of the Permanent Five and their direct involvement in peacekeeping and peacemaking would seem to offer an attractive and possibly even a cost effective way forward: better than the current US emphasis on bilateral initiatives with the Soviet Union, which however valuable in disposing of regional conflicts thrown up by the Cold War are less welcome in other respects, such as their very reserved attitude towards accepting the jurisdiction of the International Court of Justice. We ought to consider carefully whether the London Summit next summer could be the occasion for launching some ideas in this area.

I would make one small, partly semantic, plea to get away from the US habit of talking about a new world order. This appalling piece of jargon always sounds to me like a hybrid bred out of the Third Reich and the New International Economic Order. Quite apart from setting teeth on edge, it sends out the wrong signals, since it implies a kind of authoritarian world in which the Permanent Five will rule, OK. What we are really talking about is the development of a system of collective security for the twenty-first century and I hope that we can find a way of describing it as such.

❊   ❊   ❊

The two and a half years following my arrival in New York, which, perhaps not entirely coincidentally, matched the later part of President Bush's term of office, was a period of astonishing achievement for the UN. Not only was Iraq expelled from Kuwait, but the whole post-war follow-up to the conflict was placed fair and square in the hands of the Security Council. The Kurds of Iraq, although not the Shi'a, were shielded from the full effect of Saddam Hussein's wrath in a UN operation which foreshadowed the concept of the 'responsibility to protect'. The UN's biggest ever peacekeeping operation – in Cambodia – was deployed with full P5 support to a country which hitherto had been a cockpit for their rivalries, and seemed set to bring that country, however imperfectly, through elections to a state of peace and relative normality. The first hesitant steps into UN peacekeeping in the former Yugoslavia at least brought a ceasefire between the Serbs and the Croatians and the uncontested deployment of UN forces in the Serb-populated areas of Croatia. A massive humanitarian rescue operation was deployed in Somalia, with a full UN mandate despite the non-existence of any Somali government, thus ignoring the need for consent which had hitherto been regarded as a sacred principle of such operations, and saved hundreds of thousands of Somalis from imminent starvation. Mandatory economic sanctions were imposed on Libya for its refusal to hand over two men indicted for terrorist acts (the destruction of a Pan Am flight over Lockerbie in Scotland). A new, first ever African, Secretary-General Boutros Boutros-Ghali, was chosen without any particular fuss and with no P5 vetoes. A first ever policymaking Security Council Summit was held and charted a course for the organisation in the years ahead. And the Earth Summit in Rio de Janeiro marked the signing of conventions to control carbon emissions and to protect biodiversity, the first serious steps towards addressing the global threat from climate change. Quite a record, one could argue, even if some of the achievements in it contained the seeds of future failures. It was not surprising that the UN passed from being an organisation which most people, including most governments, thought could achieve nothing much beyond organising debates to one which many believed could achieve anything and could provide the solution to most, if not all, international disputes. The nemesis of over-stretch and hubris was perceptible on the horizon but had not yet arrived on the scene.

Diplomats tend to have a purely subsidiary role once hostilities in which their own countries are involved commence. And so it was at the UN in the early months of 1991. The job of the coalition's Ambassadors was to ensure that no one made a premature dash to the Security Council to call for a ceasefire before the military task of expelling Iraqi forces from Kuwait was complete. And this we achieved, with a lot of help from the coalition's Arab partners and by means of a good deal of devious procedural manoeuvring. The decision to call an end to the fighting and the ceasefire terms negotiated between the Iraqis and the coalition at Safwan a few days later were purely American decisions, about which the UN was neither consulted nor informed in advance, although the Security Council was asked and willingly agreed to rubber stamp the ceasefire agreement. In reality there was much relief at the UN that the USA had decided not to go beyond the terms of the original resolution (SCR 678) authorising the use of force by pressing on into Iraq, perhaps even to Baghdad. Despite all the subsequent controversy and the reading of history backwards after the invasion of Iraq in 2003, I am sure this was the right decision to have made. To have done otherwise would have split the coalition, would have risked the break-up of Iraq, and would have destroyed the legitimacy of what had been an astonishingly successful lesson to anyone contemplating aggression. Moreover, the coalition was no more ready and equipped to take over the government of Iraq in 1991 than it was to prove to be, with far less excuse, in 2003. What did come as a complete surprise was to be told in a hurried telephone call from Pickering early in March that Washington, London and Paris (in effect Washington, although the others went along happily) had decided that the whole of the post-war follow up to the Gulf War was to be put in the hands of the Security Council. This astonishing and unprecedented step was a gamble but one that paid off. It also plunged us into a frenetic month of negotiations between the P5 over the terms of what came to be know with conscious irony as 'the mother of all resolutions' also known as Security Council Resolution 687 (the irony being in the echo of Saddam Hussein's claim that the Gulf War had been 'the mother of all victories').

The resolution established three subsidiary international bodies; the first was UNSCOM, which, together with the International Atomic Energy Agency was tasked with removing, destroying or rendering harmless all Iraqi weapons of mass destruction (WMD) and the means of their delivery, a task whose implementation revealed a series of far more sophisticated and more advanced chemical, nuclear and biological programmes than the ones patchy pre-war intelligence had suggested. The second was to remove the supposed casus belli of the dispute over the Iraqi/Kuwaiti border by identifying the land and maritime borders between them; and the third was to establish the sums owing in compensation for damage caused in the war, not just to Kuwait and Saudi Arabia but also to a number of countries in South Asia which had had to evacuate their nationals. In addition to these three specific areas, the resolution had to reshape the sanctions regime, linking it to Iraq's performance on getting rid of its WMD programmes, deal with Iraq's international debts and its support for terrorist organisations, and decide what, if any, guarantee the Security Council would give to Kuwait against any repetition of aggression by its much more powerful neighbour. The negotiations between the P5 were not without their difficulties and moments of tension but all these were successfully resolved; together with the negotiations over the future of Cambodia they were the high watermark of P5 cooperation in the post-Cold War era. Was this due simply to the fact that, to all intents and purposes, we were now living in a unipolar world, with the United States the only global superpower left standing? Not entirely, I would suggest. It was also due to the willingness of the Bush administration to work constructively with its P5 partners and to take account of their concerns, a sensitivity that was not to be very apparent in subsequent administrations' actions. How did the SCR 687 settlement stand up in the light of later developments? Well it delivered an agreed Iraqi/Kuwaiti border, accepted, after a scare in 1994, by both parties. It paid out of Iraqi oil revenues large sums in compensation for war damages while avoiding the concept of punitive damages. And it did, however slowly and painfully, remove or destroy all of Iraq's WMD, as was finally established when nothing was found following the invasion of Iraq in 2003. But on this last issue two fundamental errors were made. The first was that the USA and the UK systematically refused to agree to honour the link between the removal of WMD and the lifting of sanctions; and instead tended to link the lifting of sanctions to the removal of Saddam Hussein. This led to an ever-widening split in the Security Council which foreshadowed the divisions in 2003; and it removed any incentive for Iraq to come clean to the inspectors of UNSCOM, and of its 2002 successor, UNMOVIC. Would a different approach, one more consistent with both the letter and the spirit of SCR 687, have delivered a better, or at least a different, result? That is far from certain because of the second major error of judgement, Saddam Hussein's determination to retain the threat of WMD and of his potential to develop them as an instrument in his relationship with his neighbours; and hence his continued pursuit of the game of cat and mouse with the UN inspectors which resulted, up to the eve of hostilities in 2003, in a universal belief that he actually was still concealing such weapons.

By the time the 'mother of all resolutions' was ready to be put to the vote in early April 1991, the repression meted out by Saddam Hussein's forces on the Kurds and Shi'a who had risen up in revolt at the time of his defeat in Kuwait was creating a major new international crisis. Whether or not this could have been avoided if the US military had not permitted the Iraqis, in the ceasefire negotiations at Safwan, to continue to fly their helicopter gunships within Iraq, will never be known. Hundreds of thousands of Kurdish refugees, men, women and children were trekking across the mountains of northern Iraq in appalling climatic conditions in an attempt to reach safety in Turkey, which was reluctant to let them in because of their problems with their own ethnic Kurdish population. Smaller numbers of Shi'a refugees were crossing the border into Iran. The political pressure in the West for action to be taken was rising sharply. The first idea (French) was to include provisions on the Kurds and the Shi'a in the big resolution, but this was quite impractical in UN political terms given that the big resolution was, and had to be, based on the mandatory provision of Chapter VII of the UN Charter, while interference in what was clearly an internal Iraqi matter was never going to be recognised by many Security Council members as falling into that category. So, as soon as the big resolution was through, we began discussion on a separate resolution for the Kurds and Shi'a. It was uphill work. By now we were testing the limits of what even a much weakened Soviet Union and a China which felt it had no direct interests in Iraq were prepared to tolerate; and, since January 1991, there had been new non-permanent members of the Council – India and Zimbabwe in particular – who were strongly opposed to any intervention in the domestic affairs of a member state. In the end we squeaked through with a bare ten positive votes and no vetoes, perilously close to the minimum (nine votes) required for a resolution. Resolution 688 called on Saddam Hussein to cease the repression of his Kurdish and Shi'a populations and to give the UN access for humanitarian assistance to the refugees. But it had only political and not legal force, it contained no follow-up provisions as to what was to be done if Saddam Hussein did not desist and there was no clear mandate for the UN. The question now was what could be built on this flimsy foundation, since no one believed that reverting to the Council for a Chapter VII resolution would work. The Americans were reluctant to get involved militarily in northern Iraq. At this point John Major took a courageous initiative and rallied his European partners at a European Council meeting in Luxembourg behind a plan to stabilise the flow of refugees on the Iraqi side of the border with Turkey and eventually to reverse it, to provide temporary security and humanitarian assistance to the refugees and to create the political conditions which would enable them to return to their homes.

I was consulted by telephone from Luxembourg and did my best, with some success, to shape the language of the initiative in such a way as to emphasise its humanitarian dimension and thus to make it easier for the UN's humanitarian agencies to cooperate. Earlier talk of 'enclaves' was dropped. At this point the Americans came fully on board. The coalition allies promulgated no-fly zones over the north and south of Iraq (but without explicit Security Council authority, although they were never challenged there); and a massive humanitarian operation, largely in the early stages under military auspices, got under way on the Iraqi side of the border. Saddam Hussein decided not to challenge all this other than verbally. Gradually the situation stabilised. The next task was to persuade an extremely reluctant UN Secretary-General (still at that time Pérez de Cuéllar) and a much more cooperative UN Under-Secretary-General for humanitarian emergencies (Jan Eliasson) to start taking over responsibility for the humanitarian operation and for getting the refugees back to their homes. Gradually and precariously this began to work. Later, much later, it proved possible to get access for the Kurdish authorities to some of Iraq's frozen financial assets and to a proportion of the proceeds of the oil-for-food scheme. When the 2003 invasion took place, the Kurdish provinces were the only ones that did not need to be freed from Saddam Hussein's yoke and which had a functioning provincial government. But none of this worked for the Shi'a who lacked the geographical propinquity to a NATO ally, and who, apart from a few unavailing attempts by the UN to get access to the refugees, were left to bear the full brunt of Saddam Hussein's wrath. It was deeply regrettable; but it was a lesson in the reality of what critics call double standards. Do you save some of the victims if you cannot save all of them?

The peace agreements, known as the Paris Accords, which brought an end to the long and bloody civil war in Cambodia were not negotiated at or by the UN, although UN Secretariat officials were closely involved, but rather between the P5 capitals and those of the main regional players, Japan, Australia and the ASEAN nations. The involvement of the P5, four of whom had been backers of different factions within Cambodia – the Soviet Union supporting the Vietnamese-backed regime of Hun Sen; the French backing the former ruler, Prince Sihanouk, living in exile in Beijing; and the

Chinese with support, however reluctant, from the USA, siding with
the genocidal Khmer Rouge – was hugely significant for the post-
Cold War UN. It involved mounting and deploying the largest ever
UN peacekeeping mission, installing a transitional administration
to run the country in the interim and the holding of free and fair
parliamentary elections. All of this would have been difficult enough
under perfect conditions. But conditions within Cambodia were
far from perfect and it soon became evident that the Khmer Rouge
were reneging on their commitments under the Paris Accords and
had no intention of disbanding their military forces, of permitting
the UN transitional administration access to the areas under their
control or of cooperating in the electoral process. The oversight of
the operation in New York fell to the P5 caucus, by now working
smoothly on a daily basis to handle the Gulf War and its aftermath.
As the only P5 member not to have had a dog in the Cambodian
fight (although we had, to our shame, supported the Americans
in continuing to recognise the Khmer Rouge as the legitimate
government of Cambodia) it often fell to me to broker compromises
over the texts of resolutions and the handling of tactical issues as
events unfolded.

The USA by this time were all for denouncing and condemning
the Khmer Rouge at every turn and imposing economic sanctions
on them, as was the Soviet Union; the Chinese wanted to do neither;
the French turned to Sihanouk as the key to resolving every problem.
Moreover, the P5 operated very differently from how it had over
Iraq; China might not yet be a global power but it was a crucial
regional player in South East Asia. My astute and suave Chinese
colleague, Li Dao Yu, was kept on the tightest of reins from Beijing.
P5 solidarity nevertheless prevailed at every crisis point and it
gradually became clear that the key decision was whether or not the
elections should go ahead in the teeth of Khmer Rouge opposition
and, if necessary, only in those parts of the country (the majority of
it) which they did not control; and, if so, whether the outcome of
those elections should be accepted by the UN, which would in effect
mean completely de-legitimising the Khmer Rouge. In the end the
Chinese joined the others on both these points, and, when the Khmer
Rouge forces were unwise enough to shell the Chinese engineering
battalion that was part of the UN peacekeeping force, they began to
do so with enthusiasm. One other unprecedented feature of the UN

peacekeeping force was that it contained military personnel from all the members of the P5, a reversal of the traditional approach under which the P5 military were never to be included in such operations. Unfortunately that was not repeated in the future. Following the elections that led to the formation of a coalition government between Hun Sen and Prince Ranariddh, leader of the royalist party, and to the installation of Sihanouk as a constitutional monarch, the transitional administration and the peacekeeping operation were rapidly wound up. When Hun Sen and Ranariddh came to New York to celebrate its completion it was not difficult for anyone sitting in the Security Council to work out which of the two was likely to emerge on top in the power struggles that lay ahead. So can the Cambodia operation really be considered a success? I would argue that it can. Certainly Cambodia 20 years on is not a functioning multi-party democracy. Human rights are under pressure. The process of bringing the Khmer Rouge leadership to justice is still not complete. But, compared to the Cambodia of the civil war period, the changes for the better are massive, particularly in the economy. Perhaps the real lesson is that the international community often has to learn to live with outcomes to such external interventions that fall some way short of the ideal. This should not preclude continuing to press for better outcomes, but it does point to the need for realism and also for avoiding too black and white an approach to the case for intervention in the first place.

At the end of the summer of 1991 the problems caused by the break-up of the Federal Republic of Yugoslavia first, rather belatedly, made their way onto the Security Council's agenda. It was to be the longest, largest and most debilitating peace operation in which the organisation had hitherto been engaged. The long delay in bringing the matter to the Council was mainly due to the Herculean efforts of the increasingly irrelevant government of the Federation to prevent it being discussed at all at the UN, since they regarded it as a purely domestic, internal dispute. As a founder member of the Non-Aligned Movement the Yugoslavs had plenty of friends at court. And in any case, as was to become increasingly evident as time went by, the UN was singularly unready and ill-equipped to address the challenges to international peace and security arising from failing and failed states. Most of its peacekeeping expertise had been focussed on handling international disputes after a ceasefire had been arranged, not on preventing hostilities in the first place. The European Community had been involved for some time in the efforts of the federal government to hold Yugoslavia together, and it was those, not particularly effective, efforts – for Europe was ill-equipped, both politically and in resource terms, to handle a crisis of this complexity on its own – that led the Luxembourg Foreign Minister, Jacques Poos, then in the European Presidency, to make the ineffably grandiloquent statement that this was Europe's hour. There was in any case a considerable reluctance by the United States to be drawn into any direct involvement in handling the Yugoslav crisis and thus there existed, from the very outset, that mismatch between US and European policies in the former Yugoslavia which was for so long to prove fatal to the chances of success. Nevertheless, with the formal secession of Croatia and Slovenia in July 1991 and the immediate outbreak of fighting between the Serb-dominated Yugoslav National Army (JNA) and the two breakaway republics, a policy of denial at the UN no longer became sustainable, particularly when, despite a rapid end to the fighting between the JNA and Slovenia, the warfare around the town of Vukovar produced scenes of violence unknown in Europe since the end of the Second World War.

So in September the Security Council unanimously decided to put an arms embargo on the whole of Yugoslavia to try to prevent the fighting spreading and involving others from outside, and encouraged the UN Secretary-General (Pérez de Cuéllar) and his Special Representative, Cyrus Vance, a former US Secretary of State, to try to broker a ceasefire, if necessary deploying UN peacekeepers to monitor it. Vance's efforts at first prospered, a ceasefire was agreed, as was the deployment of a UN peacekeeping force to the Serb-populated areas of Croatia, the Krajina and Eastern and Western Slavonia. But just as that first, relative success began to take shape, an even more serious, and ultimately much more sanguinary, conflict began to loom in Bosnia and Herzegovina. This was at least partly triggered by divisions amongst the Europeans, between on the one hand the European Special Representative, Lord Carrington, backed by Britain and France, who wanted to make recognition of the first two breakaway republics and of any others that might follow them conditional on their first peacefully resolving any boundary problems and those over the treatment of ethnic minorities, and on the other Germany, which not only wanted to recognise Slovenia and Croatia immediately and unconditionally, but favoured a process that would push the other component parts of Yugoslavia to declare their hands on secession too. Pérez de Cuéllar and Vance were of the same view as Carrington. My own efforts were deployed towards strengthening the expression of that view and to get the USA to support it too. In this I was partially successful, although an exchange at that time between me and Pickering, in which he said that we should not worry too much about the US attitude – 'we'll be right behind anything that Europe decides' – and my reply 'that's just the problem. We want you right beside us and helping to shape it' – catches the flavour of the barely submerged tensions that remained. Be that as it may, the outcome was a formal letter in early November 1991 from Pérez de Cuéllar to Hans-Dietrich Genscher, the German Foreign Minister, urging him to go slow on recognition and to make any offer of it conditional. This provoked a furious response from Bonn, and a complaint from Genscher to Douglas Hurd about my role in bringing about this démarche. Hurd brushed that complaint aside, but on the wider issue the Germans got their way during a period when the final negotiations over what was to become the Maastricht Treaty on European Union rated higher amongst the priorities of the British and French governments than did the future of Yugoslavia. Serbia and Croatia were recognised; and Bosnia and Herzegovina (where the Serbs boycotted the independence referendum and vowed to fight its outcome tooth and nail) and also Macedonia and Montenegro were pushed to take their decisions too, the former two for secession and the latter to remain, for the time being at least, with Serbia. The curtain was going up on the Bosnian war.

✳   ✳   ✳

Among all the other subjects crowding the UN's agenda in 1991 it was also an election year. The incumbent Secretary-General, Javier Pérez de Cuéllar, was completing his second five-year term and, after some hesitation, decided not to stand for a third term. When he told me of his decision – it was one of the highly discriminatory peculiarities of UN life that the Secretary-General spoke privately to each of the P5 Ambassadors – I said I thought he had made the right one. This apparently was quite unprecedented, the normal practice being to feign deep regret. But I really meant it, and not for any particularly 'British' reason. Pérez de Cuéllar had been an excellent Cold War Secretary-General, achieving far more by quiet diplomacy and gentle nudging behind the scenes than he could ever have done by taking a more assertive stance; he was to end his term with the remarkable achievement of a peace settlement in El Salvador. But he was exhausted by the ever-rising demands put on his office as the Cold War ended; and I doubted if he was quite the right person for that new era. Anyway thereafter the bizarre processes of a UN election got under way. There was nothing in the slightest democratic, transparent or accountable about it. In theory the decision was for the membership as a whole to take, with one country one vote each in the General Assembly; but the General Assembly invariably acted on the recommendation of the Security Council – and no one had ever challenged a candidate recommended by the Council – so that brought into play the potential vetoes of the Permanent Members.

When Pérez de Cuéllar was first elected in 1983 it had been a Grand Guignol occasion, with multiple Chinese vetoes of Kurt Waldheim's bid for a third term and of other Western candidates and multiple Western vetoes of the African candidate Salim Salim of Tanzania. There was a strong desire in 1991 to avoid a repeat of that, heavily Cold War-influenced, saga. Clearly there had to be some regional rotation of the holder of the office, but the approach chosen in 1991 and pursued at every election since then of developing a broad consensus around which of the UN's regional groups was to get the job before considering the whole range of candidates was about the worst imaginable, excluding as it did many strong candidates and leaving the organisation vulnerable to having to choose from a weak field once the favoured region was agreed. In 1991 that consensus coalesced around choosing amongst the African candidates, and since the P5, with only the mildest of protests, agreed, that was that. So a number of good European candidates – Gro Harlem Brundtland, the former Norwegian Prime Minister and Hans van den Broek, the former Netherlands Foreign Minister, amongst them – were barely given the time of day and gained no support. The African field was in fact on this occasion a pretty strong one, including as front-runners Boutros Boutros-Ghali of Egypt and Bernard Chidzero, the Zimbabwean Finance Minister, with Olusegun Obasanjo, the former President of Nigeria, and Olara Otunnu, a former Ugandan Foreign Minister, also in the contest.

Britain campaigned for Chidzero, who gained a good deal of Commonwealth support, and the French threw all their weight behind Boutros-Ghali, thus creating an unfortunate appearance of throwback to the days of Anglo-French rivalry over Africa. In truth our campaign was a good deal the less convincing of the two, all Chidzero's experience having been in the economic and financial field which was never, least of all at the current juncture with many of the Cold War taboos dropping away, going to be the main focus of the Secretary-General's work. So, when Boutros-Ghali emerged as the clear victor, there was no question of our vetoing his candidature, and rightly so. The Americans, who had sat on the fence to the very end, also decided not to veto Boutros-Ghali, although they had their doubts, as much as a gesture of gratitude for President Mubarak's support in the Gulf War as for any more respectable reason. In the years that followed I had my difficulties with Boutros-Ghali but I never wavered in my view that we had made the right choice. When he fell victim in 1995 to a US veto of his candidature for a second term I was delighted (it was after I had retired) that Britain did not associate itself with what was as much the outcome of a vendetta between him and Madeleine Albright, the US Permanent Representative shortly to be appointed Secretary of State, as a carefully considered act of policy. Boutros-Ghali's strengths, his deep knowledge of international affairs, his integrity and his decisiveness in my view outweighed his weaknesses, a Pharaonic management style – on being asked by a journalist early in his term how he was going to handle the built-in resistance to any change in the UN Secretariat he replied, 'As I did in Egypt, by a mixture of stealth and brutality' – a contempt for the black arts of communication management and an unwise tendency to try to operate back channels with his contacts in member state capitals, which seldom produced results but which ensured that he had a considerable number of sworn enemies among the Permanent Representatives in New York.

By the mid summer of 1991 two things were clear; first that in January 1992 the UN would have a new Secretary-General – but not yet who that would be; and second that Britain would occupy the monthly rotating Presidency of the Security Council in that same month. One always had to wait for the outcome of the election by the General Assembly of the new non-permanent members due to come onto the Council for a two-year term the following year since that could affect the alphabetical rotation. These two facts seemed to me to be both an opportunity and a challenge. It surely made sense for a new Secretary-General to get strong public support at the beginning of his term, all the more so when so much was being demanded of the UN in the new post-Cold War era; and there surely too needed to be some kind of systemic consideration of how best to equip the UN for the new role which was so far being thrust upon it in a particularly higgledy-piggledy manner with little if any thought being given to the resources required, both in people and money and in political backing. So I made the case to London for our promoting a Security Council Summit in January 1992, recognising that no decision could be taken until the Prime Minister had decided whether or not to call a general election that autumn. Complete silence ensued, which meant that I could not even begin to sound out my colleagues on what would be a completely unprecedented gathering, a Security Council Summit designed not just as a photo-opportunity but as an occasion to set the organisation's course in the field of international peace and security for the years ahead.

As the autumn months passed and no election was called in Britain, I could still get no sense out of London; and I left for a short skiing holiday in Vermont just before Christmas assuming that no more would be heard of my proposal. Then, out of the blue, a call came through to our chalet from the Foreign Secretary. Was it too late to launch my idea of a Summit in January? What had clearly tipped the balance was the collapse of the Soviet Union and the emergence of Boris Yeltsin as President of a Russian federation occupying the Soviet Union's permanent seat on the Security Council. My reply was 'Not quite'; but the United States would need to be squared in advance, and I would need to start sounding out the new Secretary-General and the other member states when, as President of the Council, I saw them one by one in the first working days of January. After that the matter would be in the public domain and, if things went wrong, we would have plenty of egg on our face. The summoning of the meeting turned out to be the least of our problems. US support was assured in advance; this was by no means a foregone conclusion because, although one potential conversation-stopper had been removed when Cuba rotated off the Council at the end of 1991, a post-Tiananmen Chinese representative would inevitably be there and the Chinese could be relied upon to cause the USA the maximum of embarrassment over the weakening of their boycott on political contacts (as indeed they did by sending Li Peng, the Prime Minister who had been directly involved in the Tiananmen repression) – but here too the emergence of Yeltsin and the attraction of an early opportunity for a bilateral meeting did the trick. Other reactions ranged from the enthusiastic to the lukewarm. A far greater problem was to determine and then get agreement on the outcome of the meeting. To my horror, but not entirely to my surprise, London had given no thought to that at all and had no ideas to offer other than the need for a prominent mention of human rights, which we could be quite sure the Chinese (and probably others) would block. I assumed from the outset that the outcome in the form of a Presidential Statement would need to be unanimous, the idea of voting through a resolution at that level against opposition being politically completely impractical.

So I set about putting together a document, and then protecting it from the naysayers of whom there were a fair number. The crucial issues of strengthening the UN machinery for peace-making, peacekeeping and conflict prevention were not too difficult to handle. Since it was inconceivable to fashion any meaningful reform in a month, I opted for a very 'Brussels' solution, a time-limited request to the Secretary-General to submit his views. This led in due course to Boutros-Ghali's ambitious but well-argued document 'Agenda for Peace', much of which was drafted by the then Under-Secretary-General for Peacekeeping and an old Diplomatic Service friend Marrack ('Mig') Goulding. In addition, it proved possible to get very clear recognition that both terrorism and the further proliferation of Weapons of Mass Destruction were threats to international peace and security and thus proper matters for Security Council discussion and action. Not surprisingly this proved more contentious, and the Indians only finally agreed when their Prime Minister had reached the VIP lounge at Heathrow en route for New York and the prospect of blocking the whole statement looked too daunting. We then had a last minute protocol crisis provoked by Chinese unhappiness over the order of speakers, which was resolved with some difficulty by Pickering persuading the White House to take a relaxed view about when President Bush spoke. The meeting itself was, as is often the case with such UN gatherings, something of an anti-climax – its style, however, being greatly boosted by the appearance of King Hassan of Morocco in national dress and accompanied by two huge, tea-pouring servants. Looking back with the benefit of hindsight there is nothing about the statement adopted of which one needed to feel ashamed. Quite the contrary. It correctly identified the main challenges that faced the international community in the period ahead, including the critical link between development and security, and the need for firm collective responses to those challenges if they were to be mastered. If its fine words had been followed up by effective action much of the disorder that followed could have been avoided or at least managed better. Where the meeting fell short was on the follow-up, of which there was virtually none worthy of the name. 'Agenda for Peace' when it arrived was left to wither on the bough and no effective peacekeeping reforms were agreed until the Brahimi Report in 2000. Thus an opportunity was missed which was not going to recur in such propitious circumstances for the foreseeable future. As is so often the case, short-term expediency and the onrush of current crises swept aside any thought of introducing the systemic reforms which the UN needed and which only its member states acting collectively could provide.

*　　*　　*

Running in parallel with the preparations for the Security Council Summit was another groundbreaking issue, taking action against specific acts of international terrorism. It was one thing for the Summit meeting, as it did, to state flatly, but in general terms, that international terrorism was a threat to peace and security, the formula needed to open the toolbox of mandatory measures under Chapter VII of the Charter, and quite another for the Council to take action against an offending government. In November 1991 the US Ambassador and I were consulted by our governments on whether we considered there was any chance of getting effective action at the UN when the indictments against two Libyan officials in respect of the blowing up of a Pan American flight over Lockerbie in Scotland some years before became public knowledge, which was imminent. For once I took a more sanguine view than Tom Pickering as to the chances of success. So, while expressing some caution as to the eventual outcome, we set out a gameplan for proceeding at the UN. This included working closely with the French whose legal authorities were proceeding separately to investigate the blowing up of a UTA flight over Niger; forming the closest possible working relationship with all the governments whose nationals had lost their lives on the two flights and publishing full details of the indictments when they were issued, and circulating them at the UN. It also included proceeding in two completely separate steps, the first calling on the Libyan government to surrender the indicted men to justice, with no reference at all to the possible consequences of defiance, and the second to impose limited, targeted sanctions on Libya in the probable event of defiance.

This plan was accepted. The first resolution was adopted by unanimity in January 1992, helped, no doubt, by the reluctance of the Heads of State and Government who were attending the Summit at the end of that month to face their US, British and French counterparts if they had dragged their feet. The second resolution, after Colonel Gaddafi had, as expected, defied the first, proved more difficult. But, with a lot of help from the Venezuelan President of the Council in March, Diego Arria, we squeaked by, the Venezuelans paying the price of seeing their embassy in Tripoli going up in flames (fortunately with no loss of life). All Libyan civil aviation links with the outside world were cut off, an arms embargo was imposed, and, subsequently, sanctions were also applied to exports to Libya of equipment for the oil and gas industry. Many years later, and well beyond the end of my time in New York, the two indicted men were handed over for trial in a specially constituted Scottish court which sat in the Netherlands; later still Gaddafi came clean on his programmes for developing Weapons of Mass Destruction and abandoned them, and also agreed to pay compensation to the families of the victims of the air disasters. There has subsequently been plenty of controversy as to whether this satisfactory outcome was more due to the cumulative effect of the sanctions or to alarm at the possibility, following the US-led invasion of Iraq in 2003, that he would be the next target for such action. Probably a bit of both. But the significance of the Security Council demonstrating that it was ready to take action against international terrorism, and the use of carefully targeted sanctions, closely related to the original terrorist acts, were both steps of considerable importance for the future.

*   *   *

Anyone who has read this chapter up to this point might be forgiven for thinking that, on going to the UN, I had turned my back on what had up to then been the main focus of my professional career, the development of Britain's role in the European Community; and they might also feel that I was unduly fixated on what went on in the Security Council to the exclusion of the other parts of the wider UN family of institutions. Both points do have some validity, but neither represents the whole story. When I arrived in New York in 1990, cooperation there between the European Community member states was not in particularly good shape. Admittedly it had proved possible to achieve a high proportion of common votes on General Assembly resolutions. But the exclusion of most member states from a Security Council which was coming to play an ever more prominent role in post-Cold War global affairs was a running sore, greatly exacerbated by the insistence of the two European Permanent Members, Britain and France, that Security Council business should not even be discussed at the weekly meetings of European Community Ambassadors. At the same time the negotiations going on in the IGC in Brussels, which were to culminate in the Maastricht Treaty, were clearly pointing in the direction of giving European foreign policy cooperation for the first time a firm treaty base and of providing some ambitious general precepts on how a Common Foreign and Security Policy (CFSP) was to be established and implemented. Unless some care was taken over the drafting of the new treaty there would clearly be plenty of scope for debilitating turf warfare in future between the two Permanent Members and the rest. What was needed in my view was a clear recognition in the new treaty that Permanent Members retained, under the UN Charter, certain rights and responsibilities that would need to be respected as CFSP developed.

My contacts with London revealed, to my astonishment, that the FCO was completely ignorant of the ban on discussing Security Council business at European Community weekly meetings and agreed with me that it was undesirable and counter-productive. They also agreed on the desirability of including in the new treaty some recognition of the continuing role of Permanent Members of the Security Council. So, on my next trip across the Atlantic, in the early months of 1991, I was sent to Paris to sound out the French on both points. At the Quai d'Orsay, the Secretary-General, François Scheer, who was an old friend from my Brussels days where he had been the French Permanent Representative, was equally unsighted and equally appalled about the ban on discussing Security Council business at European coordination meetings. He agreed that it was in our interest to brief the other member states fully and, where possible, to co-opt them in support of our policies, not to irritate and humiliate them. He undertook that, when the new French Ambassador arrived (in April 1991), he would be instructed to behave accordingly. The drafting of the new treaty I discussed with Élisabeth Guigou, at that time the lead coordinator of European policy in Paris, and later to become a senior minister. She was at first cautious about the need to incorporate some specific provision in the treaty being negotiated on the position of Permanent Members but did not dismiss the idea; and thereafter the idea gained ground in Paris as well as in London. In a typical 'Brussels' compromise the text that was finally agreed provided both for increased coordination over Security Council business between European Community members of the Council (there was invariably one – or, after the further enlargement of the Community, more – non-permanent European members) as well as recognising the rights and responsibilities of Permanent Members. This eminently satisfactory outcome has held the field until the present day; and it will probably do so for a long time to come, since the idea of a single European permanent seat on the Security Council, much canvassed in the press and at seminars, is both for political and legal reasons unlikely to materialise.

Under normal circumstances I might well not have attended the United Nations Summit meeting on the environment in Rio de Janeiro in June 1992. The unremitting pressure of business in the Security Council, where war in Bosnia had now joined the other crises of the day, was hard to escape. But the Earth Summit in Rio was an important occasion for the UN as a whole, the first time the organisation had tried to move beyond words to action to deal with the challenge of climate change and the threats to biodiversity; I had been involved in a number of the difficult preparatory discussions for the conference in New York and had become convinced that these areas were going to be, and needed to be, a major focus of the UN's future work; the European coordination process was not in very good shape under a weak Portuguese Presidency; and there were signs of wobbliness in London, largely imparted by policy chaos in Washington. Add to this our desire to see our third son, Jonathan, who was doing a year at São Paulo University and had already begun what was to later become his life's work of helping to alleviate the plight of street-children in Brazil, and the decision was made. There were moments I regretted the decision as I got up day after day at crack of dawn and fought my way through heavy traffic to the conference site 30 miles out of the city; or as I sat through seemingly endless and pointless meetings, deafened by the whirring of the air-conditioners in the giant cattle-shed-like place in which we were cooped up. Fortunately the main business of the Summit, the negotiation and opening for signature of two new international conventions, one dealing with climate change, the other with biodiversity, had been completed before the conference began.

It was the decision whether to sign both these conventions in Rio that caused the wobbles in London. In Washington the US biotechnology industry was up in arms alleging that the convention on biodiversity would ruin their commercial prospects. The pressure from Congress paid off; it was an election year; and President Bush decided not to sign the biodiversity convention. Bizarrely, given the subsequent history, no such lobbying onslaught was launched at the climate change convention, whose Kyoto Protocol was to become a major international bone of contention, and the USA decided to sign up to that one. The Secretary of State for the Environment, Michael Howard, was inclined to follow their example on both points. I argued strongly against that, pointing out that the US decision not to sign the biodiversity convention was rather absurd since the convention's main defects were not that it was liable to damage anyone's commercial prospects but that it was too weak and too loosely drafted to achieve anything very much at all (this, alas, has proved over time to be all too prophetically correct). Moreover, if we decided to follow the American example we would be the only country doing so, thus severely denting the government's green credentials. The argument continued to rage as the Prime Minister moved towards Rio via an official visit to Colombia; despite communications difficulties, it was finally settled in the sense which I had urged. The Summit segment of the Rio meeting, like all UN Summits, was something of an anti-climax, an endless succession of speeches addressed more to the speakers' domestic audiences than to the rather sparse occupants of the Rio auditorium. What was very clear was that things that had not been agreed and nailed down ahead of the conference – action against deforestation and desertification, for example – made no serious progress and remained unsettled for many years ahead. The idea that you could negotiate effectively in the hurly-burly of a summit conference with over 150 participants was shown to be totally unrealistic, a lesson which has subsequently been ignored again and again, most dramatically at Copenhagen in December 2009.

It is always presumptuous to try to divide the past up into neat time capsules and then to apply labels to them. But, just as the first half of my time in New York can be seen as a period of considerable achievement by a UN emerging from the Cold War far closer to the centre of the international stage than it had ever been before, with the crest of the wave being reached about the time of the Security Council Summit meeting in January 1992, so the second half, from roughly the spring of 1993 until our departure from New York in July 1995, was a recessional period when failures outnumbered successes and confidence in the organisation, which had reached absurdly and dangerously high levels, gradually ebbed away. An organisation which had been thought capable of anything became one which was considered capable of nothing. That was how it felt at the time and that is how it looks now with all the benefit of hindsight. The fact that those two periods of time coincided almost exactly with the presidency of George H W Bush on the one hand and the first years of Bill Clinton's Presidency on the other cannot be ignored when one seeks explanations for such a sharp turnaround, though some care should be taken when attributing responsibility since, even in the last year of Bush's Presidential term, the strong and imaginative support which he had given to the UN began to ebb away as he tried to dodge the criticism that he had been a largely foreign policy President.

The extent to which US foreign policy made the weather at the UN in New York can hardly be exaggerated at this time when the United States was the only global superpower left standing, when the Soviet Union had dissolved and its successor, the Russian Federation, was facing bankruptcy, when China was still a fairly tentative, mainly regional power, and when the Non-Aligned Movement had nothing left to be not aligned with. So the arrival in New York in January 1993 of a new US Permanent Representative and a member of the Clinton cabinet, Madeleine Albright, was seen as a major event. She did not disappoint – or at least not entirely; an effective and forceful operator, with a wide knowledge of international affairs from her time working in President Carter's National Security Council and as shadow National Security Adviser to Michael Dukakis when he ran for the Presidency in 1988, she soon made her mark, particularly in the public diplomacy which had become such an integral part of life at the UN; she was frank, warm and decisive. My own relationship with her was close, and managed to survive the vicissitudes and strains put on it by differences over policy towards the former Yugoslavia, Bosnia in particular. But it soon became clear that her own personal priorities were centred more on Washington than New York; her relationship with Boutros-Ghali, which began scratchily, slid steadily towards something close to a vendetta – there were faults on both sides; and, in any case, the skill and personality of the US Ambassador could not conceal or compensate for the chaotic foreign policy-making and incoherence which characterised that early period of President Clinton's term of office. Of course this second phase that I have identified was by no means devoid of success stories. Two major peacekeeping operations, in El Salvador and in Mozambique, were carried through to free and fair elections and successful completion. Even in the former Yugoslavia it proved possible, with the help of the preventive deployment of UN peacekeepers and with the accession of the country to the UN despite a continuing dispute with Greece over its name, to protect Macedonia from sliding into the hostilities that prevailed elsewhere. But those successes counted for little alongside the failures – in Angola, for example – and above all alongside three peacekeeping disasters, in Somalia, in Rwanda and at Srebrenica.

*   *   *

It is easy to forget just how successful the first phase of the US-led 'coalition of the willing' intervention in Somalia in December 1992 and January 1993 actually was; and also just how conceptually groundbreaking was its authorisation and legitimisation by the UN. Here was a Third World failed state in Africa, without even a modicum of a government, many tens of thousands of whose citizens were facing death from starvation as a result of the blocking of UN emergency and NGO relief supplies by the warlords who were fighting over the corpse of that state. The Security Council, acting unanimously, authorised a military intervention to remedy the situation; and within weeks, following an unopposed landing by the expeditionary force, aid supplies were flowing and the shadow of mass starvation had been lifted. This was a clear example of the international community accepting a collective Responsibility to Protect, even if that phrase had not yet been coined. The trouble began when the time came to convert the emergency humanitarian intervention into a regular UN peacekeeping mission with a mandate to help rebuild Somali state institutions. The warlords resumed fighting and the UN mission, still with a large American component, gradually became embroiled as a protagonist in the hostilities; this culminated in October 1993 in the shooting down of a US helicopter over Mogadishu and the dragging of the pilot's naked body through the streets of the city, provoking a firestorm of protest in Congress and throughout the United States. The administration panicked; the President announced that all American troops would be withdrawn from Somalia within six months; and the UN's peacekeeping mission was as good as dead from that time on, although it took a good deal longer to die. Perhaps most damaging of all, the US administration allowed it to be believed that the UN was entirely responsible for this fiasco even though the military operation in question was under US and not UN command and no UN peacekeepers were involved.

Britain's (and my own) role in all this was that of an appalled spectator. Despite my attempts to persuade London to make some contribution to the UN peacekeeping operation, it was decided we would keep our distance and have nothing to do with it apart from voting for it in the Security Council. In retrospect there was a good deal of self-congratulation about that decision, which I still believe to have been deplorable whether it was motivated by prescience at the probable course of events or by the reluctance of the government's backbenchers to get further involved in UN peacekeeping (we were already deploying troops to Bosnia). In any case, it deprived Britain of any justification for speaking up as matters went from bad to worse. Moreover, the lessons drawn from, and the knock-on consequences of, the events in Mogadishu were totally negative for the UN. The USA has never since made a substantial troop contribution to a UN peacekeeping mission. The desire to avoid what came to be called 'crossing the Mogadishu line' reinforced the timidity of the UN commanders in Bosnia, of which the Bosnian Serbs took ample advantage. The pernicious doctrine of the need for an exit mechanism before any peacekeeping mission was undertaken, a charter for spoilers of whom there is never any lack in such operations, took root. And when, six months later, a massive genocide took place in Rwanda, not one country was prepared to volunteer troops to reinforce the UN's crumbling peacekeeping operation there. Now, nearly 20 years later, Somalia remains in a state of anarchy; the threat of mass starvation again stalks the land; a major international naval operation has had to be mounted to meet the challenge from Somali pirates; and the risk of Somalia becoming a haven for international terrorism is ever present. It is hard to avoid the conclusion that a bit more determination and perseverance in the early 1990s, painful and costly though it might have been, would have produced a better outcome than that.

✻   ✻   ✻

If ever a word were to be found written on my heart at the end of my five years in New York it would have been 'Bosnia'. Britain's central role in the handling of the long, debilitating crisis in that country, as major troop contributor, as key player in the efforts to find a peace settlement and as architect of the ultimately failed policy to manage the situation without resort to full scale hostilities and without becoming a protagonist in the fighting there, meant that a substantial proportion of my time had to be devoted, week in week out, to this issue. Bosnia created tensions between us and the UN Secretary-General and the Secretariat who always wanted to be less deeply involved there than we wanted them to be and who (quite rightly) criticised some of the policy expedients to which we were forced to resort such as the establishment of so-called 'safe areas'; it set us at odds with our principal ally, the United States and it split the European Community. It also laid us open to criticism by the non-aligned members of the Security Council and by press and public opinion because the policy we supported proved inadequate to protect the civilian population in Sarajevo and elsewhere in the country from ruthless bombardment, from ethnic cleansing and ultimately, at Srebrenica, from genocidal massacre. If at any stage we and the French could have agreed with the Americans on an approach which linked action from the air and on the ground with a viable peace plan and which presented a genuinely credible threat to the Bosnian Serbs and their puppet-master in Belgrade, Slobodan Milošević, then I believe that matters could have been brought to a conclusion more swiftly, as they finally were in August 1995. But such unity of purpose and such credibility in the eyes of the Serbs continually eluded us; and the faults did not all lie on one side of the Atlantic. That was the approach put to the incoming Clinton administration following a meeting at No 10 called by John Major in January 1993 that I attended; but it fell on deaf ears. As to my own input to policy, I was continually critical to London of the fact that, whenever a crisis in Bosnia blew up, we seemed to devote more time and energy to frightening ourselves about the possible Serb reaction to a more robust policy response than we did to frightening the Serbs. At one point I wrote to the Prime Minister's Diplomatic Adviser, Rodric Braithwaite, who was also at the time chairman of the Joint Intelligence Committee, complaining that our intelligence assessments seemed to me to contain a good deal of excessively alarmist group-think about the Serb capacity for retaliation. This earned me a magisterial rebuke for traducing the objectivity of the JIC; but the course of events in 1995, when we finally called the Serbs' bluff, were closer to my complaint than to the JIC analysis. Perhaps the best flavour of my views is contained in a diary entry I made (freed by then of any constraints from my official position) while we were travelling around China and Central Asia after leaving New York on retirement and were picking up news on the BBC World Service of the final round of fighting in Bosnia which preceded the Dayton peace agreement:

> ...*no doubt the negotiating path to a settlement will be long and stony and the UN/NATO military tracks will need to be pursued in parallel. It is sad that the UK still seems to be dragging its feet over the policy of NATO airstrikes to compel the Bosnian Serbs to withdraw their heavy weapons from around Sarajevo. Plus ça change. We always end up frightening ourselves more than the Serbs; and we always travel in the guard's van with our foot hovering over the emergency brake.*

Three episodes in Bosnia stand out in my memory among what at the time seemed an unending series of Security Council resolutions, Presidential statements and visits to New York by ministers, mediators and UN troop commanders designed to shape and implement the UN's response to the rapidly changing, and usually deteriorating, situation in the former Yugoslavia. The first episode occurred quite early on, in July 1992, and was a foretaste of things to come. Fighting in Bosnia had been raging for several weeks following the country's decision to break away from Yugoslavia and to establish its independence. The siege of Sarajevo by the Yugoslav National Army, acting in concert with the Bosnian Serbs, was under way. Lord Carrington, the European Community's Special Representative, telephoned me extremely early one morning (Sarajevo being six hours ahead of New York, events there always did seem to happen before one had woken up) to speak to me in my capacity as European Community President (Britain having taken over the Presidency at the beginning of that month). Carrington said he had managed to broker a ceasefire around Sarajevo between the warring parties. What was needed now was the early deployment of military observers to the Serb artillery and tank sites around Sarajevo to monitor the ceasefire; and this only the UN, and not the European Community, was equipped to do. He had already spoken to Boutros-Ghali who had reacted sympathetically. Could I please do my best to accelerate a formal UN response? I said I would; and set to with a will, contacting Mig Goulding the UN Under-Secretary-General for peacekeeping, the small group of Security Council missions who coordinated policy on the former Yugoslavia (the USA, Russia and France), and my European Community colleagues. By the end of the day we had put together a unanimously adopted Security Council Presidential statement supporting the ceasefire and asking the Secretary-General to come forward with proposals for the deployment of military observers. So far, so good. But it then became apparent that Carrington's reading of Boutros-Ghali's initial response had been over optimistic. The Secretary-General, who had been incommunicado throughout the day in question, conducting complex negotiations with the leaders of the Greek and Turkish Cypriot communities for a settlement in Cyprus, was far from ready to see the UN involved more deeply in a new part of the Yugoslav quagmire. Indeed he was hopping mad, believing that he had been manipulated against his will and taken advantage of. So, when the time came, a week later, for the Secretary-General to report back, as requested, to the Security Council, he treated us, and me in particular, to a tirade. By that time the whole matter was in any case entirely academic since the ceasefire around Sarajevo had already broken down and there could be no question of deploying military observers. So I decided to cut our losses and simply to respond 'least said, soonest mended'. But we had all had a serious warning, if one were needed, as to just how sensitive these issues surrounding the UN's involvement in the former Yugoslavia were; and also an indication that this Secretary-General took a more independent view of his responsibilities and scope for action, or in this case for inaction, than his predecessor would have done. My own relations with Boutros-Ghali required a good deal of fence-mending which was greatly facilitated by Cyrus Vance, the Secretary-General's Special Representative for the former Yugoslavia and previous to that President Carter's Secretary of State, and a good friend with whom I worked very closely on all these matters, particularly those relating to Macedonia.

The second episode, in the spring of 1993, indeed concerned Macedonia, just about the only UN success story in the whole Yugoslav imbroglio. The UN had already taken an important, and hitherto unprecedented, step of deploying a small preventive force of peacekeepers at the sole invitation of the Macedonian government and this had helped to stabilise a very fraught situation on the border with Serbia. Getting Macedonia admitted to the UN, as Croatia,

Slovenia and Bosnia and Herzegovina had been admitted the year before, proved altogether more difficult as a result of a noisy dispute between Macedonia and Greece over the former's supposed territorial ambitions in northern Greece and a number of issues relating to the flag and name of the new country. The European Community was split, with France backing the Greek opposition to Macedonia being admitted to the UN and Britain convinced that admission to the UN was a key element in stabilising the situation and avoiding another Yugoslav disaster. For some months Macedonia's application languished in the Security Council's in-tray, the other members of the Council being reluctant to take sides so long as the Europeans were divided.

Gradually patient diplomacy by Vance whittled away the issues in dispute between Macedonia and Greece and, although the question of the country's definitive name could not be settled, a consensus began to emerge around a temporary solution whereby Macedonia would be admitted to the UN under the somewhat absurd but serviceable name of 'The Former Yugoslav Republic of Macedonia', or 'FYROM' for short. The Security Council was all set to endorse this delicate set of compromises in early April 1993. Then, the night before the resolution admitting Macedonia was due to be voted in the Security Council, I was called round after dinner to the Secretary-General's house in Sutton Place, a few blocks from our own apartment. There I found the French and Spanish Ambassadors – the other two European Community members of the Council – looking decidedly glum. It appeared that the Greek Foreign Minister, who had virtually taken up residence in New York, had told the Secretary-General that his government could no longer agree to Macedonia's admission going ahead if the offending Macedonian flag was raised outside the UN building on First Avenue. Boutros-Ghali said he had consulted his Legal Counsel, who had advised him that he had no flexibility on the matter, a new member state's flag had to be flown on First Avenue. This, of course, reopened all the old divisions among the Europeans; and Boutros-Ghali said he saw no alternative to postponement. I contested that conclusion, pointing out that nowhere in the Charter (or anywhere else for that matter) was it specified that member states' flags had to be flown on First Avenue; but the Secretary-General did have a responsibility for international peace and security. Could he not simply tell the

Macedonians that, in the circumstances, he did not intend to raise their flag when they were admitted? No doubt the Macedonians would be upset, but they were, after all, getting the main prize of UN membership, and postponement over the flag issue would be much worse for them. Boutros-Ghali thought for a moment, smiled, and said he would do just that; and to general relief everything passed off smoothly the next day.

The third episode was of somewhat wider significance than the other two and occurred in February 1994 at a key point in the siege of Sarajevo. We were spending the weekend with Felix Rohatyn (a New York banker and later to be President Clinton's Ambassador to France) and his wife in Southampton, the first of the string of Hamptons towards the eastern end of Long Island to which so many of the inhabitants of Manhattan retreated to get a bit of sea air and relaxation. The weekend had already turned into something of a busman's holiday when I was given an earful about the inadequacies of European policy in Bosnia and the damage being done to NATO by Senator John Warner who was ensconced in the Rohatyn's guest-house. Then on 5 February (Saturday) news came through of the shelling of the marketplace in Sarajevo with heavy loss of innocent civilian lives, rapidly followed by a telephone call from the Foreign Secretary. This episode was of a different dimension altogether to the daily trickle of casualties in the city. What should the response be? I said that largely depended on us. This seemed to surprise Douglas Hurd. So I explained that Britain was invariably the back marker in Security Council discussions on Bosnia and if we shifted our position now to favour a robust response, then the French and the Americans would certainly not stand in the way. We then discussed the practical options and I pointed out that there was no need to revert to the Security Council as the original 'safe area' resolution passed the year before contained quite sufficient authority for the threat or use of force in the circumstances which had arisen. Hurd agreed that a tough response was essential; and, as most of another weekend break evaporated, we headed back up the road to New York. The next day (Sunday) the French and US Permanent Representatives came round to our flat to avoid alerting the press who had staked out our mission offices. We all three agreed on the case for a tough response, and that there was no need for, and many arguments against, a formal discussion in the Security Council where we could expect the Russians and Chinese to obfuscate. Rather we should tell the Secretary-General that our three governments wanted to see a tough response and suggest that he enlist the support of NATO air power to bring about a ceasefire around Sarajevo. We decided that Merimée should speak to Boutros-Ghali on behalf of all three of us, thus once again avoiding any triggering of premature press speculation. The Secretary-General agreed and sent off an appeal to his colleague at NATO. By Monday morning the NATO Council was already meeting to consider the text of an ultimatum to be given to the Bosnian Serbs. At that point there was serious dissention in London, where a number of cabinet ministers, led by Kenneth Clarke, the Chancellor of the Exchequer, were opposed to such a robust course of action; but, faced with otherwise unanimous support in NATO for the ultimatum, the Prime Minister and Foreign Secretary's views prevailed.

For some days it looked as if the Bosnian Serbs were going to defy the ultimatum. Shortly before it was due to expire, I was approached by a troubled Boutros-Ghali in the margins of a Security Council meeting on some quite different subject to say that the UN military in Sarajevo were now by no means certain that the shelling of the marketplace had in fact been the work of the Bosnian Serbs. What should he do? Nothing, I said. The issue was no longer who had been responsible for the original incident but whether or not the Bosnian Serbs were going to accept a perfectly legitimate request that they cease indiscriminately shelling a city full of innocent civilians. No more was heard from the UN about their doubts; and then, at the last possible moment, the Bosnian Serbs, blinked, agreed to stop shelling Sarajevo and agreed too to the deployment of UN monitors to their artillery and tank positions around the city. For a few brief weeks Sarajevo's suffering was alleviated and an atmosphere of hope prevailed. But the Bosnian Serbs soon began probing the other 'safe areas' to test the UN and NATO's will to sustain a tough line; and, first at Gorazde, then at Bihac, that will was found wanting, not helped by the almost inoperable complexities of the dual key system for authorising NATO air support. The UN was gradually sliding down the slope that was to culminate the following year in the massacre of Srebrenica. I felt at the time, and I feel as strongly now as then, that we collectively missed a real opportunity following the relative success of the Sarajevo ultimatum to set a new course in Bosnia which could have brought hostilities to an end earlier than they eventually were at Dayton and in circumstances which would have inflicted less damage on the UN's reputation. But such speculation can never be proved, one way or the other.

It is not possible to justify or to excuse the UN's handling of the genocide in Rwanda in the spring of 1994. It was, quite simply, a massive collective failure of the whole international system, from which neither the Secretariat, nor the Security Council, nor the member states emerge with any credit. I was deeply depressed and ashamed by the course of events and by the inability of all those involved, Britain included, to do anything much more than to wring their hands. But one can and should try to understand why it happened and to consider what could be done to prevent it happening again. The peacekeeping operation in Rwanda began as a low priority, under-resourced operation of little interest to anyone apart from Rwanda's immediate neighbours, who were being destabilised by the continuing civil war in the country, and to Belgium, Rwanda's former colonial ruler and France which had been propping up the Hutu-led regime there for many years and wanted to be relieved of that burden. Britain was singularly ill-equipped to follow events on the ground, having no resident embassy in Kigali; and, as was subsequently to become clear as a result of the international enquiry set up after the genocide, we, like the other members of the Council, were poorly served in terms of briefing by the Secretariat. Add to this the heavy shadow cast by the failure of the UN's peacekeeping mission in Somalia which discouraged any thought of mounting an external enforcement operation.

When the massacres began, following the shooting down and killing of the Presidents of both Rwanda and Burundi, I got little guidance from London except that we were not prepared to become militarily involved ourselves in a situation which was highly confused and whose full horror was not yet appreciated in New York or elsewhere. The first American reaction was to propose the withdrawal of the whole UN mission. When a troubled Madeleine Albright consulted me, I said I really did not think that would do; the very least we should do was to try to sustain the mission, two-thirds of whose troops were in any case being withdrawn unilaterally by their governments, and hope that it could serve some humanitarian purposes. Albright managed to get her instructions changed before carrying them out. The second American attempt, which was to propose that UN efforts should be concentrated in the neighbouring countries (Tanzania, Burundi and Zaire), was not much better, since the killing was taking place in Rwanda and the floods of refugees were a consequence of that. There then ensued an agonising few weeks during which Boutros-Ghali tried unavailingly to get reinforcements for his tiny, residual force in Kigali, a period which was only brought to an end by the victory on the battlefield of the Tutsi-led Rwandan Patriotic Front and the collapse of the Hutu-led government. At that point the French intervened and sought UN cover to protect the hundreds of thousands of Hutus who were fleeing, mainly towards Zaire. This was no straightforward decision, since it was clear that among the refugees there would be many soldiers of the former Hutu-led government who had been involved in the genocide. But we nevertheless supported the request; and I still think that that was, on balance, the right thing to do. Could the Rwandan genocide have been averted, as many commentators have asserted? I am rather doubtful. The vast bulk of the killing, which it is now clear had been carefully prepared, took place in a very short period of time following the death of the President. Kigali Airport was in the hands of the Hutu-led government. It is hard to see how an enforcement operation could have been mounted in time to prevent much of the bloodshed. A more pertinent question is whether the international community can do anything to prevent a similar situation arising elsewhere in the future. Part, but only a small part, of the answer to that question was provided by the Security Council's decision to establish a Rwanda war crimes tribunal. Of much greater significance was the gradual emergence of a new norm or rule of international behaviour which would establish what came to be called the international community's collective 'Responsibility to Protect' those whose own governments are unable or unwilling to perform that basic duty; but that is a story for a later chapter of this book.

*   *   *

The enlargement of the Security Council to make it more representative of the modern world and to include some additional permanent members, drawn from those excluded in 1945 and from the main emerging powers, is the Great White Whale of international diplomacy; and, like Captain Ahab's quarry, it is still out there swimming around un-harpooned. In the early 1990s this issue became the focus of much frenzied speculation and activity at the UN. The reasons were obvious. The importance of the Security Council had increased exponentially since the end of the Cold War; and the composition and balance of the international community had already shifted a long way from that reflected in the 1945 decisions and was beginning to shift even further. The case for enlargement was therefore a compelling one, enjoying much support, and, in 1993, it was decided to take the first step towards a negotiation by establishing what was called an 'open-ended working group', which meant that all 170 plus members of the UN could participate, the ultimate decision being one for the membership as a whole and not for the Security Council alone. My own views of the chances of success were sceptical from the outset, not because I did not accept the compelling nature of the case for enlargement – I did, and have not been shaken in that view ever since; and that scepticism must have been what led me, in a mischievous moment which I subsequently regretted, to christen the group 'the never-ending working group'. So it has proved to be. The reasons for my scepticism were numerous. For every country which sincerely wanted to become a Permanent Member of the Security Council (Japan, Germany, India and Brazil and at least one African country were the main contenders) there were several more countries just behind them in their regional pecking order who sincerely wanted to prevent that from happening (Italy, Pakistan, Mexico, Argentina, Indonesia make up a non-exhaustive list of examples of those in that group). Then enlargement, which would involve amending the Charter, required not only a two-thirds majority in the General Assembly but the positive accord of the existing five Permanent Members of the Security Council. Of those, only Britain and France were publicly committed supporters of enlargement.

No US administration has ever wholeheartedly backed the project, fearing that an enlarged Council would be even more difficult to manage than the existing one. Russia, following the dissolution of the Soviet Union, feared a further reduction in its international influence. And China is in no hurry to accept the case for Japan's permanent membership, greatly preferring to keep that card in their hand for use in their mutual, often troubled, bilateral relationship. And then there were difficult trade-offs to be achieved between the increased legitimacy which enlargement would bring and the almost certain loss in effectiveness and efficiency. Although I predicted deadlock, I never believed that it was in our interest that it should persist. Enlargement did not present any major threat to our national interests; our own permanent membership could not be altered without our consent. The idea of a single European permanent seat, for all its attractions from the point of view of squaring the numerical circle, was not an even faintly practical proposition in an organisation composed of national governments who were not about to agree to their own abolition and transformation into a United States of Europe and given the current and prospective absence of a single European foreign policy (not at all the same thing as the agreed European objective of a Common Foreign and Security Policy). The trouble about continuing stasis over Security Council enlargement – and two major attempts at reaching a decision, in 1997 and in 2005, both failed – is that this undermines the credibility and legitimacy of the existing Council to an unjustified and undesirable degree.

I fear that this account of our New York years may have conveyed the impression that our life there was little more than a workaholic's paradise. That dimension was certainly not absent, with days often beginning before dawn with urgent telephone calls from London and continuing through to dictation of key reporting telegrams and recommendations by car telephone on the way out to dinner and sometimes returning to the office after that. There were many lost weekends too. But work was not the whole of our lives in New York by any means. The contrast between the social life of Brussels, which really was a European Community/NATO company town with few escapes from incessant debate about the burning topics of the day, and that of New York, a huge, bustling cosmopolitan city, full of culture, business and banking and with a window onto the American political scene, could hardly have been sharper. Not that New Yorkers ignored the United Nations; but they were not obsessed by it. So discussion of international topics, which often took the form of a single conversation around a dinner table, was set in a much wider framework and could avoid the procedural minutiae of institutional manoeuvring which tended to predominate in Brussels. Nor was it impossible to get away on holiday from time to time, blessed as I was with two excellent deputies in Tom Richardson and Stephen Gomersall and with a really strong backup team. So we were able to explore the Western hemisphere in a way we had never done before, with trips to Alaska, to Peru and Bolivia, to the Yucatán and to Brazil, which finally, and very belatedly, forced me to abandon my heavily Eurocentric world historical view. Nor was I ever called back from holiday, except once from a trip to Quebec, to which I never got closer than Montreal, when there was a crisis, one of the many, in the UN operation in Bosnia. Perhaps the closest call was when we were in Alaska. Walking across the lobby of our hotel in Anchorage on our way to catch a bus to the national park behind Mount Denali, I saw a news flash of the coup attempt against Gorbachev in Moscow. A moment's reflection led me to the conclusion that this particular saga was not going to be played out in New York; and by the time we returned from Mount Denali, the coup had collapsed.

In those days retirement at the age of 60 was the inescapable fate of every British diplomat and for me that meant September 1995. I did not particularly resent the requirement, although I certainly did not feel that I had reached the end of my capacity for useful activity. But I had spent 10 years at the head of Britain's two biggest multilateral missions; I had no wish to take on a major bilateral embassy; and I was, intellectually as well as physically, distinctly tired. So it was in no spirit of resentment nor of a desire to explain how much better the Diplomatic Service could have been run, that I sat down to write the second of my valedictory despatches in July 1995, on the eve of our departure from New York. I aimed rather to try to explain and to understand the rollercoaster ride which the UN had experienced in those first five tumultuous years after the end of the Cold War; and to argue why it was in our national interest to help it to recover from the low esteem into which it had fallen. Rather than allowing those views to be tinged with hindsight I am therefore presenting them, as they were presented then. They leave the question posed in the subtitle of this chapter 'New World: Order or Disorder?' unanswered, as indeed it was then and still is.

Valedictory despatch from the UK mission to the UN, New York

I arrived in this post almost exactly five years ago. They have been tumultuous and innovative years, with the UN in the thick of the action, in a way it had hardly ever been before and never over such a sustained period. Now, with slightly over one-third of all Security Council resolutions adopted in the United Nations' first 50 years negotiated and voted in that time and some 20,000 outgoing telegrams from this post later, it is the moment to take stock and to make some kind of overall assessment.

Three developments, which occurred far from New York and in which the UN played little direct role, fundamentally transformed the background to all its work. The end of the Cold War and the collapse of the Soviet Union brought a whole series of disparate consequences – the possibility to take effective action in the Security Council, including the authorisation of the use of force against aggression, the emergence of the countries of Central and Eastern Europe as free enterprise, Western-oriented partners, aspiring to membership of NATO and the EU, the disappearance of centrally controlled command economics as a rival to a system based on free trade and private investment, the outbreak of a rash of ethnicity-based regional disputes all the way from Croatia in the west to Tajikistan in the east, the loosening of the cement provided by the existence of a Soviet threat which had held the West together in such solidarity through the Cold War and encouraged them, and in particular the United States, to make the necessary contribution in resources and political will to handle a whole range of disputes around the world. In South Africa the fall of the apartheid system and the emergence of a multi-racial democracy was almost as revolutionary in its impact. Africa lost its alibi for saying that its woes and weaknesses came largely from the outside. At the same time a massive irritant in the relations between African countries and the West was removed. And in the Middle East the transformation of the peace process from a slogan lacking any real credibility into a reality producing steady, if painful, progress temporarily removed a threat to peace which had burst into dangerous and divisive warfare on a number of occasions.

The effect of all this on the UN was largely, if not exclusively, beneficial. When Saddam Hussein fatally miscalculated the international reaction and sought to wipe Kuwait off the map in 1990, the UN was the means chosen to reverse his aggression and it worked. The sanctions against Iraq, the subsequent coalition campaign, authorised by the Security Council, which expelled Iraq from Kuwait, and the post-war settlement with its mechanisms for ferreting out and destroying Iraq's illegal arsenal of Weapons of Mass Destruction achieved one of the most effective, and certainly the most low cost, outcome in terms of human lives and other resources of any twentieth century attempt to punish aggression. Elsewhere, in Namibia, in Cambodia, in El Salvador, in Mozambique and now, hopefully, at last in Angola too, the UN helped to broker and then to implement peace settlements which put an end to a string of civil wars, exacerbated by the interference of external powers, disputes with their roots in the Cold War and in the attempt by a white-dominated South Africa to keep its opponents at bay. In each case the UN found itself breaking new ground, overseeing the disarmament of opposing troops and their fusion into a national army, preparing free and fair elections, monitoring human rights, all activities far removed from the earlier, classical, static peacekeeping missions, examples of which are still to be found in Cyprus, in South Lebanon and on the Golan Heights. It is currently fashionable in the US Congress and elsewhere to decry such nation-building as if the UN's failure in Somalia had definitively proved that it was a mistake for the UN to get involved in these sorts of activity. The track record hardly bears that out.

But success brought with it excessive expectations and overstretch. Heady new wine was being poured into some pretty old and cracked bottles. The UN's peacekeeping machinery creaked and groaned as the number of active operations jumped to 17, the peacemakers deployed went from about 10,000 to nearly 100,000 and budgets doubled and doubled again. The time taken to deploy troops lengthened, command and control problems surfaced with a vengeance and that dread disease 'mission creep' became the talk of the town. In Somalia what began as a laudable and successful humanitarian mission to put an end to mass starvation, exacerbated by the ruthless manoeuvring of warlords, slid gradually across what has come to be known as the 'Mogadishu line', when the peacekeepers themselves became a party in the civil strife and the level of internecine warfare was actually greater when the UN was there than after it left. In Rwanda three lightly armed battalions, sent to monitor a peace settlement, suddenly found themselves in the middle of genocidal massacres which they had no means of checking; and, when no single troop contributor showed the slightest inclination to despatch troops until the military die was cast, the UN was left with part of the blame for what had happened and much of the responsibility for clearing up the mess.

But of course the UN's worst headaches have come in the former Yugoslavia, in Bosnia in particular. Here too, as in Iraq, the UN was the international community's chosen means of dealing with a major instance of new world disorder. But on this occasion it was denied the firmness of policy direction and the sufficiency of resources which characterised the handling of Iraq. The underlying problems in the former Yugoslavia were in any case far more complex and far more intractable. This was no simple war of aggression which could be ended by the expulsion of the aggressor from the territory of its victim. Rather it was a complex hybrid, a civil war with a strong dash of aggression, in which any settlement had to find an appropriate place for all the parties. The objectives pursued, of containment, of the avoidance of direct external involvement in the fighting, of humanitarian relief and of fostering a peace process were sound enough. But the insufficiency of the resources supplied for the tasks in hand, the endless, kaleidoscopic shifting in the attitudes of the main players trying to manage the crisis, the United States in particular, and above all the stubbornness, brutality and deviousness of the parties, none of whom has so far wholeheartedly sought a peaceful settlement, has resulted in an operation which looks more like a failure than it ought to. The Bosnian poison has circulated in the veins of the UN as it has in those of NATO and the EU; it may not be lethal, but it has certainly been debilitating.

Now, in the middle of 1995, the triumph of the Gulf War and the success of several other UN missions stand in the deep shadow cast by Bosnia, Rwanda and Somalia. The pendulum which swung too far towards euphoria after the Gulf War has swung too far towards despair. From being an organisation which was wrongly thought capable of solving everything, the UN now tends, equally wrongly, to be regarded as incapable of solving anything.

Beyond the field of international peace and security the picture is both less dramatic and less clear-cut. Some of the great UN gatherings of recent years have been genuinely useful; the Children's Summit of 1990 gave a much-needed impetus to securing better treatment for children in Latin America and elsewhere; the Rio Environmental Summit of 1992 for the first time addressed on a global scale the terrifyingly rapid degradation of the environment and pointed the way to the right road even if it did not take many steps down it; the Cairo Population Conference of 1994, by the very controversy it stirred up, highlighted a problem which could overwhelm our capacity to cope with many others if population growth cannot be brought under control. But others, the Social Summit of 1995, the Human Rights Conference of 1993 and probably the Women's Conference in September of this year are more in the nature of damage limitation exercises. There are simply too many of these meetings for them to be genuinely useful and followed up effectively; a cull is long overdue, but will be hard to achieve.

By far the worst generic problem facing the UN is its finances. After years of being in a state which would lead any firm to be declared bankrupt, it is now, thanks to an arbitrary cap at 25 per cent being placed by the United States on its peacekeeping contributions, about to lurch a good deal further into the red. Reform of the scale of assessments and a prompter performance by the big payers is desperately needed.

Where has Britain stood in all this? The halcyon days of 1990/91 when it almost looked as if the P5 was a <u>directoire</u> for the world have gone. That was never a very realistic prospect. But US neglect and unpredictability, Russian grumpiness and Chinese unwillingness to engage have put paid to any illusions that the P5 can be a general instrument for the conduct of foreign policy, although it remains occasionally useful and usable. Other ad hoc groupings, the Contact Group for Bosnia, the P3 for Libya, US/UK collaboration for Iraq, to all of which we belong, partly thanks to our permanent membership of the Security Council, ensure that we are at the centre of policymaking when issues come to the UN. We have always been prompt payers and, in recent years, we have, for the first time become a substantial troop contributor to UN peacekeeping, with the professionalism of our armed forces very much to the fore in Cambodia, Bosnia, Rwanda and Angola. We have been a source of many of the more sensible initiatives at the UN, to create the Department of Humanitarian Affairs, to strengthen the UN's preventive action and diplomacy, to build up an indigenous African capability for peacekeeping, to reform the organisation's finances and to reduce the duplication and waste in the economic and social fields. All this is well understood and valued, all the more so as the UN heads into the choppy waters created by US Congressional hostility and the menace of neo-isolationism.

What lessons should we be drawing for the future at the UN from this first five years of the new era which followed the end of the Cold War and which so far has only been defined in that rather back-handed way? Here are a few suggestions, selected a little at random:

1   New world disorder does not look like abating very quickly, although we may be at or beyond the middle of the stream. The very awfulness of Bosnia may deter others from going down that road. The stabilisation of southern Africa could mean that African problems will bulk slightly less large in future. The fringes of the former Soviet Union look set to provide plenty of instability. Since the United States will not and the rest of us cannot cope with new

world disorder on our own, we will need a UN which is an effective instrument for handling and containing these problems if we are to avoid the risk of spreading regional instability and economic dislocation which is against our wider interests.

2   We will need, however, to be a bit cautious and conservative about what we ask the UN to take on in future. It needs a higher success rate than it has recently achieved if it is not to be discredited. It cannot afford more Bosnias and Somalias. So enforcement should be off limits, to be undertaken either by 'coalitions of the willing', if possible with UN authorisation, or not at all.

3   But we should not revert to pure, classical peacekeeping. Some of these operations, which tend to be singularly long-lasting, become as much part of the problem as part of the solution. Nor should we rule all civil conflicts off limits. The UN has made great strides in developing a capacity to put a country back on its feet and to take it down a path leading to elections, a better respect for human rights and a return to normality. We should continue to help it to equip itself better for these tasks, as we have been doing in the last few years.

4   In Iraq we need to ensure that a job well done is not undone by messing up the end-game. We are entering the last stages of securing Iraq's compliance with the Security Council's requirements on Weapons of Mass Destruction. If and when that is achieved, and it could be only a matter of months, we should aim for a controlled shift of policy, permitting Iraq to export oil under stringently defined conditions which will ensure the proceeds go only to civilian purposes. The alternative, all too likely to be favoured by the United States in an election year, of sitting on the sanctions lid until it blows off, is fraught with risks and disadvantages. An Iraqi break-out could put at risk much of what we have gained on Weapons of Mass Destruction and also involve us in costly military actions or precautions.

5   The Bosnian imbroglio will remain to plague us, whichever way things develop. We are right to be persevering to

the bitter end with the present policy mix because the alternatives are all worse. Withdrawal of UNPROFOR and lifting the arms embargo is all too likely to lead to a spread of the war and the involvement of Muslim contingents in a European civil war. So we could find ourselves trying to operate a containment policy at a line further back than now and in even less promising conditions. The stresses all this would put on future relations with Russia could become pretty troublesome too.

6 We should continue to support Security Council enlargement without becoming attached to a particular timetable and without allowing the effectiveness of the Council to be impaired. Our own Permanent Membership remains a national asset which we should not contemplate losing or diluting. We sustain it very effectively without in fact doing or spending more proportionately on the UN than many other countries which are not Permanent Members, such as Canada or Sweden. Our Permanent Membership will be particularly crucial in the formative years of the European Union's Common Foreign and Security Policy since it secures us a discreet way of controlling that policy as it develops.

7 We should work energetically to reform the UN's finances. The proposals we and the Swedes have put forward will be bitterly resisted by all the countries who have to pay more, but the proposals, or some variant of them, offer the only hope for a negotiated outcome rather than one imposed by the United States which is liable to leave us, as well as a good many others, paying more.

8 We should press for managerial reforms in the UN Secretariat and for reform of the economic and social work of the UN and its specialised agencies so as to reduce waste and duplication. A good start was made at the G8 Summit in Halifax but the hard part remains to be done. The Group of 77 are likely to be resistant but they have no coherent alternative agenda of their own. If we are to get their acquiescence, which is essential, we will need to be seen to be working for better value for aid money, not just to pocket the savings.

9 A Secretary-General to take the UN into the twenty-first century will need to be chosen towards the end of next year, just when the United States will be electing its next President. I suggest we should approach this cautiously. We do not want a nonentity, because no international organisation we value is going to be run to our satisfaction by a nonentity. Boutros-Ghali's age will count against him but there are few Third World politicians likely to be as responsive as he has been to European interests and attitudes. The Americans may hand him the black spot; but infirmity of purpose is endemic in this administration so, again, they may not.

10 We should continue to bring home to the Americans the long-term value we and other Europeans attach to an effective United Nations. This is a lesson that needs to be absorbed on the Hill more than in the administration. Where possible we should try to find solutions and reforms which help the American body politic feel more comfortable with the UN but not to the extent of damaging the organisation's structure and viability.

Of my 36 years in the Service, 31 have been spent labouring in the vineyards of multilateral diplomacy. This may or may not reflect credit on the management but it has given me a fairly wide experience of these matters, beginning with a moribund regional security organisation (CENTO), leading on to many years of work on and in the European Community (a much pleasanter and more apposite title in my view than the European Union) and ending with the UN. What has struck me is the extent to which Britain's interests are now best protected and pursued through this network of international organisations and disciplines. During the first half of this century we learned by bitter experience how a world without such disciplines and organisations could tear itself apart. Two world wars and one world economic slump gave us plenty of lessons about the destructive capacity of the nation state if it fell into the hands of evil tyrants or if it succumbed to the siren songs of protectionism and tit-for-tat devaluation. Since the Second World War Britain's relative decline has in any case limited to a much greater extent than before our ability to defend ourselves and to further our interests by our own efforts alone. The list of issues which require a global or at least a regional response if they are to be effectively mastered grows longer every year. So I believe we have been right to have put a lot of emphasis on and resources into multilateral work and will be right to continue doing so. Our performance is often the envy of our partners and rivals and that is as it should be if we are to sustain the high standards of professionalism to which we have always aspired.

In recent years this trend towards global or regional cooperation has come in for a good deal of criticism. It is said to be wasteful and inefficient; it is usurping the powers of the nation state and assuming an unacceptable degree of authority over it. Much of this criticism springs from a mistaken belief that we are participating in a titanic struggle between the forces of world or regional federalism on the one hand and those of the nation state on the other. But that is surely wide of the mark. There are of course world or regional federalists and very zealous they are in propagating their views; but they are a minority, and they are not about to cease being one. The essence of the matter is that international organisations and disciplines exist to limit the capacity of nation states for self-destruction and for damaging each other needlessly and to enable them to handle successfully a widening range of problems which they cannot master on their own.

I must also confess that I have got through those 36 years without once being required to play a serious role in management (other than running the policy side of two large multilateral posts) so I will spare my audience the parting thoughts often lavished by others on how the Service is, or should be, run. What I should like to say a word about in parting is the pleasure and pride it has given me to serve in a body which seems to me to have adapted and transformed itself quite remarkably during the time I have been in it. The Service of 1995 is totally different from that of 1959. It is now, I believe, as close to a genuine meritocracy as one can get. The cult of the gifted amateur is dead. We set high professional standards and we achieve them (most of the time, anyway). The skill, professionalism and the willingness to work exceptionally anti-social hours of all the staff, without exception, with whom I have worked in Brussels and in New York has been beyond praise and price. The fact that this is only imperfectly understood by the majority of our countrymen is a cause of sadness to me but it does not detract from the achievement. A country like Britain needs a first class Diplomatic Service far more now than it did in the high days of empire. The fact that it has got one is good; the fact that it does not seem to realise it is not.

A fuller account of the UN's first five post-Cold War years is contained in the author's book New World Disorder: The UN after the Cold War – An Insiders View, *I.B.Tauris (2008).*

12

BRITISH SPECIAL REPRESENTATIVE
FOR CYPRUS 1996–2003

MISSION IMPOSSIBLE?

Retirement from the Diplomatic Service was a major change for my wife and I since we had spent the last 35 years within that particular cocoon. We decided that, rather than taking the quick, short, eastward route back from New York and slipping into the torpor of London's holiday season, we would take a longer, western route through China and Central Asia and devote a full two months to the journey. Although I had been once to China on an official visit, in 1975, we had seen nothing of China as a country and as a society; and it seemed to make sense to try to know a little more about a nation, which, it was already clear, was bound to become one of the great powers of the twenty-first century. As for Central Asia we were, a trifle belatedly, plugging a gap caused by the Foreign Office's ban on holiday travel by diplomats to the Soviet Union, which had frustrated our attempts to go to Bokhara, Samarqand and Khiva during our time in Afghanistan. We did not regret the decision. For one thing it provided the complete break with our professional life in New York which we both felt we needed; and, while our travels were certainly no rest-cure, we arrived back in London in September 1995 intellectually refreshed and with any vestigial nostalgia for the diplomatic circuit washed away. Our route through China, from the south-east corner to the extreme north-west, where the road crossed the frontier into Pakistan at 14,000 feet as we made our way down the Karakoram highway, while designed for purely cultural and tourist purposes, did provide an educational crash course in a country undergoing a revolutionary economic and societal transition from a command economy with a total absence of personal freedoms and choice to a mixed economy growing at a headlong pace, where discussion with foreigners of pretty well any aspect of life apart from politics itself was no longer taboo.

For five weeks we met no one but Chinese and, although pretty well every one of those Chinese was an employee of the state – tourist guides being trained in the same academies as future diplomats – we learned a lot. Every day brought not only historic sites of astonishing beauty and interest, but long discussions of the social consequences of the regime's 'one child' policy (demographically positive but pretty disastrous for future generations in the absence of any state provision for care of the elderly), of environmental pollution (quite appalling everywhere until we got to the under-populated deserts of Xinjiang, but invariably described to us as 'your problem' as if it was the West that was choking from the contaminated air and being poisoned by the polluted rivers) and of the treatment of ethnic minorities (frankly neo-colonial, particularly when we reached Kashgar, where the rumblings of Uighur discontent could already be felt, although it had not yet broken out into violence). From Pakistan we flew direct to Tashkent, the capital of Uzbekistan, passing over Afghanistan at 35,000 feet on the very day when the Kabul mob sacked the former British embassy (by then the Pakistani Embassy) in retaliation for the seizure of Herat by the Taliban. This was a reminder, if one were needed, of one of the major sins of omission during my time on the Security Council, namely the decision to wind down the UN mission in Afghanistan after the Soviet withdrawal from the country and the collapse of the communist regime. Samarqand, Bokhara and Khiva proved to be well worth waiting for, as fine examples of Islamic architecture and tile-work as can be found anywhere in the world. Politically the situation was odd rather than interesting. 'It's a bit like the Soviet Union during the Brezhnev era' was the way one Russian we met put it. The search for a historical narrative for Uzbekistan, a country which had never, as such, previously existed was taking some strange turns, a large equestrian statue of Tamerlane having just gone up in front of our Tashkent hotel impervious of the fact that his dynasty had made a hobby of slaughtering Uzbeks. And thence we came back to London and to earth.

Life in New York had not been conducive of any systematic thinking about what I was going to do next, let alone any planning on how to fill the vacuum that lay ahead. I had one or two prejudices about what I did not want to do; I did not want a full-time job; I did not want to be considered to head an Oxford or Cambridge college, which seemed to me all too similar to diplomatic life. Having spent almost all my professional career in multilateral diplomacy I did not have the sort of experience and range of contacts in particular key markets which tended to make diplomats attractive recruits to business or banking. I remained deeply interested in international affairs and in particular in the future development of what was by then (since the ratification of the Maastricht Treaty) known as the European Union and of the United Nations. But I had no clear idea as to how that interest might be pursued other than, as I began to do straight away, by acting as an occasional commentator on television and radio and undertaking some journalistic work and some writing for think-tanks.

Then, quite out of the blue, I was approached in February 1996 by Jeremy Greenstock, at that time the Political Director in the FCO, to sound out whether I would take on a newly created part-time appointment as the government's Special Representative for Cyprus. Although at that time I had never set foot on the island, I was certainly no stranger to the many attempts that had been made to resolve its problems and to reunite a country which had been divided since the Turkish military intervention in 1974 following the Greek-inspired coup to overthrow President Makarios. I had been directly involved in New York in the last two such attempts, the negotiations for a settlement between George Vassiliou and Rauf Denktash in 1992 and the subsequent negotiations over a set of confidence-building measures between Glafcos Clerides (Vassiliou's successor as Greek Cypriot leader) and Rauf Denktash in 1993–4, both of which had failed, mainly due to the obstinacy of Denktash and the unwillingness of successive Turkish governments to press him to agree to the sort of compromises that would be needed if any deal was to be struck. Indeed I had a vivid recollection of having dinner with Clerides and Denktash in one of New York's more expensive French restaurants and asking them when they were going to stop thumping the ball from the baseline and come in to the net, to be met by a joint chorus of 'but then we would be out of a job'. And I was also very much aware, because I had argued strongly against it from my position at the UN in New York, that the European Union had, early in 1995, given up most of the leverage that the Greek Cypriot membership application provided by making it clear that Cyprus would be in the next group of acceding countries and that a settlement of the Cyprus problem was not a necessary condition for accession. So I was under no illusion at all as to the scale of the challenge I was being asked to undertake and as to the probable chances of success. Nevertheless, it did seem to me that the case for making a major effort to reach a settlement in Cyprus was unanswerable given the negative consequences of a still-divided island entering the EU, not least for Turkey's own application for membership which I had by then (in contrast to my attitude in 1990) come to see as highly desirable. So I agreed to take the job. I imposed one condition and accepted another. The condition I imposed was that my work should be directed at building up a joint approach involving the USA and the main EU member states, with the UN firmly in the lead as crucial facilitator/ mediator, and that there should be no question of a solo British initiative, which, given the historical background in Cyprus, would have been doomed to failure and which would only have complicated the task of others. This approach was readily agreed. The condition imposed on me was that nothing I did or proposed should put at risk the progress towards EU membership of the countries of Central and Eastern Europe which remained one of the British government's highest priorities, that is to say that the threat of a Greek veto if a still-divided Cyprus looked like being left out of the next enlargement was to be taken seriously. Should I have contested that condition? It certainly made my task more difficult. But I shared the government's view on the enlargement priorities and the pass had already been sold about the possibility of a divided Cyprus acceding. Moreover, as I pointed out again and again to all my Turkish interlocutors and to Denktash, if the EU accession card was to be viable it required clear evidence that the Turkish Cypriots and Turkey were negotiating in good faith for a settlement; otherwise it simply amounted to giving Denktash and Turkey a veto over the accession of Cyprus. And of that evidence there was no trace for many years to come.

A few weeks later I found myself sitting next to the Foreign Secretary, Malcolm Rifkind, being presented to the press as Britain's first ever Special Representative for Cyprus. One of the journalists asked whether I was not aware that Cyprus was the graveyard of diplomats; my reply, that I was now beyond the grave in diplomatic terms, raised a laugh but underlined one major difficulty inherent in the job, which dogged my footsteps throughout, that of achieving any real credibility for a process which had failed so often in the past.

A fuller account of the Cyprus negotiations of this period is contained in the author's book Cyprus: the Search for a Solution, *I.B.Tauris (2005).*

And so began seven years of hard labour in one of the stoniest diplomatic vineyards I had ever been asked to till, by the end of which time a job which had begun as a part-time one was getting close to becoming a full-time charge. And so too began the travels of which the job was principally composed – to the inner quadrilateral of south and north Nicosia, Athens and Ankara, to the key capitals of Washington, Paris, Berlin, Rome and Moscow, and to the international organisation hubs of New York, Geneva and Brussels (both the EU and NATO). In those early months, as I built up a network of contacts and listened to what my various interlocutors had to say – mainly manipulative, alas, but I had been in diplomacy too long to be surprised by or to worry about that – I immersed myself in the detail of the previous attempts to resolve the Cyprus problem and did my best to draw the right lessons from their failure. Perhaps the most striking thing was how little had been agreed in those interminable confabulations. The Greek and Turkish Cypriot community leaders had only ever signed up in those more than 30 years of intensive negotiation to two pretty skimpy texts, the High Level Agreements of 1977 and 1979. Those agreements were not to be despised, since they did shift the two parties away from the doomed independence constitution of 1960, which established a unitary state of Cyprus, inevitably dominated by the majority community, the Greek Cypriots, with the Turkish Cypriots treated as a minority, to the concept of a bi-zonal, bi-communal federation. But that achievement concealed the fact that there was no agreement on what that magic formula actually meant, the Turkish Cypriots hankering after a confederal approach and the Greek Cypriots never really conceding the political equality that a federal approach implied.

Meanwhile, the 1992 negotiations had put onto the table a mass of UN-sponsored material required to flesh out the formula, which was known as the 'Set of Ideas'. My early contacts revealed that Clerides, who had defeated Vassiliou in the 1993 Presidential election by opposing the 'Set of Ideas', had no particular objection to the substantive content of most of those ideas, while Denktash always said that he accepted 90 per cent of them, although he was evasive over what made up the 10 per cent he did not accept. So my first broad conclusion was that a new negotiating effort needed to avoid reinventing the wheel and searching for some silver bullet which others had failed to discover, and should instead be based firmly on the High Level Agreements and the material already on the table, with adjustments to that material being worked out on an incremental basis. That conclusion stood the test of time reasonably well. The second conclusion I reached was that the earlier attempts had failed partly because they represented a halfway house to a full settlement; so, even if agreement had been reached on the 'Set of Ideas' in 1992, a mass of further negotiation would have been required before it became the basis for a comprehensive settlement. But the mistrust between the two parties, which had built up over the years meant that no two-stage approach was ever going to work. What was required was a comprehensive, self-executing set of agreements covering every detail of the new, reunited Cyprus. That became the approach of the UN after one or two false starts in 1997. And then there was, thirdly, the will-o'-the wisp of Confidence Building Measures that had consumed a huge amount of time and effort in 1993–4 and come to nothing. This too was a case of each side believing that any such measure conceded to the other side some crucial aspect of the final settlement that must be held back until an overall deal was struck. So setting off down that false trail again needed to be avoided at all costs; and it was. I also identified two much less clear-cut challenges. The first was the difficulty of ever bringing negotiations to a head and creating the conditions for an endgame. That would have been reasonably straightforward if both parties had been negotiating in good faith; but in Cyprus they never had been and they still were not. At various times in the past both sides had been led by rejectionists. When I came onto the scene there was at least one leader who fell into that category, Rauf Denktash. So the question inevitably arose whether his attitude could be influenced by Turkey and, if so, in what circumstances. The answer to that conundrum was to remain obscure for several more years. It would also have been more feasible if either side had felt under the overwhelming pressure of circumstances to bring an end to the status quo. But neither did. The Greek Cypriots were prospering economically and seemed set fair in their objective of joining the EU; the Turkish Cypriots had the shield of 35,000 Turkish troops to protect them and the cushion of a large annual subsidy from Turkey to compensate for their economic weakness. At some stage it was clear to me that the UN and its international backers, ourselves included, would have to launch a 'do or die' attempt to get an agreement, but the conditions under which that might make sense were not obvious. The second unclear challenge was a new one, which had not been present to the same degree in previous negotiations, and that was the interplay of the respective aspirations for EU membership of Cyprus and Turkey. While the concept of Cyprus joining the EU while it was still divided could not be excluded, it was quite clear that Turkey could not hope to join an EU to which both Greece and Cyprus belonged without there having been a solution to the Cyprus problem. But the straightforward approach of synchronising the two candidatures was simply not available even if there had not been deep divisions within the EU over the whole concept of Turkish membership. The question rather was whether the two sets of aspirations could be so handled as to bring about positive inputs at the Cyprus negotiating table. Not easily was the honest answer to that question; but it had to be tried.

The first priority was to get some kind of negotiating show on the road. There was at first little appetite for this at the UN, as I discovered when I met the Secretary-General in Geneva in the summer of 1996. Boutros-Ghali was still licking his wounds after a second lengthy effort to move the Cyprus problem forward (the 1993-4 negotiations over Confidence Building Measures); he had fallen out with Denktash in a big way and believed that nothing would be achieved as long as he controlled Turkish Cypriot (and Turkish) policy. He was himself facing a difficult campaign for re-election (he was in fact – in my view unjustifiably – vetoed by the USA later in the year) and, while he had appointed a new Special Representative for Cyprus, Han Sung Joo, a former South Korean foreign minister, Han was based half a world away in Seoul and was an infrequent and largely passive visitor to the region. Nor were either Clerides or Denktash or their principal backers in Athens and Ankara in any hurry to re-engage in a serious negotiation for a comprehensive settlement. The Greek Foreign Minister, Theodoros Pangalos, with memories of previous difficult exchanges between us during my time in Brussels, refused to see me; he was in any case more interested in nursing a grievance over Cyprus than in resolving it. In Ankara I met Bülent Ecevit, in opposition at the time but shortly to emerge again as Prime Minister, whose line was that he had settled Cyprus in 1974 and that there was therefore nothing to negotiate about. Cyprus was seen in Brussels as part of a purely technical accession process; and the Greek Cypriots, taking a leaf out of the previous negotiations for Greece's accession, were prepared to sign on any dotted line that was presented to them.

Washington had, as so often before and since, plenty of higher priorities than Cyprus to focus on. So I found myself, to borrow a phrase from a British politician, going around stirring up apathy. Nevertheless, little by little, some life came back into the negotiating process. When Malcolm Rifkind went to the island towards the end of 1996 – in itself something of an innovation since British foreign secretaries had tended to keep away from Cyprus for fear of creating domestic controversy among Britain's numerous ethnic Cypriots from both communities – he was able to set out in public ten points, drawn mainly from the 'Set of Ideas', which he believed established sufficient common ground to justify a further negotiating effort. I had advised him not to try to negotiate the ten points with Clerides and Denktash; and this paid off since his statement provoked only the slightest of grumbles. And, following that, the new UN Secretary-General, Kofi Annan decided to take up the baton and to pursue a more active role on Cyprus. Unfortunately that first, resumed effort by the UN hit the buffers soon enough. Annan held two meetings with the Cypriot leaders in the summer of 1997 one outside New York and the other near Montreux in Switzerland. But, instead of trying to establish a serous negotiating process, he was persuaded by his new Special Representative Diego Cordovez, a former Ecuadorean Foreign Minister who was based in Quito, almost as far away from Cyprus as Han had been, to go for a short and fairly vapid text of generalities which appealed to neither side and which Denktash rejected outright. In truth, the two meetings were doomed anyway because the Turks were deeply angered at the way the EU was handling their own application for membership (negatively to the point of insult) and also that of Cyprus (far too positively for their taste) and Denktash was never someone to miss such an opportunity to stake out an intransigent position. What was not inevitable was that the UN let the negotiating thread drop entirely. I had argued against the attempt to agree a text of generalities and against allowing the negotiating thread to drop but, perhaps somewhat handicapped by a broken ankle which I had incurred scrambling down a hillside in France a couple of weeks before, I made no impact. It was to take two weary years for the UN to pick the thread up again.

*   *   *

Working on a solution to the Cyprus problem was nothing if it was not Sisyphean; the stone was pushed painfully and laboriously towards the top of the hill only for it to roll back down, sometimes even further down that it had been before, leaving the whole process to start all over again. So those two lost years from September 1997 to December 1999, when direct talks between the parties started again in New York, required much effort for little return. A stand-off between Turkey and Cyprus over the latter's purchase of Russian S-300 missiles was resolved by the diversion of the missiles to Crete. The damage to Turkey's relationship with the EU was gradually repaired. The pressure for resumed negotiations for a Cyprus settlement was built up though the G8 and the UN Security Council. When negotiations did resume at the end of 1999 they did so, moreover, under considerably better auspices than in 1997. For one thing the departure of Pangalos as Greek Foreign Minister and his replacement by George Papandreou brought about a sea-change in Greek foreign policy that was now firmly committed to a fundamental rapprochement with Turkey, an outcome that could only be fully achieved if there was a settlement in Cyprus. As Turkey received formal recognition of its EU candidature in December 1999, so also, but not purely coincidentally, that crucial dimension of the equation came properly into play for the first time. The US administration, after a brief, cameo appearance on the Cyprus scene by Richard Holbrooke which got nowhere – the Cyprus problem was singularly resistant to the sort of meteoric, high pressure tactics he deployed

– settled down to make a serious and effective contribution as part of the international coalition supporting resumed negotiations. The EU Commission in Brussels began to cooperate closely with the UN. And the latter appointed an experienced and highly competent negotiator, Álvaro de Soto, a Peruvian who had played a key role in the El Salvador peace process, as full-time head of a small but talented negotiating team, to steer and facilitate the negotiations.

The two Cypriot leaders were the same as before. But, over time, it had become clear to me that Clerides, for all his undoubted guile and caution really was negotiating in good faith for an outcome that would require him to make some substantial compromises. He took to inviting me for a day's swimming from his yacht and our long conversations, although not directed towards negotiating detail, reinforced that view. Denktash had not changed, however, and my matching engagement with him over many a long meal offered no cause for optimism. He was completely impervious to the growing desire of many of his own people to become part of Cyprus' EU accession process; and, advised as he was by Mümtaz Soysal, a former Turkish Foreign Minister, who was a strong critic of Turkey's own EU application, he was equally impervious, indeed hostile, to the consideration that a Cyprus settlement was an essential part of Turkey's EU accession strategy. It was clear therefore that finding a way around the Denktash road-block was going to be necessary; however, given Denktash's commanding position in Turkish Cypriot politics and his popularity in Turkey itself, that was clearly going to be no easy matter. Indeed, the first major test went entirely Denktash's way. By November 2000 he was sufficiently alarmed by the progress de Soto and Annan were making in the talks and by the first signs that they were beginning to put together the elements of a comprehensive settlement that he walked out of the talks and obtained Ecevit's support for breaking off the whole process. It was another Sisyphean moment, but this time the UN did not drop the negotiating thread.

And so another lost year supervened. The wide international coalition supporting the UN pressed the Turks and Denktash to return to the negotiations. The USA believed they had brokered with the Turks the conditions for Denktash to come back to the table. A meeting between Clerides and Denktash was scheduled for 11 September 2001 in New York; but it was not only the terrorist attack on the Twin Towers which prevented its taking place (although that did leave me grounded in London); Denktash balked again. And then, quite out of the blue, in early November, Denktash wrote to Clerides (once again in New York for the interrupted session of the UN General Assembly) proposing that they resume direct negotiations and posing none of the unacceptable pre-conditions for doing so which he had presented over the preceding year. I saw Clerides as he was considering his response and he sought my reaction. Accept the offer and ignore the rhetoric in Denktash's letter, was my advice; and so Clerides did. Thereafter negotiations continued on the island on a regular basis until the late summer of 2002. What had caused Denktash to blink? No explanation for his volte-face was ever proffered, and it had to be said that his conduct in the resumed negotiations showed no more flexibility than before he had broken them off. It seemed reasonably clear that the Turks had become increasingly alarmed about the implications of a complete deadlock over Cyprus for their own EU candidature which was moving towards a decision point in late 2002. So, while the negotiations themselves produced no agreements, although they provided the occasion for Clerides to offer tentatively some important reassurance to the Turks about their security concerns and the continuing validity of the Treaty of Guarantee under which they had intervened in 1974, they did enable the UN gradually to piece together the mosaic of a comprehensive settlement plan. From the time of the European Council in June 2002 it was also clear that final decisions on Cyprus' EU application (together with those of the Central and Eastern European applicants) and an important stage in Turkey's application would both be reached at the December European Council in Copenhagen.

So at last we had what every previous Cyprus negotiator had longed for but never been granted, the conditions for moving to an endgame. But by now the timetable had switched from being open-ended to being perilously short. At that point Denktash played a wild card by disappearing into a New York hospital for heart surgery and by then prolonging his convalescence up to and beyond the December European Council. As if that was not a sufficient complication, Turkey's coalition government broke up in the summer following an economic crisis and the subsequent general election campaign presaged a major upheaval in Turkish politics, with the new and entirely untried moderate Islamist AK party predicted to come out on top. Throughout 2002 de Soto, Tom Weston, the US Cyprus coordinator, and I criss-crossed the region in a concerted effort to put together the elements of that endgame and to build up the momentum towards it. We consciously decided neither to be diverted by Denktash's temporary absence from the scene nor by the Turkish election. The Turkish diplomatic machine continued to function and indeed began to engage in a much more effective way than ever before with de Soto over the detailed content of a settlement; and Clerides, while keeping up his guard in public, privately responded with some flexibility to de Soto's probing.

The endgame began in early November when the UN Secretary-General tabled what subsequently came to be known as the Annan Plan. This comprehensive set of agreements provided for a substantial transfer of territory to the Greek Cypriot Federated State; for the withdrawal of all Turkish troops from the island by the time of Turkey's accession to the EU; for the deployment of an international peacekeeping force to oversee the implementation of the settlement; for the settlement of property disputes by a combination of restitution and compensation; for the institutions of a newly reunited federal Cyprus with extensive powers for its two component federated states; and for the reunited island to join the EU. The reaction from Clerides was muted; that from Denktash defiant. By the end of the month Annan had produced a second version, amended to take account of criticisms raised by both sides (and by the Turks, whose new AK government under the temporary leadership of Abdullah Gül showed every sign of being ready to negotiate – his mantra was 'no solution is no solution'). The key question, however, remained of how to bring matters on the Annan Plan to a decision point with Denktash sulking in his tent, or rather his hospital bed. I was in Cyprus late in November and conferred with de Soto. We were both convinced that matters must be brought to a head in advance of and not at the Copenhagen meeting. In that way, maximum pressure would be exerted on all the parties. The only way we could see of doing that was for Annan to invite Clerides within the next few days to New York where Denktash was convalescing and put matters to the test. We spoke to Weston in Washington on a secure line from an

UNFICYP hut on the old Nicosia airfield that had been put out of use since the fighting in 1974. We completely failed to convince him. He argued that the right place to bring about a denouement was at the Copenhagen meeting itself. I said that, from all my experience of European Council meetings, it would simply not work.

A meeting scheduled to deal in any case with two hugely important issues, enlargement and future Turkish accession, would simply not be able to cope with the complexities of a Cyprus endgame moving in parallel but quite separately. But Weston was not to be budged and without firm US support the UN was not prepared to move ahead with de Soto's and my New York scenario. I still believe that at that point the best chance of achieving a settlement slipped through our fingers. The Copenhagen meetings turned out as I had feared. The EU was entirely preoccupied with enlargement and with a difficult and contentious discussion over Turkey's accession; Denktash refused to come to Copenhagen and sent his intransigent foreign minister who did not even make a pretence of negotiating; and the Turks themselves were distracted over the handling of an EU response to their own candidature which, while broadly positive, fell short of what they had hoped for. It was a thoroughly dispiriting occasion that left the Greek Cypriots in an infinitely stronger position than before, with the prize of accession by a still-divided island firmly in their hands.

*   *   *

In the New Year of 2003 the Cyprus negotiations went into extra time, but they did not do so against a positive political background. Quite the contrary. A Greek Cypriot Presidential election was in full swing and it was soon clear that Clerides was losing his bid for a third term to Tassos Papadopoulos, who all who knew him, myself included, recognised was an out and out rejectionist who would look for every way of avoiding a genuine compromise agreement. The Turkish government, whose attitude was the key if some way was to be found around the Denktash roadblock, was becoming totally preoccupied by the imminent US and UK invasion of Iraq and the problem of responding to the request to allow their NATO allies' troops to use their territory in so doing. The only glimmer of light was in the north of Cyprus where large public demonstrations were taking place against Denktash's policy and in favour of joining the EU along with the Greek Cypriots; but these protests, led by the business community and by the main opposition leader Mehmet Ali Talat, who later succeeded Denktash as President, impressive and unprecedented though they were, did not alter the fact that Denktash remained the designated Turkish Cypriot negotiator.

By the time Annan visited the region and came to the island at the end of February to present a second revision of his original proposals (known as Annan III), with further adjustments on a number of sensitive points to take account of concerns expressed by both sides, the negative factors had intensified. Papadopoulos had won the Greek Cypriot Presidential election, and a vote was imminent in the Turkish Parliament on the request to allow allied troops to transit the country (it was in fact lost on 1 March). Annan's visit to the island was inconclusive, with Denktash and Papadopoulos sparring with him but not really engaging; and he therefore decided to bank everything on a make-or-break meeting in The Hague ten days later. That meeting ranks among the most depressing events of my diplomatic career. The outside players all did their best to strengthen Annan's hand. A few days before I had persuaded the British government to offer to return nearly half the territory of the UK's Sovereign Base Areas in Cyprus in the event of an agreement being reached (a concession which would have been of particular benefit to the Greek Cypriots); both the British Prime Minister and the US President weighed in with telephone calls to Ankara; the Greek government was very supportive. But it was to no avail. Denktash continued to breathe defiance; the Turks declined to put any pressure on him; and all Papadopoulos had to do was to sit on his hands. I walked around the garden of the Peace Palace in The Hague, home of the International Court of Justice, where the meetings were taking place, with Kofi Annan on the last afternoon of the negotiations; our mood matched the biting chill of the March wind blowing in off the North Sea as we contemplated the failure of several years of intensive negotiation. Much later that night Annan and de Soto admitted defeat. I do not know whether Denktash or Papadopoulos looked more pleased with themselves and with the outcome when they briefed the press.

Following the breakdown of the negotiations I took stock of my own position and consulted our ambassadors in the region with whom I had worked so closely and so fruitfully for so long. My main concern was that I risked becoming part of the problem rather than part of the solution. The Greek Cypriots, never averse to playing the man rather than the ball and never less so than when the man in question was British, were depicting me as the real author of the Annan Plan, which was thus merely the latest in a long line of conspiracies by the former colonial power to subvert Cyprus' independence and to trap it in an unbalanced deal. This conspiracy theme might be overheated nonsense, but I was not going to find it easy to controvert it; and it risked undermining any attempt by the UN to pick up the thread of the negotiations once tempers had cooled after the meeting in The Hague. Moreover, I was extremely sceptical as to whether any renewed effort was likely to be successful so long as Papadopoulos was in control of the Greek Cypriot side of the negotiation. After weighing up the pros and cons carefully, I advised the Foreign Secretary, Jack Straw, not to renew my appointment as Special Representative when it next came up for decision in May 2003, and not to replace me; and he accepted that advice. When Kofi Annan telephoned me early in 2004 to consult me and to say that he was about to resume the negotiations, I was pretty lukewarm about the prospects, while recognising that evidence of Turkish enthusiasm for reaching a deal was encouraging. I was no more than an appalled spectator of the subsequent events, as Papadopoulos first agreed that Annan's final version of his plan should be put to referendums in each of the two communities and then campaigned vigorously, viciously and successfully for a 'no' vote by the Greek Cypriots. The 'yes' vote by the Turkish Cypriots did nothing to conceal the fact that the best opportunity to settle this long-running and debilitating international dispute had slipped though the hands of the international community and was not likely to be retrieved any time soon.

Anyone involved in a failed negotiation, such as this one had been, needs to ask some searching questions about whether that failure could have been avoided and, if so, how. That mistakes were made is not in doubt. The role of the international supporters of the UN – the USA, the UK and the EU – was certainly too prominent for comfort and allowed those in Cyprus, the majority, who believe sincerely that they are treated like pawns by the great powers to nourish that illusion. Admitting that mistake does not, however, provide a viable way round the unwillingness of the two Cypriot parties to negotiate in a spirit of give and take. Also it was a mistake to have put the Annan Plan to a popular vote without making it a pre-condition that the leaders of the two communities sign up to it in advance and campaign for it. This device, which successfully circumvented the Denktash road-block, fell straight into the Papadopoulos trap. That should certainly not be repeated. But the biggest mistake was made by Denktash, in wasting years of negotiating time while the Greek Cypriots were at their most vulnerable, making their way though the intricacies of the EU accession process; and by Turkey in supporting for so long his policy of obfuscation and prevarication. I am as certain as one can be of something which is not susceptible of proof that, if Denktash and the Turks had negotiated in good faith and with flexibility between 1996 and 2002 and if the UN-led negotiations had been brought to a head during that period, there would have been a settlement and the Greek Cypriots, giving priority to the prize of EU membership, would have voted for it. Naturally there are defects in every one of the iterations of the Annan Plan. How could it have been otherwise with any set of agreements of such complexity? But it is hard to see how a deadlocked situation of indefinite duration, in which none of the territory that came under Turkish Cypriot control in 1974 is transferred to the Greek Cypriot Federated State, in which no one on either side dispossessed of their property gets restitution, in which the number of Turkish troops on the island is not reduced and in which the Cyprus problem remains a source of instability in the eastern Mediterranean can be described objectively as a preferable alternative. The fact that many on both sides of the dispute will denounce this analysis is perhaps as clear an indication as there can be of why this dispute has proved to be so intractable. Even now I do not consider that a solution is impossible. But the key requirement for it, now that divided Cyprus is inside the European Union, that Turkey should be making irreversible progress towards its own accession, looks unlikely to be fulfilled in the near future.

13

MEMBER OF THE UN SECRETARY-GENERAL'S HIGH LEVEL PANEL ON THREATS, CHALLENGES AND CHANGE 2003–2005

REFORMING THE UN

The next unexpected twist in my professional life was not long in coming. The UN had been severely damaged by the run-up to the invasion of Iraq in March 2003 and even more so by its aftermath. It was just about possible to argue that the deadlock in the Security Council in the winter of 2003 and the confrontation there between the foreign ministers of two of its Permanent Members (the USA and the UK) and the other three (France, Russia and China) together with Germany, had some positive aspects in that it demonstrated a willingness to stand up to pressure from a US administration which had clearly decided on the invasion come what may. The killing in August of Sergio Vieira de Melo, the head of the UN mission in Baghdad, and a number of his colleagues was a cloud without any conceivable silver lining. And it undermined one of Annan's greatest assets, the liking and respect that he enjoyed throughout the organisation. So, when he gave his annual 'State of the UN' address to the General Assembly that September he warned that the organisation stood at a fork in the road, one possibility being increasing disorder and descent into a Hobbesian law of the jungle, the other being a serious effort to reform the UN and to remedy its obvious weaknesses. He announced that he was appointing a high level panel to review the whole span of the organisation's activities and to make recommendations for reform to him that he would then pass on to the membership for decision. My own reaction to this was to feel that he was right to blow the whistle on the membership and warn them of the consequences of inaction. Events in Iraq had meant that a 'business as usual' approach lacked any credibility and would be a recipe for further decline. But it was also clear that Annan was taking a bit of a gamble. The road to UN reforms of any kind, let alone to a major, systemic overview of the sort he appeared to envisage, was littered with the whitening bones of previous Secretary-Generals and distinguished panels. If he ended up with empty hands his, and the organisation's, last state would be even worse than its first. The Bush administration, whose influence on the process was bound to weigh heavily, was not about to undergo a multilateralist epiphany. And there remained the unresolved issue of Security Council enlargement whose capacity to swallow up or to wreck the whole reform exercise was not to be underestimated. Those thoughts crossed my mind, but they did not stay there for long since I did not see myself playing any role in the matter. And then, a week or two after Annan's General Assembly speech, I took a telephone call from Kieran Prendergast, an old friend of many years standing and currently UN Under-Secretary-General for Political Affairs, to say that Annan would like me to serve as a member of his panel. For all my initial misgivings I did not take long to decide to accept. I liked and admired Annan and wanted to help him if I could. My conscience told me too that I had neglected, and indeed tended to be cynical about, proposals for reform when I had been in a position to influence them. The missed opportunities of the first post-Cold War decade were ones for which I, among many others, bore some responsibility. So, yet again, I found myself taking on a job which was described as a part-time activity (and this time unpaid too), but which came, over the next two years, to absorb a very large amount of my time and energy.

The membership of the panel was certainly eclectic. Being a UN body it naturally contained a careful balance of gender and of nationalities – one each from the five Permanent Members of the Security Council and representation from all the main regions. It included a substantial number of members with political experience – former Prime Ministers such as the chair of the panel, Anand Panyarachun from Thailand, Gro Harlem Brundtland of Norway and Yevgeny Primakov of Russia, former foreign ministers such as Qian Qichen of China, Gareth Evans of Australia, Amr Moussa of Egypt and Salim Salim of Tanzania. But it also included a fair number of members who had headed up international organisations, not exclusively those which were part of the UN family – Sadako Ogata of the UN High Commission for Refugees, Nafis Sadik of the United Nations Population Fund (UNFPA), Enrique Iglesias of the Inter-American Development Bank and João Baena Soares of the Organisation of American States – and some, Moussa who was Secretary-General of the Arab League, Salim who had been Secretary-General of the Organisation of African Unity and Brundtland who had been Director-General of the World Health Organization, who overlapped these two categories. And then there was a scattering of diplomats and former military figures, the latter including Brent Scowcroft who had twice been US National Security Adviser. No one could criticise the panel as lacking experience but there was a certain amount of sniping about excessive age from the nearly 200 ambassadors in New York, many of whom believed they should have been put in charge of reforming the UN. The risk of throwing together such a galaxy was that individual preferences and personalities would triumph over any collective view of what was needed and that attendance would be sporadic and disjointed. But neither of these two failings transpired. Attendance held up extremely well from the beginning to the end of the cycle of six three day meetings that were fitted into the single year of the panel's work. Most of the panellists already knew each other; and, while there were, from time to time, quite sharp tensions over sensitive issues, these never got out of control nor split the panel into different groups opposed to each other.

I myself worked particularly closely with Robert Badinter, the French representative on the panel and a former Minister of Justice, and with Gareth Evans with whom I see eye to eye on pretty well every issue and whose intellectual brilliance and driving force never cease to amaze me. Badinter and I, as the only two members from the European Union, made sure that its collective interests were kept to the fore and that its representatives in the form of the Political

Directors of the member states were kept fully informed of what was going on. The credit for the effectiveness of the panel's collegiality should go in considerable part to our research director, Stephen Stedman of Stanford University, who rapidly established a position of trust and confidence with all the members; it helped greatly that he was not an official from the UN Secretariat and was thus able to protect the panel from being subjected to the pet nostrums that such officials had accumulated over the years and which had been, as regularly, rejected by the member states.

From the very outset we were faced with a number of largely procedural choices, which, as is invariably the case in my experience with international organisations, have important implications for issues of substance. The first was a question of timing. Annan had originally wanted the panel to report within a year of his decision to establish it, so that he could submit his own views to the opening session of the General Assembly in September 2004. Not only was that timetable extremely tight but also it would have meant publishing the report and the Secretary-General's own proposals right in the middle of a US Presidential campaign. This seemed to Scowcroft, to me and a number of others, a recipe for disaster, and we said so to Annan when we met him in December 2003 at the outset of our work. Although he was at first reluctant to concede the point, Annan came round early in 2004 to accepting a November/December 2004 date for our report's submission to him. Then there was the question of our relationship with the Secretary-General while we were debating and preparing our report. All too often in the past Secretary-Generals had adapted a 'fire and forget' policy to such groups resulting in a mismatch of their and his views. We were determined to avoid that. Annan responded very positively to this and we were able to schedule four full discussions with him during the course of our deliberations. He accepted with good grace our refusal to let him have an interim report early in 2004 which would only have taken up valuable time and which, because it would inevitably have leaked into the public domain, would have unleashed a tidal wave of lobbying by interested parties. And there was the question of how ambitious we should aim to be. Should we be indulging in 'blue skies' thinking and trying to configure the UN for 20 or 30 years ahead or should we be sticking firmly to what could and should be done in the immediate future? The panel opted firmly for the second choice, although we did look carefully at some of the more ambitious ideas around, such as the establishment of a standing UN peacekeeping force. When all was said and done, we were a group of pragmatists not of visionaries. Hanging over the head of the panel from beginning to end was the issue of Security Council enlargement. There was a determination not to let it become the be-all-and-end-all of our work, not least because it was a subject that was inevitably going to divide the members of the panel. So we took the unheroic, but, in my view, tactically correct, decision to postpone any discussion of that issue until our fourth meeting, in the summer of 2004, by which time our work and views on many other equally important issues had taken shape.

The principal focus of our work was inevitably on the UN's role in achieving peace and security. That was where the greatest problems had arisen over the previous decade – the problems of peacekeeping over-stretch, of the use of force without Security Council legitimisation in Kosovo and Iraq, of the disasters in Somalia, Rwanda and Bosnia, of the weak and confused response to new threats from terrorism and the spread of Weapons of Mass Destruction. In addressing peace and security we were, however, clear from the outset that the international community needed to avoid taking too narrow a view focussing almost exclusively on the new threats, which would have been the preference of the Bush administration. We decided to take account too of the profound implications for peace and security of extremes of poverty, of gross abuses of international humanitarian law and of environmental degradation. We recommended first that the Security Council should adopt a set of guidelines that it would use when reaching decisions authorising the use of force. These guidelines drew heavily on 'just war' doctrines that had evolved down the centuries – issues such as proper purpose, proportionality, and probability of success – and were not intended to have legal force. We had no illusions that actual decisions would other than continue to be taken on a case-by-case basis. But we believed that the existence of such guidelines would increase the predictability and also the deterrent effect and legitimacy of Security Council action. On peacekeeping we proposed the establishment of a Peace-Building Commission which would help the UN to back those slipping towards failure and those emerging from hostilities, to get back on their feet and would get away from the short-termism which had bedevilled so many UN peacekeeping operations. And we recommended the strengthening of UN support for regional peacekeeping activities, particularly in Africa where so many of the operations occurred and where the African Union was beginning to act more effectively and decisively than in the past – support with training and logistics and a willingness to provide finance for regional peacekeeping operations on UN assessed contributions when the UN asked the AU to undertake them on its behalf.

We called for the Secretary-General to promulgate a counterterrorism strategy that achieved a balance between firm cooperative action and respect for individual human rights; and we put forward a legal definition of terrorism that we hoped to see enshrined in international law. On the spread of Weapons of Mass Destruction we proposed a whole range of measures designed to strengthen the nuclear non-proliferation regime and to resume progress towards multilateral nuclear disarmament, and also to provide for an inspection regime to underpin the Biological Weapons Convention. We made recommendations for the more selective and equitable implementation of economic sanctions. But by far the most ambitious idea we put on the table was what has come to be known as the 'Responsibility to Protect', a new international norm, which would establish that, when a government was unable or unwilling to protect its own citizens, the international community acting through the Security Council could intervene. This concept had already been worked up in detail by a Canadian-sponsored panel of which Gareth Evans had been co-chair, and he was determined that we should endorse it and put it forward for decision.

My own initial reaction had been cautious. I had been consulted following Tony Blair's Chicago speech in 1999, which proposed a more aggressive and far-reaching version of the same idea, and had doubted whether that would ever receive widespread international support. But, influenced heavily by my own experience of, and shared responsibility for, the tragedies in Rwanda and at Srebrenica, I came to see that the Responsibility to Protect was both necessary and viable. Agreement was not reached easily in the panel, where several members were nervous about the implications, but eventually a consensus was achieved. My contribution included using one of my regular consultations with the Prime Minister during the work of the panel to ask him to avoid any further public follow-up to his Chicago speech while we put to the test the more carefully phrased and more circumscribed concept of the Responsibility to Protect. Tony Blair readily agreed and became a strong supporter of the Responsibility to Protect when it entered the negotiating forum at the UN.

When the panel looked at the economic and social work of the UN, the perspective was quite different. The UN never had been at the heart of the international system established to regulate economic, financial and trade issues; the International Monetary Fund, the World Bank and the World Trade Organization were where the finance and trade ministers came together to do business and that was even more the case after the end of the Cold War when those three organisations became virtually universal ones as the boycott of them by the communist powers came to an end. My own attitude towards much of the UN's economic work is perhaps best captured in an analysis made at the end of 1990:

> *In 1990, as in other recent years, the economic and social activities of the UN played very much second fiddle to those involving international peace and security. The greater realism amongst the developing country delegations continued to emerge and if anything strengthened. Here or there in the committee rooms of the UN one can find the odd band of Third World ambassadors flourishing the fly-blown phylacteries of the New International Economic Order but it is an ever rarer occurrence.*

By 2003 that trend had continued, and the marginalisation of the UN in everything except some aspects of developmental work and the negotiations on climate change was even more marked. The question we faced was whether to try seriously to reverse that trend or not. There were members of the panel who thought we should do that, but they were a smallish minority. The auguries for such an approach were in any case not good. A quite recent UN Commission under the chairmanship of the former Swedish Prime Minister Ingvar Carlsson had proposed the establishment of a UN economic and social security council and this idea had vanished without a trace and without being given any serious consideration. So we settled for putting forward some fairly modest, incremental improvements in the handling of the UN's economic and social agenda. We did, however, throw our weight firmly behind the case for replacing the G8 (of course a non-UN body) by a G20 (also a non-UN body), which would bring together the leaders of the main developed countries with the leaders of the principal emerging economies such as China, India, Brazil and South Africa. The old distinction between developed and developing countries seemed to us not only distinctly out of date but also inimical to effective cooperation over the handling of the main global challenges of the twenty-first century. The G20 finally took shape in response to the great financial crisis of 2008; it should have been established some time before.

One of the other choices the panel had to make was how far down the UN food chain we should go in our search for systemic reform. This question was posed most awkwardly in the context of the handling of human rights. The Commission on Human Rights, a highly politicised and largely ineffectual body which had been trying and failing for decades to get to grips with the numerous instances of the abuse of human rights in almost every corner of the world, was not one of the UN's principal organs like the General Assembly, the Security Council and the Economic and Social Council. Should we regard it as being beneath the radar? Or should we try to reform it too? I was firmly of the reforming view; and that gradually came to be the majority view of the panel, although there were some with doubts and hesitations. And, if we opted for reform, should we, as some human rights activists wanted, propose the establishment of a principal organ for human rights or still leave the General Assembly in overall charge? We went for the incremental approach. But we had some trouble identifying the specifics of what we were going to propose, not least because neither the UN Secretariat nor the office of the High Commissioner for Human Rights were prepared to give us much guidance. So we proposed the abolition of the existing, discredited Commission and its replacement by a Council reporting direct to the General Assembly; we suggested some ways of making the new Council's work more professional and of guarding against politicisation; we tried to strengthen the separate office of the High Commissioner; and we got into a tangle over the question of membership of the new Council. Human rights activists tended to want a council made up solely of countries with completely clean human rights records but we doubted whether this was achievable or even desirable, since it was unlikely then to be particularly representative of all the regions of the world. So we aimed for a wider membership, recognising that this would inevitably bring in some transgressors. It was probably not the best of our recommendations but we had at least opened the door to a complete shake-up of the UN's human rights machinery.

The panel had postponed addressing the ever-fascinating topic of Security Council enlargement until a late stage of its deliberations but it could not duck it entirely. The question was did we simply put the ball back into the member states' court and urge them to carry on the negotiations, which had been broken off in 1997, and seek to conclude them? Or were we to put proposals of our own? I was rather of the first persuasion, believing this was the best way to ensure that, if the negotiations again reached deadlock, as I was pretty convinced they would do, that did not carry with it to the bottom of the sea all the other proposals we were going to make; but I soon found myself in a minority of one. Our research staff worked up an alternative to the earlier proposal of a Council of 24 members (up from 15) with five new Permanent Members (Japan, Germany, India, Brazil and one African country). This alternative would avoid, for the time being at any rate, appointing new Permanent Members but would create, again within a Council of 24 members, a new category of longer-term, potentially reappointable members. This could be seen as a stepping-stone towards permanent membership, although that was not how the principal aspirants to permanent membership were likely to view it. This ingenious idea was discussed at our meeting near Vienna in July 2004 and picked up a good deal of support and not just from panel members drawn from countries which did not want to see new Permanent Members created. At the same meeting Kofi Annan had urged us to make one single proposal on this vexed subject. We left Baden without having come to any firm conclusions, which we postponed until our next meeting near New York in September.

By the time we next met, the scene had changed; the alternative proposal had leaked into the press and provoked a firestorm of protest from the aspirants to permanent membership; and the Secretary-General, who had been on the receiving end of much of the protest, told us that he would, after all, like us to offer member states a choice by making two proposals and not one. The panel put up no resistance to this change of heart, not least because it avoided the need to make a choice between the two alternatives that would inevitably have split us down the middle. From then on we concentrated on refining the two options and on presenting them clearly but even-handedly. One can only speculate what would have occurred if we had presented the alternative option alone. Probably it would still not have been agreed by the member states. But putting forward two options certainly increased the chances of continuing deadlock, which was in fact what transpired.

An endemic weakness of the UN, and of its Secretariat in particular, is in communication with those outside the charmed circle of UN ambassadors in New York and diplomats in capitals around the world. This is not easily remediable given that the Secretariat has to be careful not to be seen to take sides on sensitive issues which divide the membership, and that it cannot answer back trenchantly when it is criticised by one, or a group of, its members. But there was little hope of the panel's 101 proposals for action, the most far-reaching set of reforms of the organisation put on the table since its foundation in 1945, getting traction at the highest level of government if the report could not be presented publicly in a coherent and persuasive manner at the outset. Together with Gareth Evans and our research director, Steve Stedman, I worried away at this problem through the autumn of 2004 as the panel's report assumed its final shape. We managed to keep our proposals under wraps for a month following our last meeting, while the Secretary-General became familiar with what was proposed and readied his own strongly supportive response, and while the translation of the report and its pre-positioning around the world took place. I persuaded the editor of *The Economist*, Bill Emmott, rather unusually to give Kofi Annan the opportunity to present the proposals in an extensive signed article. A whole programme of media events, in which the BBC World Service was prominent, was put in place for the launch. But, just as these carefully laid plans were being made, the Iraq oil-for-food scandal, which had been ignited that summer when many damning documents about how Iraq had evaded UN sanctions came to light in Baghdad, reached a crescendo. There were calls for Annan's resignation from members of the US Congress; the New York media went into a feeding frenzy; and morale on the UN building's 38th floor amongst the Secretary-General's entourage took a nosedive. As a result, and I never did hear a coherent explanation of the decision, the launch of the panel's report was without any warning brought forward by several days and Annan himself declined to participate, leaving the task to the panel's chairman whose public diplomacy skills were not outstanding. The result was a public relations flop. I could have wept. The campaign to muster support for the reform proposals had got off to the worst possible start.

✻   ✻   ✻

The ten months following the publication of the panel's proposals and leading up to the September 2005 UN Summit meeting which was designed to take decisions on them were given over to ponderous and reductive negotiations between the 192 member states. I had tried to persuade Annan and his Canadian deputy, Louise Fréchette, to go for a multi-track negotiating process, with institutions such as the Security Council and the International Atomic Energy Agency getting a first bite at the proposals which most directly concerned them, and the time left for the final 192 member phase of negotiations kept relatively short. But the Secretary-General's willingness to resist pressure from the New York ambassadors of the member states was at its lowest as was his influence, undermined by the continuing oil-for-food scandal. So, apart from Annan's own proposals, a document entitled 'In Larger Freedom', which came forward in March 2005 and mirrored the panel's proposals in almost every respect except for some improved ideas for the Human Rights Council, the Secretary-General's role in the negotiations was less than it should have been. The panel had formally ceased to exist with the publication of its report but I found myself even more active in speaking at conferences around Britain and around the rest of Europe than I had been when we had been consulting and listening to as wide a spread of opinions as we could reach in 2003–4. The welcome for almost everything we had put forward was general and heartening. Throughout the negotiating process between the member states the most solid support came from the EU and its member states; indeed without that support I doubt whether the September Summit would have produced anything beyond warm words, that most freely available of commodities at UN gatherings. But much was lost on the road to the Summit. The whole section of our report dealing with the strengthening of the nuclear non-proliferation regime was ditched after a bad-tempered and totally unproductive review conference of the Nuclear Non-Proliferation Treaty signatories in May 2005. The idea of agreeing guidelines for Security Council decisions authorising the use of force ran into a brick wall of opposition from most of the Permanent Members, although not, I was glad to note, Britain. The negotiations to enlarge the Security Council reached deadlock again, with the African countries unable to agree on their own representation if there were to be new Permanent Members and the least enthusiastic of the existing Permanent Members, China, Russia and the US, deeply relieved to be let off the hook. Fortunately, thanks to Annan's astuteness, these negotiations were pursued separately by the main aspirants to permanent membership, known as the G4, and did not therefore scuttle the wider negotiations as we had earlier feared that they might. There was some offset to these negative trends when Tony Blair was able to extract from the G8 summit in Gleneagles in July 2005 a number of important commitments of aid to underpin the implementation of the Millennium Development Goals. And then in the last few weeks before the Summit, New York was treated to the arrival of a new US Ambassador in the form of John Bolton, a graceless and aggressive operator who had been trying to cut the UN down to size ever since I had first come across him in George Bush Senior's State Department in 1991, armed with hundreds of amendments to the conference text. Fortunately most of these were dropped. When the dust settled after the Summit, agreement had been reached on the establishment of a Peace-Building Commission, on a new Human Rights Council to replace the discredited Human Rights Commission and, most surprisingly, on the new international norm of the Responsibility to Protect.

✳   ✳   ✳

Was it all worth it? Just about, I would suggest. If the process did nothing else it checked the drift of the UN towards irrelevance and marginalisation. The positive outcomes took plenty of time to bear fruit. The Peace-Building Commission was established, but it has been systematically under-resourced and under-utilised, even if the weaknesses it was set up to remedy have been better handled in more recent peacekeeping operations such as those in Haiti, Sierra Leone, Liberia and Southern Sudan. The Human Rights Council spent its first five years seeming to do its best to replicate the failings of its discredited predecessor, in particular turning a blind eye to the atrocities that occurred in the final weeks of the civil war in Sri Lanka. But then, in 2011, it began to show more promise in dealing with abuses in Iran, Libya, Syria, Burma and Belarus. As to the Responsibility to Protect, it appeared for a long time as if it was going to wither on the bough, an unused instrument, regarded with deep suspicion by many, particularly developing countries, as a not very well concealed excuse for Western military intervention. In the case of Kenya, although the Security Council did not get involved, it is reasonable to regard the concerted and successful efforts of the international community to prevent the violence following the elections there from sliding into open tribal warfare as an effective exercise of the new norm, all the more welcome as a case which did not involve external military intervention. Within a few weeks of each other at the beginning of 2011 the Security Council twice authorised the use of force to protect defenceless civilians – in Côte d'Ivoire and in Libya. The Responsibility to Protect could be said to have come of age and to have survived its baptism of fire. By no means everyone was pleased. And events in Syria were to demonstrate just how difficult it was to apply the norm in practice.

What conclusions did I draw from my years in the salt mines of UN reform? Firstly that an overall system-wide approach, such as we were charged with undertaking cannot be tried too frequently if reform fatigue is to be avoided. Secondly that, paradoxically, the need for reform is likely to be greatest at a time of crisis, just when the conditions for achieving it are at their least propitious because of the loss of trust and confidence among the main players, as was the case following the invasion of Iraq in 2003. And thirdly that reform might be better pursued on a sectoral basis when something close to a consensus on the need for new policy responses and procedures begins to emerge. But fourthly, as the international community discovered at the climate change conference in Copenhagen in December 2009, even that emerging consensus may not suffice to build agreement if some way cannot be found around the hopelessly unwieldy concept of a negotiating body with more than 190 members.

*   *   *

A full account of the work of the panel, its recommendations and their fate at the hands of the member states is contained in Chapters 11–13 of the author's New World Disorder: The UN after the Cold War – An Insiders View, *I.B.Tauris (2008).*

14

THE HOUSE OF LORDS AND OTHER THINGS 1995–2011

CODA

When we returned from our long journey through China and Central Asia on retiring from the Diplomatic Service, we moved back into the large Victorian house in Chiswick which we had bought in 1976 and which had been rented out while we were away in Washington, Brussels and New York. We had always loved the house, a masterpiece of that quirky, Queen Anne Revival style that had gained Bedford Park its conservation area status. It had been an ideal house in which to bring up our four sons. Even though it was a bit on the large size for two people whose children were now making their own way in the world, we never even considered moving elsewhere; its elegance, its spaciousness and its garden just made that unthinkable. Moreover, it was ideally situated for the post-retirement life that began to take shape – halfway from central London to Heathrow, rapid connections to Whitehall and Westminster and a thriving, burgeoning village of shops, restaurants and other facilities. The amount of space enabled me to convert one of the children's bedrooms into a study where I could work, surrounded by the heaps of papers and books which I tend to accumulate, and my wife to turn our dining room into the office of the charity – the Children at Risk Foundation – which she set up to support the work with street-children in Brazil of our third son, Jonathan. While we were in New York we had in addition bought a farmhouse in the south-west of France. We doubled the size of the farmhouse by converting the derelict barn attached to it and also the pigsty across the lane, which became a refuge where I could retire to write when the noise of grandchildren became too great. Le Breil, a hamlet of five houses, two of which were working farms, looking across the valley to the church at Frayssinhes, was set in the rolling, heavily wooded foothills of the Massif Central, a couple of miles outside the picturesque medieval town of St Céré in the Lot. It had a superb view, best enjoyed when swimming up and down the pool, which we had carved out of the hillside below the house. It became very much part of our lives, visited a bit less often than we had originally hoped, but a fixture at Easter and for a long five week break in the summer, which coincided with the local music festival. And so a new pattern emerged.

My first ten years after leaving the Diplomatic Service were heavily pre-empted by the work that I undertook, first on Cyprus and then on UN reform, and which is described in the two preceding chapters. But those were not the only things I did during that period and later. In 1996 I became a member of a small group called in to brief the then Leader of the Opposition, Tony Blair, on EU, foreign policy and security issues. We met on a number of occasions at his house in Islington and once only, after the new Labour government was formed in May 1997, in the cabinet room at No 10. The group, which had no fixed membership, had been assembled by Blair's Chief of Staff, Jonathan Powell; it included Robin Renwick, a former ambassador in Washington, David Simon, a former CEO of BP and destined to be a minister in the Labour government, Lawrence Freedman, professor of War Studies at King's College and a number of others. We covered a wide range of subjects and did most of the talking while Blair took copious notes on a yellow, lawyers' notepad and soaked up the views on offer. One or two impressions remain with me. The first was Blair's remarkable courtesy, which led him to send each of us a manuscript note of thanks after every meeting. Another was the fact that not once was the Shadow Foreign Secretary, Robin Cook, invited to attend; it was already clear that Blair intended to play the preponderant role in the formulation of his government's foreign policy and that whoever was Foreign Secretary would play very much a second fiddle.

As to the policy issues we covered, Blair's pro-European sympathies were evident, as was his desire to reverse the marginalisation of Britain within the EU which characterised the last years of the Major government and to play a leading role at future European Council meetings; on the question of Britain joining the euro, opinions were divided in the group of advisers and Blair had clearly not yet made up his mind, at least on issues of timing and tactics. More widely there were clear signs of Blair's interest in a more interventionist international role for Britain, born of his unease at the way Bosnia had been handled (which he had, albeit reluctantly, supported at the time). He was alerted very clearly by this group to the need to provide the armed forces with more resources if Britain was to play a more active role in international affairs; but I rather doubt whether that message really sank in. At no stage in these briefings were party political matters discussed. My own view was that the fact that the Leader of the Opposition, almost certain shortly to become the Prime Minister, was ready to sit down and listen to a group of independent experts was an admirable innovation, particularly given the fact that Blair had never held ministerial office before, and that this crossed no lines of constitutional propriety. However, I did have to fend off a suggestion from Jonathan Powell that I become Robin Cook's publicly announced foreign policy adviser, pointing out that I could not possibly at the same time continue to serve as the government's Special Representative for Cyprus, to which I was committed.

From the outset of my return to London I was involved in a number of EU-related activities. I became one of the founder members of the Advisory Board of the Centre for European Reform, a think-tank founded by Ralf Dahrendorf, whom I had known when he was a European Commissioner, by Nick Butler who was David Simon's éminence grise at BP (and then John Browne's), and above all by Charles Grant, its first, and so far only, executive director, whom I had known when he was writing for *The Economist* in Brussels. The CER has been a remarkable success story, regarded by many as one of the best think-tanks working on European issues not just in Britain but also in the EU as a whole, and that without being beholden to nor invariably supportive of proposals that come out of the European institutions. I was involved too in Britain in Europe, the organisation set up to prepare the ground for Britain to join the euro, of whose Council I was a member. A small group of former British diplomats and Commission and Council officials was established under the chairmanship of Michael Butler, my predecessor as Britain's Permanent Representative in Brussels, to prepare briefs for Britain in Europe on various aspects of EU policy with the object of encouraging a better informed debate on these matters. We worked there in close cooperation with Danny Alexander, who much, much later surfaced as Chief Secretary of the Treasury in the Conservative-Liberal Democrat Coalition government formed after the general election in May 2010.

When Britain in Europe brought its own work to an end, this group continued to provide briefing material for members of both Houses of Parliament and for the European Movement and does so to this day. To argue that the quality of the debate on European issues in Britain has improved would be hard to sustain; but perhaps it would have been even worse without our efforts. And then in 1999 when the EU was preparing to make the first appointments to the two posts which had been created by the 1997 Amsterdam Treaty, those of Special Representative for Common and Foreign Security Policy and of a remodelled Secretary-General of the Council, I agreed to my name being put forward for one of those jobs. The competition was pretty fierce, with Spanish, German, French and Danish candidates in the field; my misgivings about Britain's skills at lobbying for such top international appointments were amply confirmed. But I did not and do not for one moment think that the choices of Javier Solana and of Pierre de Boissieu for the two jobs were other than fully justified. And, while I was a bit disappointed at the time, in retrospect I have much preferred my portfolio existence to returning to a full-time, or more likely full-time and a half job.

❊   ❊   ❊

My post-New York portfolio workload was heavily weighted towards continued involvement in the public sector and did not follow the more traditional route for retired diplomats of moving into the private sector as an adviser, a non-executive director or an official in a trade association. But that route was not entirely ignored; I served as a non-executive director of Chime Communications, a political and financial consultancy, between 1996 and 2006; I was on the board too of Aegis, a media selling and management consultancy group; and I was an adviser to the board of a company which used to be known as British Oxygen but which has long since been swallowed up after a takeover by the German firm Linde. My overriding impressions were that non-executive directors tended to be kept a long way away from the key decisions being taken by the companies on whose boards they sat, with very little serious policy discussion taking place at board meetings, and that neither the newcomer from the world of diplomacy nor the company which had taken them on had a very clear idea of how best to engage with the company's work or in what ways the company wished to make use of their experience. By far the most challenging and interesting private sector job that came my way was an invitation to serve as a member of an independent advisory panel for BP on the development of a large natural gas field in the Indonesian province of Papua (also known as Irian Jaya). The Tangguh project, as it was known, presented all sorts of problems for the company. The gas field was situated under the waters of Bintuni Bay in the Bird's Head region of Papua, an extremely primitive and totally undeveloped part of what was in any case Indonesia's poorest province. The annexation of Papua by Indonesia had never been accepted by a substantial part of its indigenous population and there was a low level insurgency, mainly on its border with the neighbouring independent state of Papua New Guinea; the only technically feasible site in the Bintuni Bay region for the liquefaction plant needed to freeze the gas and load it into tankers for export to China, South Korea, Japan and perhaps even the west coast of the United States, required a large existing village to be moved to an entirely new site. The only other major international project in Papua, the huge Freeport-McMoRan gold and copper mine near Timika, was a living example of what needed to be avoided, with security problems, human rights abuses, massive in-migration and appalling environmental degradation. To help the company avoid these risks, John Browne, BP's CEO, had persuaded former US Senator George Mitchell to head up an advisory panel whose other members in addition to me were Sabam Siagian, who had been editor of the *Jakarta Post*, and the Reverend Herman Saud from Jayapura, the capital of the province of Papua. George Mitchell's acumen, integrity and international reputation, together with his capacity to engage sympathetically with whomsoever he was dealing, were enormous assets, which ensured that, from the outset and for the seven years of its existence, the panel worked together in harmony as a team.

And so, in 2002, began what was to become for the panel an annual cycle. We would foregather in Singapore for a day of briefing by BP on every aspect of the project. We would then fly to Papua for discussions with the provincial authorities (in Jayapura and then, after the province was divided, in Manokwari too), with the police and the military and with local NGO's and civil society organisations. Thereafter we would spend three full days or more in the Bintuni Bay region, visiting the project itself, the directly affected villages near the project where we would hold what the Americans would call 'town hall' meetings (except that there were no town halls and the meetings often took place in the open air so long as a tropical downpour did not intervene). From Papua we would go for a day's break in Bali (much needed as, with short nights, long days, no alcoholic drinks and both temperature and humidity edging towards three figures, the Papua leg was no rest cure); and then on to Jakarta for meetings with Indonesian Ministers, with the British and US Ambassadors whose aid programmes were involved, with the World Bank and UN representatives and with countrywide NGO's. A few months later we would meet in London to agree our report and discuss it with BP including with John Browne and members of his board. Then, after the report's recommendations and BP's response to them were published, we would hold public seminars on them in London and Washington. What was the main focus of our work? Much of it was concerned with ensuring that the company and its contractors lived up to the commitments they had entered into in advance with regard to employing a substantial proportion of Papuans, to resettling the villages that had to be moved, to avoiding environmental damage and to not harming the indigenous population's main source of livelihood, fishing for shrimp.

More ambitiously we championed an entirely novel approach to security which BP had already begun to evolve whereby the company's own security personnel (mainly Papuans) would handle everything onsite, with the Indonesian police and military remaining at a distance, in reserve in case things got out of control. This approach was designed to reduce the scope for human rights abuses and protection rackets that had been endemic in big projects in Indonesia. By great good luck, on our first visit to Jakarta, we were able to present this concept to Susilo Bambang Yudhoyono, at that time Coordinating Minister for Security and Political Affairs but subsequently a two-term President of Indonesia, who reacted cautiously but positively. Thereafter, in the face of widespread scepticism from NGO's in particular, the Integrated Community Based Security approach was put into effect and proved itself throughout the sensitive construction phase when several thousand workers were on site. We also pushed hard and successfully for the company to step up its support for health and education programmes in the villages around the project; these were the issues invariably raised with us at our 'town hall' meetings and were clearly crucial to convincing the local population that they were genuinely benefitting from the project. Over the seven-year period that the panel was involved, educational facilities and standards were improved, although they still remained pitifully low, and deaths from malaria and infant diarrhoea dropped dramatically, greatly helped by the provision of clean drinking water to which we persuaded BP to give a high priority. Ensuring that the population around Bintuni Bay were kept properly informed about the development of the project, about its implications for them and about the development programmes which BP were supporting was another area on which we put a lot of emphasis; two local radio stations were set up to serve the north and south shores of Bintuni Bay and news sheets were published in each of the villages around the bay.

In 2009, when we ended our involvement, the panel said in its last report, 'The Panel ends its charter optimistic that Tangguh will deliver many benefits to the region and will significantly improve the lives of its people'. Time alone will show whether that claim can be sustained. My only regret was that BP did not accept one of our final recommendations, which was that they should commission and publish a study of the development of Tangguh and of the interaction between the company, the panel and the local population. It seemed to us that there were useful lessons here for the way in which large multinational companies could discharge their corporate social responsibility when operating in developing countries. But Tony Hayward, who had by then taken over from John Browne as BP's CEO, had a less sure feel for these wider considerations.

✳   ✳   ✳

One other field in which I became considerably involved, somewhere between the public and the private sectors, was higher education governance. I served on the Council of the University of Birmingham for nearly ten years and chaired it between 2001–6; I joined the Council of the University of Kent in 2009; I chaired the international advisory board of one of the leading French business schools, EDHEC, with campuses in Lille and Nice; and I served on the advisory boards of the Salzburg Seminar and of the Judge Business School in Cambridge. Oddly, perhaps, the list did not include my own old university, Oxford, but then I became involved on the losing side of the debate over reforms to its governing bodies, trying to explain why having a majority of lay members on the Council of a university was an asset and not an unacceptable breach of hundreds of years of tradition. My time chairing the Council at Birmingham was particularly instructive and rewarding. I concluded that the management of a big, civic university, such as Birmingham was (and Kent is becoming), was a great deal less old-fashioned and defective than politicians and the general public seemed to believe. The reforms put forward in the Dearing Report were having their effect, as the size of Councils was squeezed down and financial management became more effective. What really was going wrong at the end of the 1990s was the lack of resources being put into the sector, as universities were forced year after year to find what were euphemistically known as efficiency savings and were faced at the same time with a massive increase in the student body. This led to low morale and an uphill struggle to maintain quality in what was rapidly becoming one of Britain's most important invisible export industries. Fortunately the tide turned with the allocation by the Blair government of considerably increased resources to the university sector and with the introduction of relatively modest tuition fees that nevertheless gave the universities a welcome increase in fiscal autonomy. By the time I stood down from the Council at Birmingham we were investing over £1 million every week in new facilities and new academic posts. Alas, this golden interlude was all too short and, following the 2010 budget cuts and strong downward pressure on student visas, the universities are once again heading into choppy waters.

*　　*　　*

Nothing was further from my thoughts when I left the Diplomatic Service in 1995 than that I might, rather belatedly, be encouraged to embark on a political career, albeit not a party political one. Former diplomats did occasionally find their way into the House of Lords, but only infrequently (and Margaret Thatcher had declined to appoint any during her long premiership). I was certainly not prepared to take the route of party membership, having voted for each of the three main parties at various moments in my life and remaining deeply attached to the British tradition of a civil service that stood apart from party politics. But then things changed with the 1999 reform of the House of Lords, which introduced the prospect of independent peers being appointed on the nomination of a cross-party Appointments Commission. I was persuaded by John Kerr, back from the Embassy in Washington and by then head of the Diplomatic Service, to put my name forward, along, I discovered much later, with 3,000 others. I filled in copious forms; and then I underwent a lengthy interview with the chairman of the Appointments Commission, Denis Stevenson and two of his colleagues, a far more challenging ordeal than the one I had survived when I joined the Diplomatic Service more than 40 years earlier or even than the viva voce interview for a first class honours degree at Oxford. Thereafter a long silence; and finally the news that my name was to be on the list of 14 for the first of this kind of appointment. Any euphoria that I might have felt, and there was a good dose of that, was soon swept away by the public relations disaster that the government contrived to make of the announcement of the appointments. It proved to be the nemesis of low politics.

For some months the No 10 spin machine, in the iron grip of Alistair Campbell, had been talking about a list of 'People's Peers' coming forward. Had he taken the trouble to read the terms of reference of the Appointments Commission, which, naturally, had been drafted by the government, he would have seen that there was no basis for this mantra, which in any case was as meaningless as it was specious. So, when the list was published, containing the country's most distinguished statistician, Claus Moser, one of its outstanding business leaders, John Browne, a leader of the medical profession, Ilora Finlay, and others of a similar kind the popular press went wild with derision. The situation was only made worse by the fact that the announcement, which it had been intended to make immediately after the 2001 general election, was brought forward into the dead period created by the postponement of that election to allow time for the foot and mouth epidemic to pass its peak. On the night of the announcement I sat helpless on the platform at a television studio as the presenter tortured Denis Stevenson with questions about why he had not put forward a hairdresser or a lollipop lady. His reply, that 'they would not have felt at ease in the House of Lords', only added fuel to the flames. Every time one of my friends, and some who are not my friends, pulls my leg at being a 'People's Peer' I feel like sticking a pin into a wax model of Alistair Campbell.

Like most of the population of Britain I had little idea of what life and work in the House of Lords would be like. I had told the Commission that I would aim to be available for three days a week; and I have held firm to that, which is more than can be said for some others who have been similarly appointed. A friend who wrote to me at the time said 'the besetting sin of the House of Lords is excessive politeness', and there is something in that, at least when European matters are not being discussed. If the House of Commons is too raucous, the House of Lords does sometimes tend towards the soporific. But the accumulated experience of its members is huge, the quality of debates is often high and the spirit of camaraderie, which I have always welcomed wherever I have been, is pervasive. As luck would have it, the subjects about which I knew something were very much to the fore within a few weeks of my arrival. The 9/11 attacks led to the recall of Parliament and thereafter to a series of debates on terrorism, on Afghanistan and, a few months later, on the handling of Iraq. I spoke quite frequently, arguing for the need to avoid Islamophobia and a drift into a clash of civilisations, for a light footprint on the ground in Afghanistan, for Pakistan to cease flirting with its own extremists and for the widest possible international coalitions and full UN endorsement to deal with all these issues.

On Iraq, my own experience at the UN led me to credit the belief that Saddam Hussein was still concealing some Weapons of Mass Destruction and that he had every intention of reconstituting his WMD programmes if ever the lifting or the erosion of sanctions allowed him to do that. It was on that basis that I took the line in the debate that immediately preceded the invasion of Iraq that such action would be justified. What I could not condone was the way in which the UN Security Council had been quite mercilessly damaged by the series of ministerial confrontations that took place there in the attempt to get a second resolution adopted to authorise the use of force. When I first heard that the British government was going for a second resolution, my reaction was 'Well they must know something which I don't know'. But they did not. And, when the invasion turned into the disaster of the occupation, for which no proper preparations had been made, I ceased to give any support to the government while avoiding speaking out so long as our troops were in harms way. Those first two or three years in the House rather masked the fact that the House of Lords does not really have much of a say on foreign policy. In particular it suffers from not having a Foreign Affairs Committee, the objections to which are obscure and unconvincing. Until that lacuna is filled I fear that the considerable accumulation of expertise, with former foreign secretaries, defence secretaries, service chiefs and diplomats in profusion, will not find a proper focus and a means of attracting the attention of the government and holding it to account, which is no doubt one of the unavowed reasons why no such committee has as yet been established.

One of the real joys of work in the House of Lords is the scope, indeed often the need, to work across party lines and to build up cross-party alliances. In the first two Parliaments in which I sat (2001–10) the Labour government needed Liberal Democrat and some Independent support to get its legislation through and to defeat Conservative opposition amendments; in the third parliament (2010 onwards), the coalition can be defeated if the Labour opposition and a majority of Independents act in concert, even more so if there are defections from its own ranks. These complexities are not well understood. They clearly completely eluded Tony Blair in 2004 when he allowed Jack Straw to convince him that, despite his large majority in the House of Commons, he would not be able to get the EU's Constitutional Treaty through the House of Lords; and let Straw tip the government into a commitment to a referendum, one of whose knock-on consequences was the defeat of the treaty in referendums in France and the Netherlands. In fact, as the voting patterns in the House of Lords on the subsequent ratification of the Lisbon Treaty showed, there were pretty comfortable majorities throughout and there is no reason to doubt that this would have been the case if the Constitutional Treaty had ever been brought to Parliament for ratification. The Lisbon Treaty was in fact a perfect example of how such cross-party alliances can work to great effect. From the outset of the process an informal grouping of the Labour government, the Liberal Democrats, a clutch of pro-European Conservatives and a substantial number of Independents worked together to defeat the large number of wrecking amendments put forward by the Conservative opposition. A similar cross-party alliance, with many of the same participants, was put together to make amendments to the coalition government's EU 'referendum lock' bill in the summer of 2011, and four major amendments were carried, although they were subsequently rejected by the House of Commons. Much smaller, less formal cross-party alliances can also influence government policy quite effectively. A group of which I was a member pressed the government constantly, through parliamentary questions, debates and representations to ministers, to ban cluster munitions; and, despite a stalwart rearguard action by the Ministry of Defence, we prevailed. The government signed the Oslo Convention; Parliament ratified it just before the 2010 election; and Britain's stocks of cluster munitions are now being destroyed. Similarly, and on an even smaller scale, I worked with Alex Carlile, a Liberal Democrat peer, to get the government to block a loophole in Britain's national legislation ratifying our membership of the International Criminal Court, which was allowing people suspected of involvement in the Rwandan genocide to escape arrest on the grounds that they were not resident in Britain. Again the government was persuaded and the loophole was blocked. A strong cross-party alliance also operates on the twin issues of multilateral nuclear disarmament and non-proliferation and I belong to a group that brings together former foreign and defence secretaries, former military leaders and diplomats to work in support of President Obama's objective of achieving a world free of nuclear weapons.

Within a few weeks of arriving in the House of Lords I was able to get myself co-opted onto one of its EU sub-committees, which work under the aegis of the main EU Select Committee to scrutinise all EU legislative proposals and to write more wide-ranging thematic reports on areas of EU policy. Since then, I have served on three of these sub-committees (economic and financial, foreign policy, defence and development, and home affairs, the last of which I currently chair). I have also been on the main committee between 2002–6 and from 2008 to the present day. House of Lords EU scrutiny procedures and output have a high reputation throughout Europe and can reasonably claim to be in the top rank of national parliamentary controls operating within the 27 member states. It is time consuming work involving weekly committee and sub-committee meetings, a considerable amount of travel to Brussels and elsewhere in Europe and ploughing through mountains of paper. Since the entry into force of the Lisbon Treaty national Parliaments have, for the first time, gained a formal foothold in the EU legislative process and have also become, to a limited extent, the guardians of the doctrine of subsidiarity (the idea that action at the EU level should only be undertaken when action at a national or regional level would not be effective) and proportionality. It is easy to mock these procedures and to argue that they are lacking in teeth; but they do offer scope for further development; and they need to be seen as part of a wider effort to bring policymaking in the EU into closer proximity with national parliamentary institutions and thus also, it must be hoped, with their electorates.

A focus on EU business has not distracted me from my other main area of expertise, the UN. From 2006 to 2011 I chaired the board of the UN Association of the UK, a membership organisation that exists to support, but also to act as a friendly critic, of the work of the UN. This involved a good deal of public speaking around the country; and it fitted well with my parliamentary work since I was able to secure debates in the House of Lords on UN issues, to ask questions about the whole range of UN business and to use the All Party Parliamentary Group on the UN, which I now chair, as a platform for visiting speakers from overseas. Attitudes in Britain towards the UN are in sharp contrast to those towards the EU. The latter tend to be sharply polarised, with debate deteriorating rapidly into exaggerated confrontation and raised voices; the UN, for its part enjoys wide support, but that support is shallow and often not very well informed. So, when things go wrong at the UN, it is regarded as capable of nothing and when they go right it is expected to do everything. With the help of the tiny hard-working staff at UNA it has proved possible through advocacy to have a greater impact on government policymaking and to be recognised as the foremost NGO working in that field. As usual the problem is a shortage of resources to support the work of the UNA and also the greater salience of single-issue NGOs in the modern world.

No member of the House of Lords can entirely escape the issue of reform of Britain's upper house, although I have never been as fascinated by it as are many of my colleagues. With the coalition government having tabled a project for a much smaller, largely elected house, the subject is clearly not going to go away any time soon, even if one can doubt whether it comes very high up the list of burning issues which concern ordinary people. Also unlike many of my colleagues I do not have very black and white views on the subject. It seems clear to me that a bi-cameral parliamentary system is better than a uni-cameral one but that a bi-cameral system with houses that have equal powers as in Italy and Japan is undesirable given the scope then for deadlock. This points towards changes that do not disturb the present balance of powers between the Commons and the Lords. It seems doubtful whether the coalition government's proposals meet that criterion. There are perfectly good arguments for keeping an all-appointed house on the principle of 'if it ain't broke don't fix it'. But there are also powerful arguments against it. I have never been of the view that the inclusion of a modest elected element should be a make-or-break issue. Nor do I believe that such an outcome would or should alter fundamentally the way in which the House of Lords functions; there is a remarkably strong element of cultural tradition which has carried the present chamber through some quite substantial changes in the past; for example, when life peers were introduced and when most of the hereditary peers left. About one thing I do have strong views. If the coalition's plan withers on the bough, as it may well do, then the government should allow a bill introducing some modest incremental reforms getting rid of the worst anomalies, like the House's inability to expel members convicted of crimes, and to provide for retirement to pass into law. It would be sad indeed if such common-sense reforms could not be enacted just because agreement on more far-reaching reforms is elusive.

15

THE QUEST FOR A ROLE

I have so far narrated the story of my professional career in a straightforward manner, avoiding, I hope, too much recourse to hindsight and too many instances of self-justification. I have also, I trust, avoided betraying the invisible bond of mutual respect and confidence that binds together elected politicians and their senior professional advisers. But it is now time to draw together the threads that run through this story and to look at the evolution of Britain's foreign policy over a period of a little more than half a century. Some of the main themes – the European dimension, the relationship with the United States – are clearly discernible as part of this personal account and that is as it should be since they have been the two principal axes along which Britain's foreign policy has been defined and operated for the last 50 years. I have attempted to avoid forcing the successive episodes I have described into any overall pattern or imposing some kind of template on the events. That method would not only be untrue to life but would have been alien to the whole way in which a country's foreign policy evolves. The academic conceit which presents foreign policy as a realm where blueprints can be drawn up and imposed by a single country is totally removed from the reality of foreign policymaking by a middle-ranking power with worldwide interests such as Britain has been throughout the period covered by this account. Most of the decisions that influenced foreign policy were made in response to unexpected events and to actions by players over whom we had no, or little, influence or control. To an increasing extent, as Britain's capacity for individual action has waned, those policy choices have had to be modified to take account of the policies of allies and partners without whose cooperation there would have been no chance of effective action being taken. And all that has to be fitted into a framework of rules-based international activity which has grown exponentially since the Second World War and which successive British governments have concluded, correctly in my view, that it is in Britain's national interest to nurture and to strengthen. So, even looking into the rear-view mirror the picture is far from clear, and ahead of us, as usual, lie foggy conditions into which we are driving at a speed we cannot control.

The two series of events which did more than any others to shape British policy during the period we are looking at – the fiasco of the Anglo-French Suez adventure and the decision by Britain not to join in the process of European integration at the outset – had both taken place shortly before this story begins. The far-reaching, medium and long-term consequences of those events are with us still. They lie at the heart of what I have chosen to call Britain's quest for a role, a quest which continues to this day and which looks little nearer to a definitive conclusion than it was at the beginning. The Suez adventure was to a considerable extent an expression of post-imperial nostalgia, driven by a Prime Minister, Anthony Eden, whose formative foreign policy experience had been in the 1930s and during the Second World War, when Britain still saw itself and acted as one of the few 'Great Powers', capable of projecting its power and influence around the world. Suez destroyed those illusions utterly; and thereafter, British foreign policymaking suffered less from that post-imperial nostalgia than might have been expected – less than the foreign policies of some other departed empires have done, as a glance at the foreign policy of Vladimir Putin's Russia would seem to demonstrate. But in its place emerged a resolute determination among British policymakers never again to get at serious cross-purposes with the United States and to hew as closely as possible to US policy initiatives; that determination imposed its distortions too. And the contrast with the French reaction to Suez, which was to look to Europe for an alternative pole in the foreign policy firmament, could not have been sharper; moreover, it was to complicate the establishment of a settled relationship between Britain and the Europe of the six original members of the European Community.

Looking back on those British and French reactions to Suez it is clear that both were excessive and not very well thought through; and both tended to lead their two protagonists down blind alleys. The French for a long time pursued a vision of an independent European foreign and security policy identity which would not only be autonomous, but which would consciously set out to distance itself from, and on occasion to oppose, US policies. The French departure from the military command structure of NATO was only the most prominent manifestation of that policy. But, while France's European partners supported the idea of greater European foreign and security policy cooperation, none of them was prepared to construct that cooperation on the assumption of separation from and opposition to their main NATO ally and the guarantor of their defence against the threat of Soviet domination. Britain on the other hand gave a degree of primacy to its relationship with the United States which made cooperation with other European countries on foreign policy issues quite difficult to achieve and also led to Britain's independent voice being discounted in many parts of the world, for instance, by the Soviet Union.

The legacy of Suez was, however, less of a burden for British policy than the legacy of the decisions not to join the European Coal and Steel Community when it was established in 1952 and the European Economic Community when it too was established in 1958. Those two decisions have taken a toll on Britain's relationship with the other European countries and, above all, with its partners in the European Community when it did eventually join in 1973, which it is hard to exaggerate. Britain thereby lost any chance of having a say in the shaping and formulation of some of the Community's main policies – those for agriculture and fisheries and for the financing of the budget, for example. But it also lost the chance to join the Community during a period of generally rising prosperity and economic growth that did so much to consolidate broad political support for the European project in the original six member states. By the time Britain did join in 1973, following two bruising vetoes by General de Gaulle in 1963 and 1967 which severely damaged the political image of Europe in Britain, the global economic climate had taken a sharp turn for the worse and the early years of British membership coincided with a period of high inflation, rising unemployment and stagnant growth; accession therefore brought with it to Britain none of the boost to prosperity and to morale which the founding member states had enjoyed. When one reflects now on the considerations that led to those opportunities to join the European project at the outset being missed it is surprising that they carried the day. The sacrosanct nature of the British coal and steel industries is hard to appreciate in a country where those industries have now shrunk to a tiny fraction of their former size. This was not through any imposition of European rules and regulations but simply thanks to market forces; and the fact that the two industries were at that time in public ownership turned out to be a complete red herring when we came to negotiate the terms of our accession to the Coal and Steel Community in 1970. The failure to join the European Economic Community seems with hindsight even more egregious and inexplicable.

It is clear that the policymakers in London simply did not understand what was going on among the Six and grossly underestimated the chances of it proving successful and moving on to more ambitious objectives. The responsibility for those missed opportunities has to be widely shared across what would now be called Britain's political class. Both the two main political parties were implicated in the decisions, Labour having been in power when the Schuman Plan for coal and steel cooperation was first mooted, and the Conservatives being in office when the European Economic Community treaty was negotiated and established. But the responsibility went wider than that. The weight of the advice from the senior civil servants was against British involvement in Europe. There were honourable exceptions both among politicians and civil servants who understood that crucial opportunities were being missed, but they were few and far between. The negative consequences of those missed opportunities were to dominate my own professional life and that of several generations of British politicians in both main parties.

Only once those initial mistakes had been made, did the search for alternatives get under way. Each one turned out to be a false trail. The first was the idea of a Europe-wide industrial free trade area. This quickly ran into the obstacle that the Six had already negotiated a customs union amongst themselves and were setting to work on an agricultural policy; and did not want to conclude a free trade agreement limited to industrial goods. So, when the European Free Trade Area came into being it included only Britain and the small countries around continental Europe's periphery. These were too small to provide the sort of large barrier-free market that Britain needed; and, moreover, several EFTA members from the outset regarded membership of that organisation as very much a second-best option to joining the Community, a view that Britain itself came to share. The attempt to build bridges between EFTA and the Community also fizzled out. Then there was what some saw as a Commonwealth alternative. But the Commonwealth as a whole had no provisions for regulating trade (although the members of what was called the 'white' Commonwealth did have preferential trading arrangements between themselves). Many of the developing country members of the Commonwealth were far more interested in getting duty free access to and aid from the relatively rapidly growing European markets, which they were only likely to do if Britain itself joined the Community. Moreover, the idea of the Commonwealth as any kind of effective political entity was soon being tested to destruction over the issues of Rhodesia's Unilateral Declaration of Independence and of the apartheid policies of South Africa. So that too turned out to be a false alternative for Britain. Much later some interest was aroused in what was called a North Atlantic Free Trade Area. But this never gained governmental support on either side of the Atlantic. It was hard to see either the US administration and its Congress or some members of the European Community reaching agreement on provisions that would necessarily have had to include the vexed issue of agricultural trade. And, as the European Community moved beyond the concept of a customs union and began to build a genuine single market, the idea of a NAFTA as an alternative to EU membership seemed less and less attractive. Successive US administrations had in any case attached a great deal more importance to their relationship with, and access to, the Community; it still remains something of a mystery how so many British policymakers managed to close their eyes to the fact that the preferred US option, from the early 1950s onwards, was for Britain to be firmly embedded in the European Community, influencing the formulation of its policies. So the search for alternatives led nowhere and, as time passed, it became clear that the alternatives that had been canvassed were often not really alternatives at all.

Europe-wide free trade was achieved through the European Economic Area negotiations at the end of the 1980s; and the majority of EFTA's original membership joined the Community. Many of the developing members of the Commonwealth benefitted substantially from the evolution of the Community's policies after Britain joined; and countries like India became major players in the new multipolar pattern of world governance arrangements that began to emerge after the turn of the century. And the sectoral approach to economic relations between the USA and the Community seemed likely to be more fruitful and more practical than any overarching framework.

The decisions taken by the Macmillan government in 1961 to explore whether terms for Britain's accession to the European Community could be agreed and, to an even greater extent, the uncluttered application for membership made by the Wilson government in 1967, represented a strategic choice of far-reaching significance. However, unlike the position in the founding member states when they established the Community, those decisions did not reflect a nearly universal national consensus. The 1961 initiative was criticised and opposed by the Labour party, then in opposition. The 1967 application, while supported by the Conservative opposition, in effect divided the cabinet, several prominent members of which were opposed to it; their opposition was merely swept under the carpet for the time being. Then, when the time came in 1971–2 for Parliament to ratify the terms of Britain's accession, the Labour party, once more in opposition, split again and smaller divisions began to emerge in the Conservative party. The 1975 referendum, while registering a 2:1 majority in favour of membership, notably failed to end the argument, which divided the Labour cabinet in the 1974–9 Parliament whenever an important decision on Europe came to be taken. By the time of the 1983 general election, the Labour party was campaigning on a policy of withdrawal from the Community. From that moment onwards the fever in the Labour party began to subside; and, when Labour came to power again in 1997, it was on a platform of solid support for Britain's involvement in Europe. By then, however, the contagion had spread to the Conservatives and the 1992–7 government was handicapped by continuous backbench revolts and the greatest possible difficulties in ratifying the Maastricht Treaty. This Euro-scepticism, as it was now euphemistically called, established an increasingly dominant grip on the Conservatives in opposition and led them to vote against ratification of the Lisbon Treaty. Now the fault line runs down the middle of the 2010 coalition government. This short description of the domestic political history of the European issue in Britain should suffice to demonstrate how far the strategic choice made by both main parties successively in the 1960s was from being consolidated and from being carried forward as a firm bi-partisan basis for policymaking on European issues. On the contrary, every British government since Britain joined the Community has had to negotiate in Brussels while continuously glancing behind it at its own supporters and continually conscious about the electoral consequences at the next general election of what was being decided in Brussels.

When parliamentary majorities were small or non-existent (as they were between 1974 and 1979 and between 1992 and 1997) this resulted in something close to paralysis in Britain's European policymaking. At other times it tended to be reflected in governments using a very different vocabulary and tone of voice when addressing European issues abroad and in Britain, thus confusing the national debate and undermining support for the choices being made. It is a sorry story and one that does little credit to those involved, sincerely held though the views they expressed may have been. Above all it meant that British ministers travelling to European meetings dragged a heavy ball and chain behind them.

In the circumstances it is not surprising that the prevalent impression in Brussels and other Community capitals is that Britain is, at best, a half-hearted member of the enterprise; nor is it surprising that, at home, European issues have been poorly explained and almost invariably seen through a crude prism of pro or anti-European sentiment, this tendency having been exacerbated as the press, particularly the tabloid press, swung from the heavily positive coverage of the 1960s and 1970s to an overwhelmingly negative approach. And yet, throughout the 40 years now of Britain's membership, there has in fact been a positive British European agenda pursued by successive governments of both parties, and pursued with considerable success. The shift from a customs union, still incorporating thousands of non-tariff barriers, to a single market, still admittedly incomplete in sectors like services and energy policy, owed much to British advocacy. The same is true of the European contribution to a series of global trade liberalising negotiations in the GATT (now the World Trade Organization). And Britain's role in supporting and overcoming the obstacles to a whole series of enlargement negotiations which have transformed the small, tight, Western European organisation of the 1960s into the genuinely pan-European organisation of today, foreseen dimly by the original founding fathers when they signed a treaty to be open to 'any' European country, has been unwavering. These successive enlargements, which provided the countries of southern Europe with a path away from fascist dictatorships and the countries of Central and Eastern Europe with the route from Soviet domination and communism to multi-party democracy and market economies, have been at the heart of the most successful peaceful transition in Europe's long and often blood-stained history. Sadly that positive agenda has all too often been overlaid by the domestic 'noises off'. But it remains there as a sound foundation for a Britain that can finally come to terms with its European demons.

The two themes which I have identified as being at the heart of Britain's international role – its relationship with the rest of Europe and with the United States – naturally ran in parallel over the decades covered by this memoir and often overlapped and interacted on each other. As the members of the European Community became collectively more involved in foreign policy coordination and as its member states, particularly the larger ones amongst them – Britain, France, Germany and Italy – sought, not always successfully, to concert their policy responses to international crises and challenges, the US interest in Britain as an international player shifted from a purely bilateral approach to its role as an influence in Brussels on any emerging European consensus. Unfortunately British leaders were often reluctant to recognise this shift and even more so to profit from it. In this respect the talisman phrase 'the special relationship', so treasured and often also ridiculed by the media, and invariably figuring in Presidential speeches when the US leader of the day wished to gratify and flatter his British opposite member, was a genuine obstacle to a more mature and sophisticated understanding of the evolving nature of the relationship. No one could sensibly deny that Britain and the United States had, and still have, a special relationship based on history, culture, language and many other factors; no one could even reasonably deny that there are some elements of exclusivity in that relationship – for instance, in the cooperation over nuclear weapons and intelligence. But to jump from that to the claim of overall exclusivity, which is encapsulated in the use of the definite article linked to the special relationship is to fly in the face of reality. The United States has had to balance its Atlantic/European and its Pacific/Asian strategies since the time of the Second World War, and the rise of China makes it inevitable that this will continue. Moreover, the United States has a whole range of special relationships with countries in all four corners of the world – not least with possibly the most genuine claimant to the talisman phrase, Israel. So the sooner Britain moves away from that spurious claim to exclusivity the better. Recent signs of an attempt to define the relationship as essential rather than special are to be welcomed in that respect.

Having said that, Britain does need to avoid, what I would regard as a false choice, between its links with the United States and its links with the rest of Europe. From time to time over the years it has been suggested that Britain should decide definitively that it is going in future to give absolute priority to European foreign policy cooperation over its links with the United States or, on the contrary, that it should attach little or no importance to European cooperation unless, miraculously, that reflected US choices and priorities. No other European country, not even France, for all the occasional bluster of its leaders, can be said in reality to have made that choice. None can afford to ignore the indispensability of cooperation between Europe and the United States if they are successfully to protect and further their shared values and common interests in a world where their relative weight is diminishing. Sometimes that will involve disagreement and, when disagreements do arise, the Europeans are a lot more likely to be able to sustain their side of the argument if they stand together. Surprisingly enough, one of the best, perhaps slightly unwitting, exemplars of this was Margaret Thatcher, when she stood up to attempts by the USA in the early 1980s to prevent the building of a gas pipeline from the Soviet Union to Western

Europe and when she argued against the USA moving beyond the research phase of ballistic missile defence. She demonstrated that there was no contradiction between a robust defence of common European interests and a continuing role as a close ally of the United States. Unfortunately she failed to draw the conclusion that a more vigorous and proactive British involvement in European foreign policy cooperation was actually likely to enhance Britain's influence in Washington. And, just as unfortunately, both her predecessors and her successors failed to find the right policy mix for the successful handling of Britain's key relationship with the United States.

❈   ❈   ❈

Nothing contrasts more sharply the period we have lived through since the end of the Second World War with the centuries of diplomatic history before 1945 than the emergence of major global and regional multilateral institutions and the beginnings of a rules-based international order where previously none existed. This massive expansion in multilateral activity has transformed the practice of diplomacy, as well, incidentally, as providing the stage upon which the present writer acted out his professional career. There was nothing inevitable about this development. After all the first tentative and flawed effort at moving in that direction, the establishment of the League of Nations following the First World War, had foundered amidst the protectionism, the beggar-my-neighbour currency devaluations and the acts of aggression of the 1930s, weakened from the outset by the refusal of an isolationist United States to participate. It had been a shaming failure. Nevertheless, the conclusion drawn by the victorious allies, and above all by the US President, Franklin Roosevelt, and the British Prime Minister, Winston Churchill, was that a renewed and more determined effort must be made to 'rid the world of the scourge of war' as the preamble to the UN Charter signed in San Francisco in June 1945 so eloquently put it. The founding of the UN was matched in the economic field by the establishment of the International Monetary Fund, of the World Bank and, somewhat later, of the General Agreement on Tariffs and Trade. In the early stages of this commitment to multilateral cooperation the British role was second only to that of the United States in significance and intensity. A number of Britons played key parts in the establishment and operation of the new international organisations – Gladwyn Jebb and Brian Urquhart at the UN, John Maynard Keynes in the case of the IMF and Eric Wyndham White at the GATT; and successive British governments with only brief lapses – the Suez crisis in 1956, the import surcharge of 1964 and the confrontation in the Security Council over the handling of Iraq in 2003 being the most flagrant examples – gave consistent support to them. Moreover, this support was not seriously contentious domestically in the way that almost everything to do with the European Community proved to be. Backing for the UN was initially certainly stronger on the left of the political spectrum than on the right, but this never became a partisan issue in any lasting way. British support for these international organisations was not purely altruistic, although there certainly was an element of idealism involved, particularly in the case of the UN. It also reflected a hard-headed judgement that Britain, whose relative weight in world affairs was on the wane, had much to gain by strengthening these international organisations, in whose councils its role as a founding father had given it a strong position, and much to lose if they failed again as they had done between the two world wars.

Indeed Britain's support was a good deal less fickle than that of the United States where successive administrations zigzagged between backing and undermining the UN and where UN issues acquired something of the toxic quality of European ones in Britain. None of these international organisations functioned as fully or as effectively as they had been intended to do, so long as they were affected by Cold War paralysis, but all survived; and with the end of the Cold War much that had been taboo throughout that period became acceptable. The UN reversed an aggression in Kuwait and presided over a massive expansion in peacekeeping operations, the three economic organisations became genuinely universal ones, with the GATT metamorphosed into a World Trade Organization which had genuine rules-based functions for handling trade disputes. Therefore, it is not unreasonable to suggest that, in this area of international diplomacy, Britain did find a role which was commensurate with its interests and its resources; and then stuck to it with commendable perseverance.

*   *   *

What then of the prospects for the future? It is easier to reply with some confidence in respect of the fields where Britain can be said to have already successfully found a role than it is elsewhere. It is hard to foresee circumstances in which Britain's interests will not best be served by a strengthening of multilateral organisations and disciplines and indeed their extension to new fields such as handling climate change. Pretty well every global trend that is discernible – the emergence of new powers in Asia and Latin America, and perhaps one day in Africa, the declining relative economic weight of Britain, Europe and indeed the West, the increasing dependence of even the most powerful nations on each other, the growth of threats and challenges to our collective security and prosperity which only concerted action at a global level can hope to master – all these point in that direction, and underline the futility of seeking to deal with them on our own or in some loose framework, sometimes now called a 'network world', without any set of internationally agreed rules. But we will not succeed in strengthening these organisations and these disciplines by simply camping on the status quo and by defending Britain's own position within them as if nothing had changed. Ensuring that the emerging powers become responsible stakeholders will mean giving them a proper say in the councils, and in formulating the policies, of the great multilateral organisations. That will necessarily involve some dilution of our own influence though not, I believe, our displacement. It will also involve throwing our full weight behind efforts to reform these organisations where their present performance is inadequate or wasteful.

Clearly the strengthening of these rules and of the organisations which underpin them and are charged with carrying them out – a trend which I believe it is in Britain's national interest to encourage and to support – will require a lot more than just making some institutional changes designed to give the emerging (or, in some cases like China and India, re-emerging) countries a greater say. It will require building a broader consensus than exists now on a whole range of global issues – on the maintenance of peace and security, on nuclear disarmament and non-proliferation, on trade policy, on climate change. That will not be achieved easily, and it will not be achieved without making difficult compromises and without diverting scarce resources to any joint endeavours we collectively agree on. There are considerable tensions over all these issues and will continue to be, between developed and developing countries, however outdated those labels may seem to be; between those with one view on the need to intervene in countries whose governments are unwilling or unable to protect their own citizens and those who place greater weight on non-intervention; between nuclear weapons 'haves' and 'have nots'; between free traders and protectionists; between environmentalists and climate change deniers; and, naturally, also between powers jockeying for position in a shifting world pecking order and calculating how best to place themselves in any international disputes which arise. It is tempting to regard this agenda as simply too difficult, too complex and too costly to address. But such a conclusion, particularly if it came to be shared by other middle-ranking nations such as Britain, who tend to be the engine of international cooperation, would be only too likely to lead to a new world disorder, with even those rules which are already in place fraying and atrophying, a situation in which we would be poorly placed to defend our continuing worldwide interests.

Questions of international peace and security will always be among the most difficult to handle, all the more so during a period when major shifts in power are taking place. Such periods can be extremely dangerous for world peace, as was clearly evidenced by the experience of the early twentieth century. The rise of major powers in Asia and elsewhere is almost certainly achievable peacefully but it would be unwise to assume that this will happen naturally and without any close shaves with conflict. So, much will depend on how the UN and its Security Council, those most imperfect of vehicles, will evolve; and how its, currently five, Permanent Members handle international crises as they come along and whether they can work together rather than cancelling each other out. Much too will depend on how the Security Council interprets and applies the emerging norm of the Responsibility to Protect, no longer a vague, academic conceit but, since the interventions in Libya and Côte d'Ivoire in 2011, a reality whose scope and definition still remain vague and disputed. And while one may hope that the demand for UN peacekeeping will dip over time, it would be wiser to prepare for an increase or at least for the continuation of the present high level of need. The winding down by the USA and NATO of the major military deployments in Iraq and Afghanistan, and the unlikelihood of their being repeated in the near future, will merely increase the burden on the UN and other forms of international cooperation, more often than not regional cooperation, particularly in Africa. Britain will necessarily have a role to play in all this. We will need in particular to consider how best we can support UN and regional peacekeeping, to which our contribution has recently been remarkably modest. As peacekeeping operations become more complex, more dangerous and more multifaceted it could well be that our best contribution will be through the provision of specialist services which are often so lacking when infantry battalions are deployed without proper support and through the strengthening of regional peacekeeping forces by training, logistics and finance.

The Nuclear Non-Proliferation Treaty which came into force in 1970, discriminatory though it undoubtedly is, has made a major, if largely unrecognised, contribution to international peace and security over the last 45 years, but it is now under greater strain than it has ever been before. The failure of the five recognised nuclear weapons states to move further and faster towards fulfilling their disarmament commitments entered into in particular when the treaty was prolonged indefinitely in 1995, the existence of three nuclear armed countries – India, Israel and Pakistan – outside the provisions of the treaty, two of whom at least are continuing to build up their nuclear arsenals, and, above all, the attempts by North Korea and Iran to break out of the regime, mean that we are at a tipping point in the efforts to prevent the geographical spread of nuclear weapons and to make progress towards a world free of nuclear weapons. All three of those elements will need to be addressed successfully in the period ahead if the world is not to become a much more dangerous and insecure place, with a strong likelihood of nuclear arms races developing in such already fragile and conflict-prone regions as North East Asia, South Asia, the Gulf and the Middle East. Once again Britain will have a role to play in avoiding such an outcome that would be seriously damaging to our interests. We will not simply be able to sit this issue out, arguing that our own nuclear arsenal is at an irreducible minimum. But nor, I believe, would a revival of unilateralism in this country be either effective or desirable. So we will need to apply ourselves with determination, perseverance and imagination to the multilateral agenda, being ready to reduce the salience of nuclear weapons in our own national defence strategy and to work with others for the spread of nuclear weapons-free zones, to the Middle East in particular, and for measures to ban the production of fissile material and to bring into force the Comprehensive Nuclear-Test-Ban Treaty. As to the cases of North Korea and Iran, neither the pre-emptive use of force nor a fatalistic acceptance of their emergence as fully-fledged nuclear weapons states are likely to prove the best way to proceed; which leaves a major challenge for that combination of collective diplomacy and economic sanctions that has so far yielded meagre results.

The global financial and economic crisis which began in 2008 is severely testing the international machinery which was gradually built up during the decades after the end of the Second World War with a view to avoiding the wave of trade protectionism and beggar-my-neighbour devaluations which had such disastrous political as well as economic consequences during the 1930s. So far those kinds of mercantilist responses have been largely resisted, but the world is far from being out of the woods yet. The new restricted grouping, the G20, which was, very wisely if belatedly, conjured up to bring together the world's largest economies, accounting currently for more than 80 per cent of global economic activity, and to bridge the gap between the old G8 grouping of industrialised countries and the major emerging economies from the developing world, after a promising start seems now to be degenerating into a series of photo-opportunities with little in the way of concerted actions coming out of recent meetings. That needs to be remedied if the temptations of national or regional protectionist responses are to be resisted during the period of austerity that lies ahead. The latest in the rounds of multilateral trade negotiations that have done so much over the last 60 years to fuel economic growth, the Doha Development Round, has stalled. Britain's role in such trade negotiations is exercised through the EU, where it has played a formidably effective part in promoting a trade liberalising stance in trade policy negotiations. Anything that weakens Britain's influence in Brussels will damage the effectiveness of that effort and, in a period where it is hard to see from where else leadership for freer and fairer world trade rules will come, this could be very damaging for both the EU and Britain. Were the World Trade Organization's machinery for resolving trade disputes, the sole fully rules-based element in the global economy, to come under threat that would be even worse.

The best way ahead may lie in the EU enlisting, more purposefully than has been the case in the past, the support of the major emerging economies for freeing up world trade. These countries seem gradually and reluctantly to be appreciating that, as major exporting countries of both goods and services, they have a lot to lose in a situation where creeping protectionism takes over. And the best antidote to protectionism is not to stand still but to move ahead. In this field of trade policy, as well as that of overseas aid, the EU and its member states are key players who, by exerting their collective weight, can provide the sort of leadership which has recently been in such short supply. It will be important that Britain does not come to regard vigorous export drives in the world's most rapidly growing markets, necessary and desirable as these may be, as in some kind of way a substitute for the strengthening of multilateral trade liberalisation. The two are complementary and it is a successful combination of both that will produce the best results for our and other European economies.

It is hard to deny that the drive to combat climate change and to hold the increase in carbon emissions, and thus the consequent global warming, below a level that will cause major worldwide damage has faltered since the onset of the financial and economic crisis of 2008. But the science has not changed, despite blanket coverage of some fairly marginal errors in the presentation of global trends; and the scientific analysis shows that, for all the talk at Rio in 1992, at Kyoto and then in Copenhagen and Durban, carbon emissions are still rising, and that in a period when the economies in many parts of the world have either been in recession or are growing very slowly. It is easy enough to say that a period of austerity is not the moment for taking the costly long-term decisions needed if climate change is to be checked, but those decisions will always be long-term ones and the costs of not taking them will mount as time passes, as will the costs of trying to remedy the consequences of unchecked climate change. Here too, as with trade policy, Britain's principal role and most effective influence is through the EU; and Europe has indeed led the way, and continues to lead the way, in the search for legally-binding measures to be applied worldwide to deal with climate change. Yet again anything that diminishes or marginalises Britain's capacity to influence the formulation of EU policy will be damaging to the overall effort; and Britain on its own, responsible for a tiny proportion of world carbon emissions, cannot hope to or afford to influence the outcome in any serious way by acting separately.

Those four policy areas – collective efforts to achieve peace and security, nuclear disarmament and non-proliferation, trade policy and climate change – are ones where Britain can reasonably be said to have found a role and to be exercising it in a responsible manner. They are by no means the only ones. Issues over human rights and over the strengthening of the international machinery for breaking down the culture of impunity for breaches of those rights, in particular through the activity of the International Criminal Court, are higher up the international agenda than they have ever been before, and rightly so. None of these issues are passing fads or fashions, although some critics would like to persuade us that they are. They will be the bread and butter of international diplomacy throughout the present century. One common feature that almost all of them share is that the United States, as much for reasons of Congressional politics as because of the policies of successive administrations, is at best a reluctant participant in the international efforts to handle them, at worst obstructive; and another common feature is that the countries with which Britain shares most common ground are the other European countries with whom we are partners in the EU. If that is the case, there are surely important conclusions to be drawn for the future conduct of British foreign policy.

The geopolitical context within which Britain's relationship with the United States has to be shaped changes all the time; and those changes are currently as fundamental in nature as the ones that took place 20 years ago when the frozen certainties of the Cold War period melted away after the fall of the Berlin Wall. A number of important trends are affecting the US end of the equation. America's relative weight and influence in the world, both in terms of hard power and of soft power, are coming down from the dizzying heights they reached in the last decade of the twentieth century and the first decade of the new one, when the USA was quite simply the only superpower left standing; and that shift will continue over the period ahead. The USA is directing increasing attention and resources to its relationships with the main emerging powers in Asia. The appetite in the USA for major military interventions overseas has been blunted by the experiences of Iraq and Afghanistan. And the polarisation of US domestic politics, combined with the rather dysfunctional workings of its constitution, are making it hard for the USA to give a consistent lead in handling the major global challenges of peace and security, nuclear proliferation, trade and climate change. But none of these trends are increasing at the speed and to the extent that the more excitable commentators would have us believe. So the USA will remain the predominant military power in the world for as far ahead as it is wise for any sensible observer to look. It would be unwise, too, for anyone to assume, as Saddam Hussein did when he invaded Kuwait in 1990, that the USA, traumatised by its experiences, would never again deploy a major military force and be prepared to use it. And the hard fact remains that if the USA and the countries of Europe ever get at serious cross-purposes none of those global challenges will be effectively addressed.

So the relationship between Britain and the United States will inevitably remain a crucial one for Britain. Whether it also remains an important one for the United States will depend as much on Britain's relationship with its other European partners and allies as on any other factor. If Britain's influence on the formulation of EU policy wanes, if it becomes either a semi-detached member of the EU or leaves the Union altogether, then Britain's influence in Washington and elsewhere in the world will count for far less. It will be assumed that Britain will simply tag along behind the USA or will fall in with any deal the USA strikes with the principal shapers of policy in the EU. That, after all was the pattern that was beginning to emerge in the years immediately preceding Britain's accession to the European Community in 1973. Moreover, Britain's capacity to influence the often Byzantine processes of policy formulation in Washington will be greatly enhanced whenever it is able to act in concert with the other European nations. All these trends point towards Britain putting a greater premium on achieving a degree of unity among the Europeans in their dealings with the United States than has often been the case in the past. They also suggest Britain giving a lead, working particularly closely with France, when threats and challenges arise in Europe's neighbourhood, that arc of insecurity that runs from Archangel to Agadir. Given the differences of perspective and attitude amongst Europeans, especially when consideration has to be given to the use of force, those will be uphill tasks, as we have seen recently in the case of the response to events in Libya; but the alternative is likely to be the increasing marginalisation of both

Britain and Europe and a decreasing willingness by the United States to pull the Europeans' chestnuts out of the fire when things get out of control in their own backyard, as they were compelled to do in the Balkans in the 1990s.

*   *   *

There are no prizes for identifying the aspect of its foreign policy where Britain has most signally failed to identify in any settled manner its proper role and set of objectives, namely its relationship with its fellow European countries, first in the European Community and then in the European Union. The reasons why this should have happened are set out in various chapters of this memoir and most extensively in the overall look at the relationship that I took on leaving my post as Britain's Ambassador to the European Communities in 1990 and which is included at the end of Chapter 10. Some of those reasons are historical, the difference between our experience and those of most of the other member states in the crucible of the two world wars and of the Cold War which followed it; the contrast between the benign global economic context in which the original six member states passed the formative years of their membership and the turbulent period in the 1970s when Britain followed the same path. Some of the reasons amount to what in tennis would be called unforced errors by Britain itself: the original decisions not to join the Six at the outset of their journey, when Britain's international prestige was high and when its relative economic weight was greater than when it actually joined; the viciously raucous tone of the public debate about European issues, which to some extent reflects, but often exceeds, that in which we conduct our own, domestic political battles and which has over the last 20 years been orchestrated by a predominantly blatantly Europhobic press; most recently, in December 2011, the decision to walk away from the negotiations of new treaty-based disciplines for the members of the Eurozone. The role which domestic politics has played in defining Britain's stance on European issues has been almost invariably negative. Despite the fact that at any given moment during the 40 years of Britain's membership there has been a substantial majority in Parliament in favour of it, often across party lines, and despite the two-thirds majority for it in the 1975 referendum, which was supposed to settle the matter once and for all but which did not, there have been lengthy periods when governments – the Labour government from 1975–9, the Conservative government from 1992–7 and now the Conservative-Liberal Democrat Coalition government which took office in 2010 – have been held hostage by a noisy and determined minority. Along with the errors of judgement there has been plenty of bad luck too, but no nation can afford to count on an unbroken run of good luck; and the way it handles bad luck when it comes along will be the real test of the sustainability of its policies.

It is of course perfectly legitimate in the democratic society in which we live for individuals to assert that Britain would be better off outside the European Union and that its proper role is as a country making its way on its own. But the arguments for that course seem, to me at least, even less convincing now than when successive governments turned their backs on them in the 1960s. To go right back to basics, the belief that Britain is not itself a European country has, in historical terms, no validity of any sort at all. We are clearly ethnically, culturally and politically just as European, no more so and no less so, than other European countries, almost all of whom are now members of the European Union. We have been involved, whether we liked it or not, in intra-European wars over many centuries and our interest in ensuring that such disastrous occurrences never happen again is as great as that of any other European country; the fact that, in the past, we ruled an extensive colonial empire is not something that differentiates us from other European nations but something we have in common, even if it is our national conceit that we had a more successful record than others did. Nor do the alternatives look any more beguiling than they did before. The Commonwealth has real value but not as either an economic or a political alternative to Europe. The United States is not looking in our direction, and would, quite frankly, be appalled and mystified if we were to walk away from the European Union. The idea that we could transform ourselves into a kind of 'greater Switzerland', receiving our orders on regulatory matters by fax from Brussels, without any chance to influence them, in order to maintain our access to the single market, is inconsistent not only with our historical record and our view of our place in the world but also with the hugely exaggerated claims of the benefits from withdrawal advanced by its advocates. Nor is withdrawal likely to be reconcilable with maintenance of our own union within the British Isles, already under considerable strain. What that adds up to is that the policy of withdrawal, despite protests to the contrary, is a 'little England' policy which, I would argue, should not and cannot achieve any sort of national consensus and which is not in our national interest.

What then should Britain be doing about its troubled relationship with the rest of Europe? What shape should that rather large part in the jigsaw of Britain's external relations take, that piece which has to fit in with, and which influences, so many other pieces on the table? On both sides of the Channel there needs to be recognition that pursuit of the European venture is a form of politics not religion, requiring an ability to compromise in the common interest. The European Union has already recognised that some extensive variations in the application of individual policies are acceptable even on a lasting basis – thus there is no need to revisit the opt-outs (or potential opt-ins) for membership of the Eurozone or of Schengen. But we do need to avoid any systematisation of groups of 'ins' and 'outs', any emergence of two leagues, with Britain on the outer fringe losing the capacity to influence from the outset a wide range of policy options as they emerge. We need to accept that the concept of solidarity is not purely transactional, although it clearly cannot stray too far away from a publicly acceptable perception of an equitable outcome. We need too to be willing to set out confidently and compellingly a vision for the future of the European Union which takes account of the visions of others and which does not solely consist of a long list of negative propositions, red lines and no-go areas. Can we not take the lead in developing a European security dimension, with Britain and France its key members, now that it is clear that our own capacity for independent military action is ever-more limited, that this will not damage the Atlantic Alliance and that the USA would actually be likely to favour some such evolution? We do need to recognise that a necessary, if not a fully sufficient, condition for ensuring that the EU develops in ways consistent with Britain's national interests is an unbroken policy dialogue with the other large member states, Germany and France in particular, in which some give and take occurs alongside the vigorous assertion of our own priorities. But the single most important element of Britain's European policy will need to be a willingness by the leadership of all three main political parties to go out and explain publicly why making a success of Britain's EU membership is a vital and an achievable national interest. In all likelihood that will involve facing down those whose claim to the euphemistic label of Euro-sceptic is merely a camouflage for their real objective of withdrawal. The idea that this group can be successfully appeased by concessions often damaging to Britain's chances of playing a full and successful role in EU policy formulation, is a dangerous illusion.

16

ENVOI

I am naturally an optimist. I suspect many diplomats are; it helps them to handle the often difficult conditions in which they have to live and work and to address successfully the daunting challenges that arise in the international arena. So, if I end these memoirs on a note tinged with pessimism, it does not reflect my habitual approach; nor, I hope, does it reflect elderly grumpiness, which I try to hold at bay.

My principal concern is that we may be at a point when the main international structures which have been so laboriously built up since the end of the Second World War, and even more so since the end of the Cold War – the UN, the IMF, the World Bank, the WTO, the EU, NATO to name the most prominent – may begin to fray and crack and to lose their relevance. The world has been in this situation at least once before, in the 1930s when the League of Nations, the disarmament conferences, the attempts at worldwide economic cooperation were swept aside in a Gadarene rush by individual countries to protect themselves from the consequences of a financial bust, high unemployment and a world slump, and when the leaders of the main nations turned in on themselves and neglected even the few weak instruments they had for collective security and prosperity. The international structures and instruments we have now are far more elaborate and resilient than the ones that formed such a feeble barrier then to the mayhem which was to follow; but they are not immune to centrifugal tendencies and to a process of unravelling should their main member states drift towards isolationism and reject mutual solidarity. First reactions to the financial and economic crisis of 2008 seemed to show that the lessons of the 1930s had been well learnt. But the handling of the aftershocks and of the second wave of sovereign debt crises has been less impressive. And all this is occurring during a period of shifts in the tectonic plates of world power, when new players are gaining in weight and significance and old players need to make room for them and to co-opt them as equals and full partners in global governance. So there are two sets of challenges overlapping each other; and the prosperity and security of all of us will depend on the outcome of the responses to both. Either the world will surmount the current crises and continue the painful process of edging towards a more rules-based international community capable of mastering, or at least managing, the main global challenges which face us; or it will drift towards a new world disorder, with pretty unpleasant consequences for all concerned (and that is a truly British understatement). My hope is that Britain will play a substantial role in working effectively for the first of these outcomes, will overcome its European doubts and demons, and will reject the siren songs of 'little England'. But I cannot say for sure that this is what will happen.

My other worry is rather more parochial, and concerns the relationship in this country between politicians and those who staff the public services, the military, the civil servants and the diplomats. Throughout my own professional career (up to 1995) that relationship was close and I believe beneficial to both sides. The British public service ethos, founded in the great reforms of the nineteenth century, may not have produced perfect results but it did provide the foundation from which impartial advice could be offered to ministers, who then took the responsibility for accepting that advice or for discarding it. It was a system which compared favourably with the much more politicised public services of many other democracies and which was fully consistent with the model of representative parliamentary democracy which had first been pioneered in this country. In general the advice offered by civil servants was not mediated through or dominated by a filter of what are now called special political advisers. In recent years the number of such advisers has markedly increased and their role has become more pervasive. I fear this is not a positive development and is one whose consequences are not well understood. There are signs of disenchantment, and occasionally of disloyalty, on both sides of the divide between politicians and civil servants which cannot be good for the health of the body politic; nor in the long run will it be compatible with the maintenance of the highest professional standards in the civil and diplomatic services. So I hope that recent trends will be checked and perhaps modestly reversed before more damage is done to structures that provided the framework of what I always found to be a deeply satisfying professional career.

INDEX